Living
Morally

Living Morally

A Psychology of Moral Character

LAURENCE THOMAS

Temple
University Press
Philadelphia

To my aunt, Mariam Lupeter Dobson,
an ole-fashioned Jamaican woman
who never allowed me to wallow
in the valley of despair.

Temple University Press, Philadelphia 19122
Copyright © 1989 by Temple University. All rights reserved
Published 1989
Printed in the United States of America

The paper used in this publication meets the minimum
requirements of American National Standard for Information
Sciences—Permanence of Paper for Printed Library Materials,
ANSI Z39.48-1984

Library of Congress Cataloging-in-Publication Data
Thomas, Laurence, 1949–
    Living morally : a psychology of moral character / Laurence
Thomas.
        p.   cm.
    Bibliography: p.
    Includes index.
    ISBN 0-87722-602-4
    1. Ethics, Modern—20th century.   2. Altruism.   3. Social values.
4. Motivation (Psychology)   I. Title.
BJ319.T46 1989
170—dc 19   88-28275
                                                    CIP

Contents

Preface

A theory of morality is about what is right and wrong. This book is not about what is right and wrong: it does not attempt to offer such a theory. Nor does it attempt to bring into sharper focus any existing account of what is right and wrong—either by examining a rich theoretical account such as Donagan's or Gewirth's or by trying to give structure to our pretheoretical intuitions in the way that Thomson, with great skill and ingenuity, takes up an issue in moral and social philosophy. Rather, I am interested in moral motivation; and I assume without really much argument that to be moral is to be altruistic—that the true morality is an altruistic one, that is, an other-regarding morality. Specifically, then, I am interested in the extent to which people are motivated to act in accordance with an altruistic morality.

Interestingly, most contemporary writers—Baier (1958), Darwall (1983), Gauthier (1986), Gewirth (1978), Nagel (1970), and Rawls (1971), to name a few—defend an altruistic conception of morality yet, presuppose a self-interested conception of human motivation. Thus, as these writers conceive of things, being moral turns out to be very much a matter of going against the grain of what we are as human beings, in that self-interested individuals are called upon to follow the requirements of an altruistic morality. Accordingly, much moral philosophy has struck me as a kind of philosophical sleight of hand, a kind of moral magic: starting with quintessentially self-interested creatures, one then proceeds to show by some very elaborate, sometimes ingenious, argument that they can be moved to act in accordance with the requirements of an altruistic morality. I think that Sidgwick (1907) saw as clearly as anyone that self-interest and altruism do not sit comfortably together, suggesting that a person could be both an egoist and a utilitarian only in a world rather unlike this one, namely, one where every act that maximized the individual's happiness also maximized the total amount of happiness.

Believing that there is no gainsaying Sidgwick on this matter and also believing that the true morality is an altruistic one, I am ineluctably drawn to the idea that there has to be more altruism in our bones, so to speak, than contemporary moral philosophers have allowed— if, that is, there really is much to be said for the view that we should act in accordance with the requirements of an altruistic morality. To make good this idea is essentially the aim of this project. My view is that while human beings are perhaps not entirely altruistic, we have a considerable capacity for altruism, and, what is more, our having this capacity is due to our biological make-up. Indeed, I regard the capacity to be altruistic rather like a natural gift or talent to sing or to play the piano or to draw or to do mathematics. Like any other natural endowment, whether our capacity to be altruistic flourishes is contingent upon the nature of our social environment. Those who have a gift for singing must take care of their bodies and they must practice; they do not sing well come what may and regardless of how they live. In a like manner, our altruistic capacity is most fully realized when social conditions are as they should be. I attach enormous weight to the parent-child relationship, companion friendships (assumed throughout to be between adults), and the beliefs that we have in general about how others will treat us. I believe that when these things are as they should be, our capacity to be altruistic flowers; and by acting in accordance with the demands of an altruistic morality, a person can thus obtain a purchase on living well.

In a word, this essay is a defense of a very old ideal, one that goes back to Plato and Aristotle. The ideal can be simply stated: moral flourishing and human flourishing are inextricably linked.

This ideal can be defended from so many different directions and quarters that it is extremely difficult to know when to leave well enough alone. My focus has been upon social interaction as played out through a biological and psychological make-up that is congruent with the claims of an altruistic morality—so I believe. Biology is my point of departure because I believe that if, indeed, we are quintessentially self-interested—if this quality characterizes our motivational structure through and through (Gauthier 1986), then there really is no chance of the traditional virtues' ever obtaining a secure footing in our lives. If we are self-interested to the core, no Kantian argument will render us otherwise (contra Darwall 1983; Nagel 1970). If we are self-interested to the core, a profound alteration in our motivational structure would have to take place in order for an altruistic morality to hold an attraction for us. But I write in the hopes that we are not. A great deal of altruism can be found in the biological and psychological make-up of human beings—so I believe and argue (cf. Brandt 1976, 1978).

There is surely much that remains to be dealt with, as a complete defense of the view that moral and human flourishing are tied together would have to deal with the traditional moral virtues in a systematic way. I have not given all the areas of psychology that bear upon the themes of this essay the attention they deserve. The issue of self-deception comes readily to mind here: a complete account of human flourishing would have to speak to the ways in which we are susceptible to self-deception, the ways in which we can minimize self-deception in our lives, and so on. I have not done so here. Nor do I say as much about the role of the emotions in our lives as perhaps one might (cf. de Sousa 1987; Greenspan 1988). While I discuss various emotions, I have not attempted to offer a systematic account of the human emotions generally or, for that matter, any particular emotion.

A mark of maturity is knowing when to leave well enough alone, as John Cooper once told me. I have tried to exhibit that maturity throughout this book. This work is not complete, but I shall be most content if I have managed to say something that serves to keep alive the ideal that moral and human well-being are inextricably connected.

It may seem to some that this work amounts to nothing more than an exercise in pop psychology, floundering in a sea of intuitions about our psychological make-up and social interaction. Well, unsubstantiated intuitions are just that, whether they appear in game theory, where they do appear in abundance (cf. Gauthier 1986; Rawls 1971), or anywhere else. The fact that one set of intuitions admits of mathematical rigor and another does not hardly shows, in and of itself, that the latter intuitions are unacceptable; for mathematical rigor and truth are not one and the same. In the end, we must judge the plausibility of our intuitive assumptions by the extent to which they illuminate their subject matter—human beings, in the case at hand. I have been guided by the following intuitions: (i) social cooperation is the key to human survival; (ii) there can be no genuine cooperation in the absence of altruism; (iii) the very nature of both parental love and friendship would suggest that human beings are capable of considerable altruism; and (iv) the realization of altruism in our lives contributes to our living well. My hope is that when these considerations are reflected upon jointly, they will provide us with a new vantage point —one that departs from the economic model of humans as relentlessly self-interested maximizers—from which to take the measure of humankind. I believe that love gives morality a place in our lives that it would not otherwise have. If you will, love anchors morality in our lives; for it is in virtue of love that doing what is right has ontological priority in our lives. It is not because we are moral that we love, as perhaps Kantians would have it; rather, it is because we love that we are moral. And if love is a good, then the right, namely morality, is anchored in the good.

The topic of evil is not addressed in this book. But I endeavor to do so in another work now in progress: *Vessels of Evil: Philosophical Reflections on Slavery and the Holocaust.*

I provide no direct commentary in the present work. There is much in the literature that I should like to have explicitly discussed, but I bowed to considerations of length. This work brings together ideas that I have developed in a number of papers over the years, especially: "Morality and Our Self-Concept" (1978); "Ethical Egoism and Our Psychological Dispositions" (1980a); "Law, Morality, and Our Psychological Nature" (1983); "Morality, the Self, and Our Natural Sentiments" (1983a); "Love and Morality: The Possibility of Altruism" (1985b); "Beliefs and the Motivation to Be Just" (1985a); "Justice, Happiness, and Self-Knowledge" (1986); and "Friendship" (1987a). I trust that I have taken what was good from these essays and ignored what was bad.

In writing this book, I have been so fortunate as to receive institutional support on a number of occasions: an Andrew W. Mellon Faculty Fellowship at Harvard University (1978–79); a fellowship at the National Humanities Center in North Carolina (1982–83); an office campus assignment from the University of North Carolina at Chapel

Hill (1982–83); a grant from the Earhart Foundation for a research assistant (1985–86); and a research appointment from Oberlin College (1987–88). Without the freedom from normal teaching responsibilities and duties, it would not have been possible for me to give my inchoate ideas what little structure they now exhibit. I am very, very pleased to acknowledge the support of these institutions.

On a more personal note: I must mention Bernard Boxill, Lawrence Thomas Ellis, Jr., and Howard McGary, Jr. Each, in his own way, forced me to take the philosophical implications of the black experience more seriously than I might ever have been willing to do, and in doing so helped me to grasp more clearly the character of my own thought. Likewise for Christine Lee. Brad Goodman, Terrence McConnell, and David Weissbord have been privy to the many highs and lows of writing this book, and each always responded in the appropriate way. Robert Audi, Kathryn Jackson, Alasdair MacIntyre, Michael S. Pritchard, and Judith Jarvis Thomson have offered very encouraging words at some quite crucial junctures. Thanks are owed to my former colleagues at the University of North Carolina at Chapel Hill—especially E. M. Adams, William G. Lycan, and Jay Rosenberg.

Over the years Thomas Nagel has listened to and read many of the ideas in this book. For this I am most grateful; he has been a natural sounding board for my thought because in many respects, our views about moral motivation have often differed at just the right junctures. John Rawls has been an enormous source of philosophical inspiration; in particular, it was conversations with him (1978–79) that rekindled my interest in (socio)biology.

I should like to mention just a few others. When I joined the faculty at Oberlin College, I met Norman Care, Michael Stocker (who was visiting), and Ira Yankwitt. Their enthusiasm and interest in my work could not have been more propitious. With one exception, no other undergraduate has (to this date) contributed as much to my moral and intellectual flourishing as has Yankwitt. Care listened to my various germinating ideas, and often made it possible for me to separate the wheat from the chaff. In general, my colleagues at Oberlin were extremely tolerant of my moods and fits as I labored to complete this book; and it was Alfred MacKay, in his role as dean, who made it possible for me, in only my second year at Oberlin, to be free from teaching duties. Stocker read the manuscript in its entirety and commented on it with great wisdom. His groundbreaking work (see, for example, Stocker 1976, 1981) was pivotal in shaping my philosophical interests. Jane Cullen, Senior Acquisitions Officer in Philosophy at Temple University Press, was a godsend. I could not have asked for a better or more encouraging and supportive editor to work with. My student Steven A. Friedman proofread, and commented upon, all but two of the chapters of this book. He was never reluctant to tell me when he thought poorly of what I had written—but then again, he was never reluctant to tell me when he thought I had done a wonderful job. Jane Barry and John Ziff did an excellent job of copyediting the manuscript.

Last, but certainly not least, I want to mention Kurt Baier (with whom I wrote my doctoral thesis) and Annette Baier. Having read their Aristotle, they have so very often said the right thing to me at the right time and in the right way. My intellectual and spiritual debt to them, individually and collectively, is greater than words can tell. So is my gratitude.

Few things are more precious than the good will of others, especially their confidence in one. The harsh reality, however, is that for women and minorities this confidence has not always been easy to come by. To the various individuals—some mentioned above, some not—whose confidence in me has made my writing of this book possible: THANK YOU.

Laurence Thomas
Oberlin, Ohio

Living
Morally

CHAPTER ONE

Moral Character and Moral Theories

Social interaction is the thread from which the fabric of moral character is woven.[1] For it is social interaction that informs the way in which
each of us conceives of both ourselves and one another. Indeed, it
is such interaction that makes it possible for us to conceive of ourselves as agents among agents; and only beings who so conceive of
themselves can have a moral character of any kind. My aim in this
essay is to offer an account of how individuals come to have and to
maintain a good moral character. That is, I want to offer an account of
the wherewithal necessary to lead a moral life and of how this wherewithal is acquired and sustained. As the beginning sentence suggests,
I shall be particularly concerned to show that social interaction plays
a pivotal role in this regard. Friendship and parental upbringing are

---

[1] In *A Theory of Moral Sentiments*, Adam Smith wrote: "Were it possible that a
human creature could grow up to manhood in some solitary place without any communication with his own species. He could no more think of his character, of the propriety
or demerit of his own sentiments and conduct, of the beauty or deformity of his own
mind, than of the beauty of his own face. . . . Bring him into society, and he is immediately provided with the mirror which he wanted before" (III.i.3). Before him, David
Hume wrote: "The minds of men are mirrors to one another, not only because they
reflect each other's emotions, but also because those rays of passions, sentiments, and
opinions may be often reverberated." (*A Treatise of Human Nature*, II.ii.5).

3

the two forms of social interaction that figure most prominently in the theory I shall offer.

A rich description of the subject of this essay, namely, the morally good individual, is initially presented. An attempt is made to give some structure to our basic intuitions about the morally good person. Along the way, I do some refashioning. Thus, the description offered is not without normative import.

1. Persons of Good Moral Character

Doing what is morally right, that is, leading a morally good life, is an abiding and overriding concern of persons of good moral character. But while such persons may be of one heart, they are not necessarily of one mind. Perhaps one of the most fascinating observations that one can make is that persons of good moral character do not all hold identical moral views, even with respect to substantive moral issues.

Currently, there are some substantive moral issues over which morally good persons may, and sometimes do, hold widely disparate views, the issue of abortion being a case in point. From the fact that a person is a decent and upright individual, it hardly seems that one can infer whether she is a liberal, conservative, or moderate on the abortion issue (Wertheimer 1971). Again, some morally good individuals believe that if we refrain from helping someone, then we are just as culpable for the harm that the person experiences as if we had actually taken steps to cause that harm. Others do not believe this.[2] And again, it does not seem that one can infer where any given decent and upright individual stands on this issue.

Lest there be any misunderstanding, I am not suggesting that these matters do not admit of a correct answer. Perhaps they do; and surely some people think that they do. The point, rather, is that having a good moral character does not seem to be tied to subscribing to that answer. For not only are we unable to infer where a person stands on such issues, but we are often reluctant to say that a person's moral character is blemished on account of her stand.

---

[2] Reference here is to the debate over whether or not there is a morally relevant difference between acts and omissions. For a discussion of these issues, see, for example, Bennett (1981), Foot (1984), Rachels (1975), and Trammell (1975).

Now, it might seem that the explanation for this is that our moral views are simply not settled concerning abortion or the moral equivalency of harming someone and of refraining from helping him. It might be thought that when it comes to settled moral views, at least concerning issues of great significance, a person's moral character is immediately called into question if he fails to subscribe to the correct moral view. But this conclusion is too hasty.

Tradition has it that Socrates, Abraham Lincoln, and Martin Luther King, Jr., are exemplars of good moral character.[3] And if there is any settled moral view nowadays, it is that slavery is wrong. Yet Socrates was more accepting of slavery than Lincoln, who was more accepting of it than King, who was against not just the peculiar institution of American slavery, but all forms of slavery. Undoubtedly part of the explanation for why their views concerning so important a moral issue as slavery differed is that they lived during quite different eras. Still, as exemplars of good moral character Socrates and Lincoln present a problem for the thesis that persons of good moral character subscribe to the correct view concerning settled moral matters. That is, this thesis will have to be suitably modified if we are going to insist, on the one hand, that all three of these individuals are persons of good moral character and, on the other, that it is incontrovertible that slavery is morally wrong. And that modification notwithstanding, the observation that persons of good moral character can differ concerning their moral views will remain unvitiated.

There can be no doubt that historical contexts do make a significant difference in how people think about matters. And it might be tempting to say that people of good moral character will not differ on substantive moral issues, provided that they live in the same time period. However, this would seem to be nothing more than an ad hoc move designed to save appearances. Different historical contexts represent nothing more than different social milieus. But the social milieus of contemporaries can vary widely; and there is no in-

---

[3] See Lawrence Kohlberg (1981), for example, "Justice as Reversibility: The Claim to Moral Adequacy of a Highest Stage of Moral Judgment." That all or any one of these individuals should in fact have considerably less of an anchored moral character than tradition makes them out to have had does not militate against the point being made here. For the view, whether truth or myth, that these were all individuals of exemplary moral character certainly makes sense to us. I have learned much from Kurt Baier's excellent discussion of Kohlberg's views. See K. Baier (1974).

principle reason to suppose that they cannot vary widely enough to account for the fact that people of good moral character differ in their moral views concerning some matter.

This last remark brings us back to the issue of abortion. This moral issue shows that different historical contexts are not always the explanation for why individuals of good moral character sharply differ on substantive moral issues. People of good moral character with quite similar social backgrounds as determined by wealth, education, and so forth disagree about the moral status of the fetus, though they in no way disagree on matters of fact, such as its origin, biological make-up, and so on. Some take the fetus to be a full-fledged person from the outset; others think the very idea is absurd.

My claim has been that not all people of good moral character hold identical moral views, even with respect to substantive moral issues. I regard the issues of abortion and slavery as jointly providing formidable support for the truth of this view. The latter reveals that from a historical perspective persons of good moral character cannot be identified solely by the content of their views. At least this holds so long as we continue to regard Socrates, Lincoln, and King as exemplars of persons of good moral character despite their differences concerning the morality of slavery. The issue of abortion shows that people cannot be so identified among contemporaries with similar social backgrounds and with no disagreement over the facts as such.

At first blush, the idea that a person of good moral character need not subscribe to the correct set of moral views might seem counterintuitive. One might be inclined to think that a person has a good moral character only if all or, at any rate, enough of the moral views to which he subscribes are (objectively) correct. The problem with this criterion is that it is too stringent. It ties having a good moral character to having moral knowledge. By this criterion, a person lacks a good moral character, no matter how defensible his moral views might be, if these moral views should turn out to be wrong. Insufficient weight is attached to the defensibility of a person's moral views.

Necessarily, reasoning and reflection occur against a particular backdrop of views, attitudes, and so on. What we are justified in believing, what we find plausible, and what we find manifestly obvious are tied to the circumstances of our lives (cf. Simon 1983, ch. 1). Moral reasoning and reflection have no immunity in this regard. This fact cannot be completely irrelevant in our assessment of whether or not a person has a good moral character. We must judge a person's moral character not by the shortfall from what he might be, but by the distance he travels from the beginning. Barring a world that is particularly hostile to their good intentions,[4] persons with an abiding concern to do the right will, by and large, actually do what is right insofar as they are able to discern it. This is very much part and parcel of having a good moral character. But through no fault of their own, persons may fail to discern the right. And when this is the case, their failure to do the right cannot plausibly reflect negatively upon their character. To establish that a person's character is flawed, it does not suffice to show that she or he failed to do what is morally right, any more than establishing that a person's solution to a mathematical problem is incorrect suffices to show that she or he is not mathematically inclined.

Consider the following. Dolphins are now considered to be very intelligent animals, capable of sophisticated social interaction. Just how intelligent is unclear. But given that the depth of our moral regard for other creatures depends on the extent to which social interaction is essential to their proper development (cf. Goodpaster 1978), it would seem that dolphins are deserving of far more moral regard than anyone could have had reason to think some two hundred years ago. Back then, probably no one had any reason to believe that there might be a moral difference between dolphins and other creatures of the sea. And neither the failure to discern such a difference nor, a fortiori, the failure to have the proper moral regard for dolphins can be attributed to a defect in the moral character of people then. It does not seem possible that individuals who lived two hundred years ago could have had the appreciation that we have today for the social sophistication of dolphins. Our moral regard for a (kind of) creature is indissolubly tied to our beliefs about its capacities; and it is wildly implausible to suppose that our failure to have the correct beliefs in every instance can be attributed to a defect in moral character.

We can now state succinctly and with greater force why having a good moral character cannot be made to turn upon subscribing to the correct moral views, and therefore why persons of good moral character cannot be identified solely by the content of their moral

4 Obviously enough, my use of the expression "good intentions" owes its inspiration to Kant's idea of a good will. See his *Fundamental Principles of the Metaphysics of Morals*.

views. The very notion of a good moral character cannot be articulated independently of how we should treat other creatures (human and nonhuman). But how we should do that is contingent upon the beliefs that we are justified in having about other creatures; and the simple truth of the matter is that we may be quite justified in having morally relevant beliefs about a (kind of) creature—albeit beliefs that turn out to be false, as was the case with dolphins two hundred years ago.

Undoubtedly, what is most troubling about the claim that persons of good moral character cannot be identified solely by the correct content of their moral views is that nowadays, at any rate, we most definitely want to say that no such person fails to have the deepest moral disapprobation for both American slavery and Nazi Germany. And this, it would seem, we cannot say if persons of good moral character are not to be identified solely by the content of their moral views. I shall return to this apparent difficulty momentarily.

The view that all persons of good moral character do not hold identical moral views, even with respect to substantive moral issues, receives support from another quarter. Observe that while utilitarians and deontologists, especially rights-based theorists, have been at loggerheads down through the centuries, neither side has contended that persons in the other camp have a bad moral character on account of the moral theory to which they subscribe. This is no accident. A moral theory has to yield terrible consequences in a quite systematic way before we are inclined to think that only those of bad moral character could subscribe to it. There is much that can be said in defense of utilitarian theory, although it is not a rights-based theory; and rights-based theories, for all that can be said in their defense, are not without their shortcomings (Sumner 1981). It cannot be said that only a person utterly lacking in moral sensibilities would subscribe to either kind of theory.

By contrast, note that the one moral theory that is often associated with the immoral person is ethical egoism (see Gauthier 1970b). And this, again, is no accident. Ethical egoism readily lends itself to a characterization according to which a person who subscribes to it is systematically lacking in moral sensibilities (Section 14) because he is concerned only to maximize his self-interests.[5]

---

[5] See, for example, Murphy (1972). Jesse Kalin (1970) has gone a long way toward rescuing ethical egoism from this characterization. I should mention that some liber-

I suggest, then, that a defining characteristic of persons of good moral character is not the correctness of their moral views or the possession of moral knowledge, but the (moral) defensibility of those views.[6] When can it be said that a person's moral views are defensible and, therefore, compatible with his being a person of good moral character? This question admits of both an objective and a subjective answer. The objective answer is this: when (i) a person's moral views call for treating all innocent (full-fledged) persons in a minimally altruistic way; and (ii) the criteria by which a living being is determined to be a full-fledged person are grounded in the best scientific and sociological considerations available, and the criteria by which a person is determined to be noninnocent are not contrived. A view or piece of behavior is minimally altruistic if it takes into account the good of another without flowing from affection for that person or from a plan of life wherein one's primary aim is to do good for others—wherein one's mode of flourishing is defined primarily in terms of activities of this sort. With minimal altruism, the very point of one's actions cannot be to harm others, and the gratuitous harming of others is always deemed morally repulsive.

The subjective answer is the same as that given above, save that condition (ii) is adjusted to reflect the reality that as children we get our initial beliefs about the world and others from our social environment, especially our parents (Sections 8 and 22). Our social environment may deliver false beliefs about others to us; and our experiences (including the acquisition of new information) may be such that reflection upon and critical examination of them gives us no reason to correct these beliefs or, in any case, to question their plausibility. Subjectively, then, a person's moral views are defensible although mistaken if they are the best that one can expect of him given both his initial beliefs and the experiences (including the acquisition of new information) that he has to reflect upon and examine critically. This subjective answer speaks to the reality that a person's assessment of

---

tarians have also been concerned to rescue egoism from its unsavory connotations. See, for example, Machan (1987), Mack (1971), and Regis (1979). I am very grateful to Tibor Machan for reminding me of this.

6 Thomas Nagel (1980) observes: "The idea that the basic principles of morality are *known,* and that all the problems come in their interpretation and application, is one of the most fantastic conceits to which our conceited species has been drawn" (emphasis in the original).

others may, through no fault of his own, not be informed by the best scientific and sociological evidence available.

It is not possible for a person living in an urban center such as New York City to suppose that blacks find the epithet "nigger" other than offensive. Whatever the individual might in fact think of blacks, he would certainly know that they strongly resent this word. By contrast, suppose that a child was raised in a newly formed and entirely racist community of adults that was completely isolated from society: there was no television, daily newspaper, and so on. The child only saw pictures of blacks doing the most morally despicable things, and blacks were only referred to as "niggers." This child would come to regard blacks as morally despicable people who are properly referred to as "niggers." Of course, it would have to be true—and this begins to defy the imagination—that none of the adult members of this community acted in morally despicable ways toward one another. On the account given of the conditions necessary for moral defensibility, this child's views of blacks would be morally defensible, albeit quite wrong. In particular, the child could not be considered a racist in the way that the adult members of a community could be. For to be a racist is not just to believe wrongly that a group is inferior along some dimension, but to be committed to viewing the group in that way regardless of the evidence (Nozick 1981, p. 325). As I have told the story, the child is not so committed, although the adult members of this community are.

Now, if this child was, as a young adult, to relocate to a major urban center such as New York City, his views about blacks would rapidly become indefensible. True, he would encounter (or read and hear about) blacks doing morally despicable things; but he would quickly discover that the morally despicable was hardly the purview of blacks only. One would not expect this young adult's beliefs to change overnight, but one would expect them to change. This raises a very important question: How quickly do persons of good moral character adjust their views in the light of corrective experiences? I shall not attempt an answer. A satisfactory one would surely be contingent upon a multitude of factors. Not least among these would be the extent to which their mistaken beliefs are constitutive of their self-concept (Section 22). The more central a role beliefs play in this regard, the more difficult it is for individuals to adjust them or to jettison them entirely in the light of corrective experiences. Constitutive beliefs are foundational: we understand and interpret who we are and our experiences in light of them. For this very reason, we are naturally inclined to dismiss an experience or event that is at odds with our constitutive beliefs rather than to see it as a reason to reevaluate the beliefs themselves.

To take a straightforward example, until very recent times many women have dearly believed that motherhood was their only true calling, that above everything else they were ordained by God or nature to be mothers. This belief was so central to the self-concept of many women that it was extremely difficult for women to take seriously their artistic and intellectual talents. Even if a woman had considerable talent in these areas, she would not, under this belief, be doing what she was truly called to do—she would not be actualizing her truest self—were she to realize either her artistic or intellectual talent. From a motivational standpoint, this belief was deadly, as it is very difficult to be motivated to pursue ends different from the one whose realization one dearly regards as an expression of one's truest self. My intention in this example has not been to justify or excuse sexist arrangements, but to illustrate the extent to which mistaken beliefs that are central to our self-concept may resist corrective experiences. In times past, rather than seeing the talented women of their day as a reason to rethink their views about women, many (women and men alike) discounted the contributions of such women for one reason or another (see, for example, A. Dworkin 1983, pp. 39–43). For example, such women were said to be frustrated because they had missed out on the opportunity to have children. Or their work might be characterized as exceptional for a woman, but not up to the standards of a man. Indeed, what were dismissed as mere ramblings when written by a woman were praised as deep insights to be mined by future generations when written by a man.

Any satisfactory theory of persons of good moral character must take seriously the fact that (i) even persons of good moral character can have mistaken morally relevant beliefs that are sufficiently constitutive of their self-concept that these beliefs have a high immunity to corrective experiences; and (ii) because of a host of factors having to do with both personality and other beliefs, different persons will respond differently to like corrective experiences regarding the same constitutive belief. One man's encounter with an obviously brilliant female mathematician will shame him. He will wonder how he could let her do better than he did. Another man will be suitably humbled, his belief that women cannot do high-powered mathematics having been seriously shaken. I do not see that a general theory about these matters is possible. Let me just state that because persons of good moral character are morally autonomous, in the way that I shall explain below, they are better than others in responding appropriately to corrective experiences.

It is clear that the account of a morally defensible view that has been offered is compatible with sharp differences on substantive moral issues. It does not, for instance, settle the issue of whether abortion is right or wrong. But the account is far from empty. For, on the other hand, it entails that American chattel slavery and the extermination of six million Jews must be wrong. Regarding American slavery, we know the following to be true (Genovese 1974): (i) some slave masters kept black women as mistresses; (ii) upon occasion the wives of some masters were jealous of some black female slaves; (iii) slaves cared for and suckled the children of whites; (iv) sexual liaisons between slave master and female slave sometimes resulted in fertile offspring; and (v) slaves were known to be speakers of the language. From these scientific—as in the case of (iv)—and sociological considerations, it is utterly implausible to suppose that slave masters could have truly believed that blacks were anything but full-fledged human beings, or that anyone could come to believe this. Hence, any moral view that made the practice of chattel slavery a part of the right is unacceptable by the account given of a morally defensible view. The same is true of any moral view that has it that Jews might be or have been deserving of genocide; for we know that there are no considerations available now or at any other time that could warrant anyone's holding such a view.

It is in light of the foregoing considerations that we must view the differences between Socrates, Lincoln, and King concerning slavery. Their points of reflective departure were radically different. In view of Socrates' life circumstances and moral vantage point, it would be absurd to blame him for not reasoning about slavery in the way that King did, though it would have been very nice if he had; and in view of King's life circumstances and moral vantage point, it would have been inexcusable had he reasoned about slavery in the way that Socrates did. That is, it would have been inexcusable for King to accept any form of slavery. Although Socrates was quite accepting of slavery, he did not think it natural that the slaves should be black. Moreover, he did not hold that, as a matter of principle, a person who was a slave lacked the intellectual and moral wherewithal of a free person.[7] The judgment that Lincoln was a person of tremendous moral character rides primarily upon one's interpretation of his performance as president of the United States during the conflict between Northern and Southern states over the issue of slavery. It would seem, or so the myth would have it, that Lincoln masterfully rose above his own personal beliefs and considered the good of the nation as if he were an ideal observer standing between the present and the future United States. This is most commendable given a few assumptions. One is that among his constitutive beliefs was certainly the belief that blacks were naturally inferior to whites. Another is that the justification of chattel slavery was erroneously thought to be a natural consequence of this view of blacks—erroneous because from the fact that one group is morally or intellectually superior to another, it hardly follows that the superior group is justified in enslaving the inferior —and that it is in light of this assumption that Lincoln had to consider the issue of chattel slavery. Lincoln, then, did the astounding thing of seriously questioning—indeed, agonizing over—the justification of slavery, although he continued to believe that blacks were inferior to whites. He is to be commended for having the wherewithal to separate these two issues in a moral climate that invariably ran them together.[8]

The discussion of the preceding paragraph is consistent with the observation that, given (i)–(iv) above, it was not possible for anyone to believe that blacks were less than full-fledged human beings. It will be remembered that slavery did not just deny that blacks were

[7] I am indebted here to Kraut (1984).

[8] Charles G. Finney, an Oberlin College president (1851–1866), saw no difficulty in opposing slavery on religious grounds but favoring racial social segregation. See Horton (1985). I am grateful to Anthony Marshall for bringing this article to my attention. To see just how much credit Lincoln deserves for making this distinction, recall that many people (whites and blacks alike) objected to Arthur Jensen's work (1969), which purported to show that blacks were inferior to whites because on the average blacks scored lower than whites on IQ tests, as if it followed from these results that vicious discrimination against blacks was thereby justified. No such justification followed, since no one was proposing to discriminate against whites with below-average scores, which were no better than the average scores of blacks. I am much indebted to Norman Care for discussions about Lincoln.

as intellectually capable as whites; it denied that blacks were human beings. By abolishing slavery, the Thirteenth Amendment declared that blacks were no longer three-fifths persons; it did not speak to their intellectual powers. Whatever people may have been justified in believing about the intellectual abilities of blacks, they were never, given (i)–(iv), justified in believing that blacks were less than full-fledged human beings.

I have said that the defining characteristic of persons of good moral character is the defensibility of their moral views. But given how this idea has been developed, it is clear that another defining feature of persons of good moral character is that they have an altruistic nature, as I shall say. Aristotle remarked that the virtuous person is one who does the right thing, at the right time, in the right manner, toward the right objects, and so on (*Nicomachean Ethics* 1106b20). As we shall see, having an altruistic nature goes a long way toward explaining why this is so. The claim that persons have an altruistic nature is not to be understood as just so much hand waving; I shall offer a sustained defense of it in Chapter 2.

Another defining feature of persons of good moral character is that they are morally autonomous. I shall bring out what is meant here by contrasting the morally autonomous with the morally nonautonomous. While there are many variations on the theme, the heart of the difference between the morally autonomous and the morally non-autonomous can be put as follows.[9] For the former, correct behavior is defined by a decision of conscience in accordance with self-chosen ethical principles that, at the very least, satisfy logical comprehensiveness, universality, and consistency. The morally autonomous are very much concerned to do what is right for the right reasons. By this, I mean the following: In addition to wanting to believe and do what is

[9] As should be obvious to anyone familiar with Kohlberg's writings (1981), my debt to him here is enormous. While I do not accept his account of moral development, I believe that his characterization of the difference between stage 4 and stage 6 persons goes as far as any discussion in giving us a handle on the difference between the morally autonomous and the morally nonautonomous. See Kohlberg (1971, 1973). See especially the appendix to Kohlberg (1981), which contains Kohlberg's six stages of moral judgment. One reading of Gilligan (1982) is that there is more to moral development than being morally autonomous. I do not take issue with her, as my discussion of friendship (see, especially, Sections 12 and 13) will make evident. Again, I have profited from K. Baier (1974).

morally right, it matters greatly to them that they can grasp why their moral views and behavior are defensible. Thus, it is very important to them that they themselves are able to furnish justificatory reasons for their moral views (and moral behavior [I shall not always bother to make this explicit]); hence, neither appeals to numbers nor arguments from authority suffice to settle moral matters with them. The actions of the morally autonomous stem from a deep conviction concerning the rightness of what they do, and that conviction is not tied to obedience to the authority of another. It is in this respect that they are morally independent in thought and action.

By contrast, the very opposite of these claims holds true for the morally nonautonomous. For them, right behavior consists in doing one's duty, showing respect for authority, and maintaining the given social order. Their moral views are strongly influenced by social institutions. Indeed, they are not prepared to put too much distance between their own moral views and those of their fellow citizens (or the group of individuals with whom they identify). In fact, the morally nonautonomous are quite concerned that their own moral views meet with social approval; accordingly, they are prepared to alter them in the face of widespread disapproval. The morally nonautonomous are concerned minimally, if at all, with being able to offer justificatory reasons for their moral views and behavior. In other words, although the morally nonautonomous may be very much concerned with believing and doing what is right, they are unlike the morally autonomous in being relatively unconcerned with doing what is right for the right reasons, where this notion is understood in the way that I have explicated it above. A paradigmatic example of a morally nonautonomous person thus understood would be the deeply religious individual who, on moral matters, uncritically accepts the teaching of his religion. In fact, if such a person is a strict fundamentalist, for instance, he may very well pride himself on accepting uncritically his clergy's biblical interpretations.

Unlike the morally nonautonomous, the morally autonomous critically examine their own moral views from time to time and, of their own accord, revise them in light of newly perceived weaknesses and strengths. This is why their moral views evolve in the absence of a change in the prevailing moral attitudes of society. This observation also helps us to understand how it is possible for both the morally autonomous and the morally nonautonomous to have the same points of departure and yet come to think in radically different ways about various moral issues. Everyone's moral views are influenced by social institutions. It is just that whereas the morally autonomous are prepared to question and examine critically their points of departure, the morally nonautonomous are not.

Needless to say, the idea is not that, as a matter of principle, the morally autonomous hold moral views that differ from those that are widely shared. After all, there are some widely shared beliefs that are surely right, such as that the wanton killing of innocent persons is morally opprobrious. Rather, the point is that because the morally autonomous critically examine their moral views, their moral views evolve as reflection reveals the need for further refinement or revision; in contrast, because the morally nonautonomous do not critically examine their moral views, they invariably fail to see where refinement or revision is in order.

At this juncture, I should like to bring out the importance of one distinction that I have drawn between the morally autonomous and the morally nonautonomous, which is that the moral convictions of the former are not tied to obedience to authority. Religious fundamentalists are often impervious to widespread public opinion. For instance, some believe that dancing and attending the cinema (regardless of the nature of the movie) are morally objectionable because they are sins; and they believe these things although the overwhelming majority of their fellow citizens society think such beliefs patently absurd. So, in light of what has been said, it might seem that these individuals have a claim to being morally autonomous if any do. But not so.

The reason for this is not just that such individuals uncritically accept the teachings of their church, but also that their steadfastness in their convictions owes its existence to, first, their belief that God requires such behavior of them and, second, their belief that disobedience to God will result in eternal damnation. In the final analysis, then, fear of divine punishment is the primary reason why fundamentalists adhere to their convictions in the face of widespread rejection of them. Their commitment to their views is underwritten by fear of authority.

The case of strict fundamentalists shows that the mark of the morally autonomous cannot be steadfastness alone. The explanation for why a person stands her ground is of the utmost importance.

Our discussion of the difference between the morally autonomous and the morally nonautonomous points up an inadequacy in our taxonomy of the moral character of persons. Roughly speaking, persons are said to have a saintly (or heroic), a good (but not saintly), a bad (but not evil), or an evil moral character, with each category naturally admitting of gradations, where the assessment is a function of both a person's moral behavior and his good will. The taxonomy does not acknowledge any fundamentally important differences among persons of good moral character. But as the preceding discussion reveals, at least one important difference needs to be singled out, namely, the distinction between morally autonomous and morally nonautonomous persons of good moral character. With this difference in mind, I propose to expand our taxonomy of moral character in the following way. Let us say that persons in the former category have an anchored or virtuous moral character and those in the latter category have a good but unanchored moral character. A person has an anchored moral character if (and only if) he has a good moral character and is morally autonomous. I shall expound upon this distinction in what follows.

(I should prefer to use only the word *anchored*, but I suspect ordinary usage will not be very accommodating in this regard; hence, for the sake of clarity—especially later in the text—my use of the word *virtuous*. I have argued that morally autonomous persons of good moral character are morally better than morally nonautonomous persons of good moral character. And the connotations of "virtuous" are such that to be virtuous is to be better than good. While "virtuous" has no adjectival parallel to the word *unanchored*, one can say that something —a performance, for instance—was a good but not a virtuoso exhibition. Further, a display of virtuosity means a display of great technical skill. So, with regards to moral character, I shall either speak this way or use the word *anchored*. There would seem to be sufficient precedent in ordinary language for this usage.)

There is all the difference in the world between, on the one hand, the person who desires to do what is right and who uncritically accepts his religious leader's teachings in the belief that the leader has a proper understanding of moral matters and, on the other, the person who has no desire to do what is right, but does what is said to be right in order to enhance his public image, to avoid guilt feelings, to escape punishment, or whatever. In a very straightforward sense the former clearly does have a good moral character, though he is not morally autonomous, whereas the latter does not. However, the morally autonomous person who is also morally good exhibits a very important moral excellence, which is not to be found in the life of the merely morally good. The life of the person who is both morally good and morally autonomous exhibits greater moral depth, if you will, precisely because the person has a greater understanding of why he subscribes to particular views; and this understanding, in turn, enhances the person's commitment to those views.[10] His moral character is anchored by an understanding of why his moral views are defensible in a way that the moral character of the morally nonautonomous person is not, and cannot be, anchored by his moral views, since it is more on the strength of authority than understanding that the morally nonautonomous individual subscribes to a given set of moral views.

Notice that I do not deny that the morally nonautonomous can be deeply committed to their moral views. The contention, rather, is that their commitment is not born of a depth of understanding. This is because the morally nonautonomous person is like someone who, having memorized all the solutions to a mathematics exercise, is able to give the correct answer when questioned but does not grasp *why* in each case the given answer is the correct one.

To exploit this analogy a bit, it is clear that a person who does understand why her answers are correct has a better grasp of mathematics than one who lacks this understanding. And this would mean that the former is more likely than the latter to better understand new problems in mathematics. In particular, she will have a better sense of how to approach them. Accordingly, in this discipline her grasp of previous problems will serve as something of a beacon in hitherto uncharted waters. Likewise I maintain that in the realm of morality, the understanding of one's moral behavior that comes with being reflective constitutes a beacon in the face of new moral experiences. For how we respond to any new situation, moral or otherwise, is directly a function of the understanding that we can bring to bear upon it.

As was noted earlier, tradition has it that Socrates, Abraham Lincoln, and Martin Luther King, Jr., are exemplars of good moral char-

---

[10] Cf. MacIntyre (1981): "The educated moral agent must of course know what he is doing when he judges or acts virtuously" (p. 140).

acter. This is so because each is regarded as having an anchored moral character: not only were they morally good, but, according to tradition, they were also morally autonomous.

It should be obvious that a person can be morally autonomous, and so have an anchored moral character, only insofar as she is proficient at moral deliberation; otherwise, her confidence in the defensibility of her moral convictions would be unwarranted, especially when they are at odds with prevailing moral sentiments. After all, the mark of the morally autonomous is not that they are intransigent, but that they are independent in their thinking about moral matters. And a person who held to his moral convictions in the face of widespread opinion that they were wrong, though he could not defend them in the least, would be displaying sheer recklessness of mind rather than independence of moral thought.

Now, proficiency at moral deliberation does not come easy. To put the matter most simply, moral deliberation involves the application of general principles to specific instances. We deliberate about which general principles are applicable to the situation at hand, how much weight each should receive, what exceptions the principles admit of, whether we have an exception to any of the relevant principles in the case at hand, and so on. There is hardly anything like a recognizable series of steps that one can follow in order to accomplish this. And on the assumption that moral deliberation is successful only when it yields a morally defensible answer, it is all too obvious that there is no litmus test for determining whether or not one has arrived at such an answer.[11]

Indeed, one reason why this is so is that moral deliberation is nothing like means-end deliberation, as these two notions are normally understood. For with the typical piece of moral deliberation, it is not supposed that we already know what is the morally right thing to do, and so need only ascertain how to do it; rather, the deliberation is about what *is* the morally right thing to do. What moral deliberation yields is not a way in which to pursue a course of action, but an evaluation of one or more courses of action. For example, if the issue before us is whether we morally ought either to keep our promise to have dinner with an old friend or to comfort a new neighbor whose

---

[11] Here I am much indebted to Burch (1974). See also John M. Cooper's (1975) provocative Aristotelian account of moral deliberation (ch. 1, sec. 5).

house was just burglarized, our deliberations surely will not be about how to *do* either of these things. They will be about which one of these courses of action morality recommends. The point being made here is obscured by the fact that if we are persons of good or anchored moral character, then we do what we conclude to be morally right. But, needless to say, we do not engage in moral deliberation in order to come to the conclusion that we should do what is morally right. Quite the contrary, it is because we are already steadfastly committed to doing what is morally right, and, therefore, have a firm disposition to do so, that we engage in moral deliberation. The fact that moral deliberation is not a species of means-ends deliberation means that we cannot test the adequacy of our moral deliberations using the criteria applicable to means-ends decisions. The ease or difficulty with which a view can be executed is hardly a sign of its moral defensibility.

Although I have made it clear that such moral deliberations involve the application of general principles to particular circumstances, this is not a matter of performing deductions in the logician's sense of the word. Moral deliberation is nothing like this. And even if it were, things would still not be simple: not just because deductions themselves can be quite difficult to perform, but for a rather different reason as well.

There is what we may call the problem of moral opacity.[12] With any moral theory—and I take moral theories to embody a set of principles—there is the problem of recognizing how the moral theory applies to a particular situation and what acting in accordance with the theory amounts to. Consider a moral theory according to which only behavior satisfying the criterion of universalizability counts as acceptable moral behavior (cf. Hare 1963). There still remains the task of arriving at the correct description of our moral circumstances and,

[12] I am much indebted here to Catherine Z. Elgin's (1983) discussion of exemplification in ethics. See also Sabini and Silver (1982, pp. 43–44). As I have explicated it, Aristotle was clearly on to the problem of moral opacity. He writes: "However, we do not blame a man for slightly deviating from the course of goodness, whether he strays toward excess or toward deficiency, but we do blame him if his deviation is great and cannot pass unnoticed. It is not easy to determine by a formula at what point and for how great a divergence a man deserves blame; but this difficulty is, after all, true of all objects of sense perception: determinations of this kind depend upon particular circumstances, and the decision rests with our moral sense" (*Nicomachean Ethics*, Bk. 2, Sec. 9).

hence, the conditions under which we universalize. Or, in the case of a theory that calls for maximizing some end such as happiness, there remains the task of deciding what does that. Or, finally, suppose that right action can be defined in terms of the cardinal moral virtues: kindness, honesty, courage, and so on.[13] Well, it is inarguable that not every act of helping someone constitutes an act of kindness. A person who insists on helping someone who has made it unequivocally clear that she wants no help is hardly being kind. And while honesty, of course, involves telling the truth, there are any number of ways that one can go about doing that; and there is also the question of timing. One can be ruthless in one's truth telling. Not every truth should be told. For example, suppose that a student's term paper is the worst that one has read in thirty years of teaching. Naturally, the student should not be led to believe that he has written a masterpiece. Nevertheless, there is absolutely nothing to be said for telling the student that his is the worst paper of one's career, however true that might be.

In a word, then, it would seem that there is no way of carving up the moral landscape so as to eliminate the problem of moral opacity and thereby make proficiency at moral deliberation something that comes with ease.

The importance of distinguishing between persons of good moral character and persons of anchored moral character is underscored by the foregoing discussion of the nature of moral deliberation. For if anything is incontrovertible, it is that there are morally good people who are not very good at moral deliberation. These are people who are very much concerned to do what is right, but who are either reluc-

---

[13] Adam Smith, in *A Theory of Moral Sentiments*, writes: "The general rules of almost all the virtues are in many respects loose, vague, indeterminate, admit of many exceptions, and require so many modifications that it is scarce possible to regulate our conduct entirely by a regard to them. . . . If your benefactor attended you in your sickness, ought you to attend him in his? Or can you fulfill the obligation of gratitude by making a return of a different kind? And if you ought to attend to him, how long and in what ways ought you to attend to him? It is evident that no general rule can be laid down by which a precise answer can in all cases be given to any of these questions. The differences between his character and yours, his circumstances and yours, may be such that you may be perfectly grateful and justly refuse to attend to him" (III.vi.9).

These words were echoed by George Eliot in *The Mill on the Floss*: "The complexity of our life cannot be totally subsumed under the following and application of general maxims; moral judgments must remain hollow unless they are checked and enlightened by a perceptual reference to the special circumstances that mark the individual lot."

tant or unable to deliberate about moral matters. And, of course, one explanation for such reluctance is that, as we have observed, there is no litmus test for determining whether or not one's moral deliberations have yielded a morally defensible answer. Finding this unsettling, a person might very well prefer to subscribe to the prevailing moral views of his society or to accept uncritically the moral teachings of his religion rather than to deliberate on his own about moral matters. That is, a person might prefer to take comfort in either numbers or authority. Even so, such a person might be very much concerned to do what is morally right.

At this point, a qualification is in order regarding our distinction between morally anchored and morally good persons. I have said that the former are proficient at moral deliberation, whereas the latter are not. But it is possible that a person may be able to perform a task well and yet not be confident in his ability to do so. A person may be *able* to hit a certain high note—that is, his voice range permits it —but he may be without confidence that he can do so. Similarly, a person may be able to reason adequately about moral matters and yet not be confident in his ability.[14] So, while it is true that a morally autonomous person is proficient at moral deliberation, it is not always true that a morally *non*autonomous person is incapable of this proficiency. Nor is it true that if a person has this proficiency, she must be morally autonomous. Among the morally nonautonomous, there are those who lack the ability to reason adequately about moral issues, and those who have this ability but cannot exercise it with confidence. The morally anchored and, hence, the morally autonomous possess this confidence. The independence of their moral thinking is born of it. Having made this refinement, I shall not be much concerned to press into it service. For simplicity's sake, I shall generally employ the unrefined characterization of the difference between the morally autonomous and the morally nonautonomous.

With the distinction between the morally good and the morally

---

[14] Kohlberg (1981) observes: "You have to be cognitively mature to reason morally, but you can be smart and never reason morally" (p. 138). A paragraph later he writes: "Stage 6 [he identifies six stages of moral development] may be the cognitively most advanced morality, but perhaps those *capable* of reasoning that way do not wish to be martyrs like Socrates, Lincoln, or King, and *prefer* to reason at a lower level" (p. 139, emphasis in original).

anchored now before us, I should like to point out that the latter are ✓
exceedingly good monitors of social behavior, both their own and
others'. This should be apparent given much of what has been said. A
person sorely lacking in social monitoring skills could not be morally
autonomous, at least not as I have characterized the idea. What I
called the problem of moral opacity clearly calls for tremendous social
monitoring ability, since the proper display of this or that moral virtue
is very much a function of one's circumstances. In general, successful
altruistic behavior calls for considerable social monitoring skills, since
doing the right thing at the right time, and so on, simply does not
reduce to the application of a finite set of well-defined rules to the
circumstances of life. By contrast, having an altruistic nature, as such,
does not call for great social monitoring skills. Having a profound
desire to help others is perfectly compatible with going about things
in the wrong way, with doing more harm than good. A person who is
generally unable to grasp the subtleties of social interaction could very
well have a most altruistic nature and yet not display much successful
altruistic behavior.

I have identified three salient features of morally anchored persons: they have an altruistic nature, are morally autonomous (and
therefore proficient at moral deliberation), and are excellent at monitoring social behavior. The distinction between the morally good and
the morally anchored makes it clear that with respect to the issue of
moral character, rigorous standards of excellence are being applied.
In fact, it might be thought that the standards are too rigorous precisely because so much significance is attached to powers of reasoning. Succinctly put, the objection might be that too much importance
is attached to powers of reasoning and too little to having an altruistic
nature pure and simple.

The following consideration serves to strengthen this objection.
Some of the most moving displays of altruistic behavior, such as a
child's expression of affection to her parents or a lover's expression of
affection to the beloved, are spontaneous and in no way the product
of any exercise in reasoning. These acts constitute altruistic behavior
at its best, notwithstanding the fact that they are not a product of
some profound reflective act. Indeed, it might very well be argued
that if they did result from such thinking, that would take something
away from the altruistic character of the act (cf. Blum 1980).

This objection is not, I think, well taken. The implicit premise is that altruistic behavior is most purely altruistic when it is spontaneous. But this is to make a sweeping generalization from a very narrow range of altruistic behavior, where the object of the altruistic behavior (one's parents or beloved) is well identified and what counts as altruistic behavior well defined and, moreover, the nature of the relationship serves to explain, at least in large measure, the altruistic behavior of the person in question. Finally, in situations of this sort, the altruistic behavior usually does not, and is not meant to, speak to some important material need (such as food or clothing); rather, it is intended simply as an expression of love. Obviously enough, it is easy to be spontaneous in one's displays of altruism in cases of this sort. However, it should be just as obvious that cases of this sort are limited to relationships between family members, lovers, and friends —familiar relationships, as we may call them. While it is true that there are many familiar relationships in the world, most of us do not bear a familiar relationship to most other people. And being altruistic toward a person outside such a relationship is an entirely different matter.

It is in the context of nonfamiliar relationships, then, that powers of reasoning become important to being altruistic. For surely, being altruistic to the right person, at the right time, and in the right manner is anything but easy in nonfamiliar relationships, at least when we move beyond well-defined cases of eliminating imminent danger, such as saving a drowning person. Our earlier remarks about being kind bear out this point. People do not always appreciate assistance even when it would seem to be obvious that they need it. Or one's assistance can be disdained if one's altruistic motivations for providing it are not made clear. This latter point no doubt derives much of its force from the fact that not all motivations for performing a specific altruistic action are themselves morally commendable. This is the case, for example, when a man's only motivation for helping a woman who enquires whether he has solved the quadratic equation is that he believes (wrongly) that women are not the intellectual equal of men, or when an individual's motivation for helping a handicapped person is not respect but pity.

It is undoubtedly a good thing to help people, but our motivations are of the utmost importance both morally and in terms of how others feel about our providing them with assistance. And communicating to people that our motivations are morally commendable can require quite subtle behavior and thus considerable reasoning.

The point of these remarks has not been to deny that having an altruistic nature is itself a good thing. Surely it is. However, from this it in no way follows that being altruistic in one's behavior is a simple matter—so simple, in fact, that it requires no thought. I have tried to make clear that except in familiar relationships or instances when a person is in imminent danger, this is hardly the case. It turns out, surprisingly perhaps, that being altruistic often calls for considerable thought. The unthinking may very well have their hearts in the right place; but when it comes to displaying the right behavior in complex moral situations, they will often fall short of the mark. Accordingly, it is a mistake to think that powers of reasoning are peripheral to being altruistic.

The difference between being a morally good person and a morally anchored person underscores what has just been said. Because the latter are more reflective, they will, other things equal, be better at displaying altruistic behavior, since that is, as I have tried to show, very much a matter of doing the right thing, at the right time, in the right manner, and so on. There can be no doubt that powers of reasoning are important to being a morally anchored person. This is not because spontaneity of good will is unimportant. Nor is it because good will without reasoning is empty. Nor, again, is it because being a morally good person is a matter of being able to ingeniously apply some principle, such as the categorical imperative, to the circumstances of life. Rather, it is because responding adequately to the complexity of life's circumstances demands considerable reasoning.

However, although I have attached considerable importance to being able to reason well, at no point have I claimed that this capacity is more important than having an altruistic nature. I do not hold that if we had to choose between good will and powers of reasoning, then the cause of morality would be best served if we held on to the latter and gave up the former. On the contrary, if anything, I imagine that deliberative powers without good will would serve neither human beings nor morality well at all. This is so, at any rate, if, as Hume observed, it is not contrary to reason for a person to prefer the destruction of the whole world to the scratching of his finger (*A Treatise of Human Nature*, ii.iii.iii).

This work, then, gives expression to the Kantian insight that there is nothing that can be regarded as wholly good save a good will, and Hume's insight that reason is the slave of the passions.[15] However, I shall not be concerned to develop the insight of either in accordance with the theoretical machinery of their views. It may very well be that what I shall say can, at various points, be made to square with their views. But the success of this project is not to be measured by the extent to which such a fit is achieved.

2. Moral Theory and Altruistic Motivations

We can bring into sharper focus the aims of this essay by looking briefly at the contemporary debate between neo-Kantians and Humeans with regard to the motivation of persons to act in accordance with the requirements of an altruistic morality.[16] The former hold a reason-based conception of motivation; the latter, a desire-based conception. Neo-Kantians maintain that it is possible for a person to have a moral reason to perform an action required by altruistic morality, and for that reason to be efficacious, in and of itself, in motivating the individual to act, where the desires of the person do not in any way figure into the explanation of the behavior in question (Darwall 1983). Humeans will accept nothing of the kind; they insist that desires, and only desires, motivate a person to act.

Obviously, if neo-Kantians are right, then when it comes to acting in accordance with the requirements of an altruistic morality, it matters not whether humans are by nature essentially self-interested

---

[15] Respectively, *The Foundations of the Metaphysics of Morals* and *A Treatise of Human Nature*.

[16] Kant's is undoubtedly the most distinguished of the pure reasons-based accounts of motivations. The latest defender is Darwall (1983). Recent defenders of a desire-based account of motivations include Foot (1972) and Williams (1980). It is tempting to place Rawls in the former camp, but I believe that this temptation should be resisted. This way of viewing Rawls (1971) is incompatible with what he says in part 3 of *A Theory of Justice* and, in particular, with what he says concerning egoists. He writes: "Given their aims and wants and the peculiarities of their nature, the thin account of the good does not define reasons sufficient for them to maintain this regulative sentiment [of justice]. It has been argued that to these individuals one cannot truthfully recommend justice as a virtue. And this is surely correct, assuming such a recommendation to imply that rational grounds (identified by the thin theory) counsel this course for them as individuals" (p. 575).

(egoistic) or altruistic in their desires—or neither, since on this view reasons can motivate independently of desires. Nor, if altruistic desires should turn out to be characteristic of the human make-up, does it matter that such desires are readily extinguishable, since, again, reasons can motivate people independently. In short, the neo-Kantian view of moral motivation speaks to two issues at once, namely, the content of our desires and their entrenchedness. For, on this view, it matters not whether we have entrenched self-interested desires or fleeting altruistic ones. Moral motivation is possible all the same. On the neo-Kantian view the morally anchored person is, among other things, one whose rational self is such that moral reasons are capable of moving her to do the right thing (at least often enough).

On the other hand, if Humeans are right, then of course it matters greatly whether humans are by nature essentially self-interested (egoistic) or altruistic in their desires, or neither. If acting in accordance with an altruistic morality is to be in keeping with our human nature—indeed, is an activity whereby our human nature is realized—then we must be sufficiently altruistic in nature. And the morally good person is, among other things, one whose altruistic nature is sufficiently realized.

I am not especially concerned to show that neo-Kantians are wrong in their view of motivation, though I very much believe that they are, and I shall speak to that briefly. The more interesting question for our purposes is this: What follows if they are wrong? This is a very serious question because the evidence that they are right would not seem to be forthcoming. And it is certainly worth knowing that not all is lost if they are wrong. My answer is that a satisfactory account of human nature can be proffered from which it follows neither that the desires that characterize our motivational structure are essentially self-interested nor that such desires are fleeting if they should be altruistic. I believe that such an account can be gotten from a proper rendering of evolutionary theory. Neo-Kantians might object here that moral motivations that are grounded in human nature are neither necessary nor inescapable. The idea here is that desires cannot suffice as the springs of moral motivation, either because it is a contingent feature of our lives that we have the desires we have, even if they are universal, or because we are left without a rational basis for saying that we should have one set of desires as opposed to another.

As to the first prong of the objection, I believe that it rests on an ambiguity between something's being necessary, in this case a desire, and its being fleeting. That which is not necessary is not, on that account alone, fleeting. This is shown by the existence of the human species itself. If evolutionary theory is both sound and suffices to explain our existence, then it follows that our being the way that we are is not a matter of necessity, since it is very much a contingent truth that human evolution has taken its present course. Yet it is manifestly clear that there is nothing fleeting about our being the way that we are. The contingent can be quite resistant to change.

As to the second prong of the objection, it succeeds in part only if human beings are sufficiently plastic that they cannot be said to possess a human nature according to which some desires and not others are appropriate to humans. If human beings are a tabula rasa, especially with respect to desires, and thus any desire a person might have is a natural desire, then there is surely a point to the second prong of the objection. But there is no reason to suppose that human nature is so plastic in this regard, and evolutionary theory surely does not support this view.[17] As we shall see below (Section 3), the capacity to love, and so to desire the well-being of another, is very much a part of human nature. It is no more natural for a human being to live without any regard for the well-being of another than it is for him to live without wanting to advance his self-interests at least some of the time.

If I have understood correctly, there are two separate issues fueling the reservations of the reason-based theorists (neo-Kantians) about a desire-based (Humean) conception of moral motivations. One is whether there is anything that can properly be called human nature, or whether a proper characterization of it can be rendered if, in fact, there is. The other is that if humans do have a human nature, then it is essentially a Hobbesean self-interested one. The Humean conception simply tells us that desires, and nothing but desires, can motivate a person to act. Thus, it is formally compatible with persons' being motivated by anything from the noblest to the basest of desires, and

---

[17] See Midgley (1978). At one point she writes: "The very idea that anything so complex as a human being could be totally plastic and structureless is unintelligible" (p. 19). Cf. MacIntyre (1981): "Yet moral arguments within the classical, Aristotelian tradition—whether in its Greek or its medieval versions—involve at least one central functional concept, the concept of man understood as having an essential nature and an essential purpose or function" (p. 56).

with these desires' being as fleeting as the moments or as permanent as the ages. So understood, a Humean conception of the motivation structure of persons is compatible with a Hobbesean self-interested view of the content and entrenchedness of desires. The idea that human nature does not provide us with a vantage point from which to assess rationally at least some of our desires makes sense only if one holds either that we have no human nature to speak of or that, if we do, we are unable to give it adequate characterization. I believe that this skepticism is unwarranted—that we have a human nature, and that a rich characterization of it can be given. Moreover, I believe that our human nature is congruent with an altruistic conception of morality. The contribution of this project to the study of moral character will lie, I hope, in making good these claims, especially the latter one. As I have noted, one difficulty with a desire-based conception of moral motivations is that we are at the mercy of our desires when it comes to whether or not we act morally. If the arguments I hope to make are sound, then being at the mercy of some of our desires is not such a bad thing, after all. This project is a response to neo-Kantian skepticism, and on both accounts.

Still, it must be admitted that from none of this does it follow that altruistic motivations have an inescapable grip upon us. However, if altruistic motivations are a deep part of our human nature and if, because of this, such motivations are essential to the full realization of human beings as we understand them, then what should follow is this: In some way or another, individuals who do not have their altruistic motivations manifestly realized in their lives flourish less than those who do. I want to make good this claim in Chapter Seven. For, as I shall endeavor to show, self-knowledge is one of the fruits of the moral life.

If the neo-Kantians cannot make their case and, what is more, it turns out that altruistic motivations are not a deep feature of our human nature, then acting in accordance with the requirements of an altruistic morality could scarcely be something we could readily or easily do. Morality would surely be a burden to us. Indeed, if such were the case, our human nature itself might be the excuse for our immorality—if, that is, our human nature should turn out to be radically antithetical to the requirements of altruistic morality. This means, obviously, that I accept the precept that ought implies can (cf. Hare 1963, ch. 4). Given a suitable characterization of what we can and cannot do, we cannot be required to do what we cannot do, nor, a fortiori, can we be blamed for not doing what we cannot do.

Supposed counterexamples to the precept that ought implies can —namely, that sometimes we morally ought to do what we cannot do—are not convincing. Consider. There is a remarkably simple explanation for why people cannot perform some tasks. It is that the tasks are beyond the reach of human powers, that is, powers characteristic of the biological species called *Homo sapiens*. This is why no one can (completely unaided) leap tall buildings with a single bound, run faster than a speeding locomotive, swim on the bottom of the ocean floor, and so on. This is also why no one can avoid being somewhat affected by his parental upbringing, or feeling some rancor and resentment if he believes that he has been continually wronged by others, especially those whom he has loved and trusted (Strawson 1962). A moral theory requiring that we be able to do any or all of these things would be unsatisfactory on that account alone. This is not because it would not be a wonderful thing if we could, but because in no way could we be reasonably expected to measure up to the theory and, therefore, our not doing so could not be viewed as a moral failing on our part. It is no accident that there has never been a moral theory that requires a person to save another by outrunning a speeding locomotive, as such a theory would be immediately dismissed as untenable.

(A) There is what a person cannot do because his specific natural endowments prevent it (as with a person born blind who cannot be proficient at driving), or because he has been rendered permanently unable to do it through no fault of his own (as in the case of a person who cannot walk because he was paralyzed from the waist down by a stray bullet). (B) There is what a person cannot do because he is temporarily unable to do it, either (i) because he voluntarily performed a prior action (as with a person who is too intoxicated to walk a straight line) or (ii) because something happened to him (as in the case of the person who has been knocked unconscious) or because he involuntarily performed an action rendering him unable to do it (as in the case of the person who thought he was consuming a nonalcoholic punch when, in fact, he consumed a quite potent fruit-flavored alcoholic drink). Of course, in some instances of incapacitation (temporary or otherwise) due to involuntary action—depending on how knowledgeable we take the person to be about the matters at hand—we maintain that the person ought to have known better and avoided the action that resulted in his incapacitation. (C) There is what a person cannot do because no human being has the wherewithal to do it—such as leaping tall buildings with a single bound. Finally, (D) there is what some person might be able to do, but what in general it is not reasonable to expect people to do. For example, it is possible that someone might lead a life completely devoid of any voluntary sexual (including masturbatory) activity, but it is not reasonable to expect this of anyone. Again, it is possible, but highly improbable, that a person should go through life without ever experiencing shame. (C) and (D) define what we may call the range of human powers; (A) and, especially, (B) are rough guidelines for when a person is *not* accountable for the permanent or temporary curtailment of this range in his own case. This range, while hardly immutable and well defined throughout, is fixed enough and clear enough to form the backdrop against which human behavior can be assessed with respect to matters of responsibility and culpability. That there is this range is readily conceded when it comes to physical abilities and limitations. But it is surely there, as well, in terms of our psychological abilities and limitations. As I have noted, no one can help but be affected by her or his parental upbringing. This fact is due to our psychological make-up, and not our physical constitution as such. For good or ill, all children bear the imprint of their parental upbringing regardless of their physical make-up. Imagine a teenager who is not deeply saddened by the simultaneous deaths of his very loving parents. This response would not be just a statistical oddity, like the precocity of a two-year-old, which we might attribute simply to a fortuitous combination of genes. Rather, we would suppose that in some profound way the teenager was not well adjusted, as his behavior would be contrary to our understanding of human nature.

The precept that ought implies can should be seen as circumscribed by the range of human powers as specified by (C) and (D) above, plus any further limitations on that range, in the case of a particular individual, as specified by (A). Presumably, there will always be further limitations, since no one can do all that humans can do. When understood in this way, the precept would seem to be immune to counterexamples. If a given act, such as leaping unassisted over a tall building, is unequivocally beyond the range of human powers, then no sense can be made of the idea that a person morally ought to do it; nor, in any event, can any sense be made of holding a person responsible or accountable or blameworthy for not doing so. I do not suppose that a complete account of the powers of *Homo sapiens* is available, but only that we have a rich enough conception of what these powers come to that we can assess whether or not there is congruence between our human nature and altruistic morality. It is worth mentioning that (C) and (D) might also serve to fix our intuitions concerning the saintly or heroic person. The former, such as Mother Teresa, lives a life the altruism of which, at the very least, is widely regarded to be beyond what can be reasonably asked of a person; the latter performs an action or series of actions that is likewise regarded.

My aim in the preceding remarks has been to show in an intuitive way that the precept that ought implies can is hardly an indefensible view. Because I subscribe to this precept (and I have suggested that everyone does, at least implicitly), I believe that it makes no sense to suppose that human beings with an essentially self-interested motivational structure can act in accordance with the requirements of an altruistic moral theory (Gauthier 1986). Thus, I hold that we must reject either an altruistic conception of morality or the view that the motivational structure of human beings is essentially self-interested. Being ineluctably drawn to the former, I reject the latter.

As I have said, I do not believe that neo-Kantians can make a reasonable case for their view that reason alone can motivate a person to act in accordance with the requirements of altruistic morality. In a word, here is why. It would appear to be a consequence of their view that no fully informed and fully rational creature can make an immoral choice; and this seems contrary to the facts. The manifestly wicked person is not a moral fiction (Milo 1984). Neo-Kantians might explain such a choice by pointing to problems of weakness of will or some such thing. But none of this seems to be convincing. Immoral people can act with extraordinarily firm resolve, as accounts of the moral atrocities committed by the Nazis leave no room to doubt. Or, neo-Kantians might attempt to account for this sort of immoral behavior by arguing that social upbringing and other factors can bear upon how receptive persons are to moral reasons. They might argue that just as one has to be in the proper state of mental health to be moved by reasons for behaving in certain ways, one has to be in the proper frame of mind to be moved by moral reasons. But surely this is to concede too much. For if one has to be in the proper frame of mind, then it follows that moral reasons are not sufficient in and of themselves to motivate persons to do what is morally right. However, it is precisely the claim that moral reasons are so capable of moving people that is the distinctive feature of the neo-Kantian position.

In accounting for immoral behavior, the Humean view does considerably better. Quite simply, this view tells us that if altruistic motivations are not sufficiently realized in a person's life, then he will not be disposed to act in accordance with the requirements of an altruistic morality. Thus, in this regard the Humean view, unlike the neo-Kantian one, places a premium upon moral training and the factors of our social environment that would give rise to and sustain our altruistic motivations.[18] And for this very reason it is a more intuitive view. Traditionally, moral training refers to the practices and forms of behavior the very point of which is to ensure that individuals acquire a firm disposition—that is, become firmly motivated to act in the morally appropriate ways. The value of moral training is thought to lie in the fact that precisely what it delivers is sufficient motivation to act morally. Thus, on the Humean view, it is neither an accident nor a mystery that a person sufficiently bereft of moral training is not moved by moral considerations, since the power of these considerations to move is deemed to be contingent upon an individual's receptiveness to them, which, in turn, is maintained to be a function of the effectiveness of his moral training.

Moral training speaks to the importance of shaping our desires and habits very early in our lives. It embodies the view that moral motivation cannot be sustained independently of the desires and habits that are constitutive of a person's life and self-concept (Sections 22, 23). Given the central place that moral training has in our lives and the view that it embodies, we should hope that a non-Kantian argument for the possibility of altruism, and thus moral motivation, can be made out. Such an argument will have a most secure foundation if it is grounded in our biological make-up. This is our point of departure in the following chapter.

---

[18] No one could be clearer about the importance of moral training than Aristotle, who maintained that we acquire the disposition characteristic of virtue by first merely performing the sorts of acts that are characteristic of that virtue. He wrote: "Moral virtue comes about as a result of habit" (*Nicomachean Ethics*, b. 2 , Sec. 1).

CHAPTER TWO

The Biological Basis of Altruism

Love is surely a form of altruism. Morality can be grafted upon the natural affection of parental love. The capacity to love is essential not just to the survival but to the very flourishing of the human species. Parental love, in particular, is indisputably important to the flourishing of the child; and this love, I argue, has been selected for. With an eye toward showing its relevance to morality, an account of the nature of parental love is offered. This kind of love is characterized as transparent, which I contrast with opaque love. On the view being presented, then, morality has biological foundations. Understandably, there is a reluctance to view morality in this way. This reluctance stems from two sources. One is the threat of biological determinism. The other is the fear that if morality is given biological underpinnings, then the altruism is taken out of morality, and altruism thus becomes a mere illusion rather than a reality. For the idea of genes maximizing their own numbers in the gene pool is at the heart of sociobiological explanations; and, prima facie, it would not seem that altruism can be squared with a maximizing notion of this sort. While I shall address the first concern briefly, my primary aim in this chapter will be to show that biology is not incompatible with an altruistic morality. I begin, though, with a few remarks concerning the former. Needless to say, I cannot hope to settle the issue of biological determinism here. However, I hope to dispel a few worries.

3. Morality and Sociobiology

Crudely put, biological determinism is the view that most, if not all, aspects of human behavior are controlled or, at any rate, strongly influenced by our genetic make-up. We may think of this as thoroughgoing biological determinism. That some aspects of human behavior are so influenced is too obvious for words. What should be noted, though, is this: From the fact that some aspects of a given kind of human activity may be biologically determined, it is a mistake to infer that all aspects of that activity are biologically determined; hence, it is a mistake to invoke thoroughgoing biological determinism with respect to that activity. For example, consider the sex drive, the presence of which everyone regards as purely a matter of biological determination. This drive is known for manifesting itself, upon occasion, quite independently of our wishes. Still, by no stretch of the imagination does it follow that people have no choice as to when or why or whether they engage in sexual activity. When people do so clearly depends upon, inter alia, tastes, preferences, and opportunity. Reasons abound for why people engage in or refrain from sexual activity: personal ones (for example, to get even or to prove themselves), religious ones, political ones, and so on. Finally, a person may opt for celibacy and thus avoid sexual activity with others entirely.

Obviously enough, none of this entails that thoroughgoing biological determinism does not obtain. But on the strength of the foregoing considerations, what can be said with complete confidence is this: We have no reason to suppose that just because some aspects of a given human activity are biologically determined, then thoroughgoing biological determinism obtains with respect to that activity. For in view of what we now know, it is clear that a person would be maintaining a false view if he held that since the sex drive is biologically determined, all sexual activity is.

Now, I have not addressed, and shall not address, the general problem of determinism—namely, whether human action is free or determined. And, of course, to diffuse the threat of biological determinism is not in any way to resolve the general problem of determinism. But given our concerns, that should not be necessary. The issue for us is whether we straightaway have an objection to morality's having biological foundations on the grounds that thoroughgoing biological determinism holds, as I have developed this notion. It suffices for our purposes, then, if it can be shown that we do not. To put the matter another way, it might be thought that taking a biological approach to morality thereby makes one especially susceptible to the difficulties of thoroughgoing determinism. As we have seen, however, this surmise is mistaken.

I turn now to the second reason why people are reluctant to allow that morality can have biological foundations, namely, that the altruism is taken out of morality, so that seemingly altruistic acts are, in the final analysis, really selfish ones. It is not difficult to see how one might come to think this. On a typical reading of a sociobiological account of human behavior, the ultimate motivating force behind each human being's behavior is the drive to maximize her or his gene pool.[1] All manifestations of altruism are to be thus explained, even parental altruism in human beings, since the sociobiological argument is that parents best maximize their gene pool by caring for their children until the latter are in turn able to have progeny (grandchildren). Yet on the face of it, not only does this explanation for parental altruism seem manifestly false, but it would also seem that altruism toward non-kin does not neatly admit of a sociobiological explanation.

Consider a typical instance of parental love. Two parents hear their five-year-old child screaming desperately. It turns out that the child is being attacked by several vicious dogs. We suppose that if the parents genuinely love the child, then without any regard for their own well-being they will attempt to rescue her. In particular, we suppose that the parents will be motivated to rescue their child simply out of their love for her, and that in no way will a desire to maximize their gene pool figure into an explanation of their attempt. Most parents would surely regard it as the cruelest of statements if someone were to claim that in the last analysis what motivated them to rescue their child was the desire and hope that she would give them grandchildren, thereby contributing to the survival of their (the parents') genes. The problem is that a sociobiological account of human behavior would seem to commit us to saying just that—or so it is objected.

As for altruism toward non-kin, Mother Teresa would seem to be a tremendous embarrassment to the theory. Whatever else is true, her altruistic behavior does not serve her gene pool in any way at all. To be

---

[1] Cf. Dawkins (1976), Trivers (1985), and Wilson (1975).

sure, Mother Teresa represents an extreme display of altruism. Still, it would not seem that less extreme displays of altruism admit neatly of a sociobiological explanation. Consider helping a stranger who has just been robbed, or making a substantial and anonymous donation to charity. Is there any reason whatsoever to suppose that such acts serve the gene pool of the agents who perform them, let alone that people perform such acts with that thought in mind? Surely not.

I believe that with regard to human altruism, a sociobiological explanation of human behavior does not present the sort of difficulties that many have attributed to it. True enough, sociobiologists have not helped matters by describing genes in metaphorical ways, as having intentions, purposes, and the like.[2] But I hope to show that notwithstanding this abuse of language, sociobiology does not take the altruism out of altruism. That is, I hope to show that it allows for genuine altruism.

Let us begin by distinguishing between motive altruism and unwitting altruism, on the one hand, and motive selfishness and unwitting selfishness, on the other. With motive altruism, a benefit is intentionally bestowed upon someone at some cost or risk to oneself without regard to future gain (keeping in mind that simply foregoing a benefit can count as incurring a cost [see Trivers 1971], and that from the standpoint of sociobiological theory, to do something at a risk to oneself is to do something at a cost to oneself). With unwitting altruism, while it is true that someone has benefited from one's behavior (which was at some cost to oneself), the benefit was in no way intended; indeed, unwitting altruism does not make reference to intentions or motives of any sort. Motive altruism is what is generally regarded as genuine altruism. It is the kind of altruism required by altruistic moral theories. Motive selfishness and unwitting selfishness are to be understood in analogous ways with respect to the term selfishness. Thus, motive selfishness is what is generally regarded as genuine selfishness.

---

[2] As the very title of his book, *The Selfish Gene*, might indicate, Dawkins (1976) is quite guilty of this. He writes: "I shall make use of the metaphor of the architect's plans, freely mixing the language of metaphor with the language of the real thing" (p. 23). In his *Ever Since Darwin* (1977), Stephen J. Gould alerts the reader as follows: "I do not mean to attribute conscious will to creatures with such rudimentary brains [ants]. I use such phrases as 'he would rather' only as a convenient shortcut for 'in the course of evolution, males [male ants] who did not behave this way have been placed at a selective disadvantage and gradually eliminated'" (pp. 264–65).

Of significance is that while unwitting altruism entails neither motive nor unwitting selfishness, unwitting altruism is compatible with unwitting selfishness. That is, individual X may gain from having unwittingly benefited individual Y, since benefiting someone at a risk to oneself does not entail a loss to oneself; indeed, it is compatible with a gain. An illustration of this will be given below. The charge that sociobiology takes the altruism out of altruism holds only if what is presented as motive altruism in fact turns out to be motive selfishness. Unwitting selfishness does not take the altruism out of altruism.

Sociobiologists frequently talk about animals (such as calling birds) and insects (such as ants and bees) benefiting others. And the theories of kin selection and reciprocal altruism are currently two of the most basic ways of explaining altruism in species. Roughly speaking, kin selection tells us how natural selection tends to operate upon social groups who interact with a fair degree of frequency; reciprocal altruism tells us how natural selection operates upon individuals with a degree of dependence upon one another, of whom longevity is characteristic, who tend to interact over a reasonably long period of time.[3] The latter is meant to explain altruism between different species and non-kin. With neither, however, does motive altruism turn out to be motive selfishness. Each explains how unwitting altruism might come about as a result of natural selection, and how this unwitting altruism results in unwitting selfishness in that the individual's gene pool is benefited. If so, then the claim that sociobiology takes the altruism out of altruism turns out to be false. A brief discussion of the two theories will render these points more perspicuous.

A most important consequence of the theory of kin selection is that it makes possible a very satisfactory evolutionary account of parental altruism. But even here it is important to realize that the altruism that the theory of kin selection is intended to capture is primarily unwitting altruism rather than motive altruism. The intuitive idea behind the theory of kin selection is this: The degree to which an individual is disposed to help another is directly a function of the degree of genetic relatedness between the two individuals. So, other things equal, we are more disposed to help our siblings than our first cousins, our first cousins than our second cousins, our second than

---

[3] The theory was introduced by W. D. Hamilton (1964): the theory of reciprocal altruism was introduced by Robert L. Trivers (1971). My understanding of the former owes much to Maynard-Smith (1976, 1982).

our third, and so on. Full brothers and sisters, on the one hand, and parents and children, on the other, have the same degree of genetic relatedness, the members of each pair having half of their genes in common. Only identical twins have a greater degree of genetic relatedness, since both have exactly the same set of genes. Other things equal, then, the theory of kin selection tells us that parents should be just as disposed to help their baby siblings as they are to help their own offspring. We rarely have siblings who are completely in our charge and who are the same age as our own offspring, so we rarely feel a conflict between the two.

It is easy to see why the theory of kin selection makes possible a very satisfactory evolutionary account of parental altruism. Given a choice between helping any two creatures, an individual does more to ensure the continuation of his gene pool by helping the one whose gene pool is more in common with his own. The greater the degree of genetic relatedness, the more disposed the individual to ensure the continuation of his own gene pool. In terms of genetic relatedness, the score is tied between an individual's siblings, his own offspring, and his parents. But in terms of who is most likely to need help and where providing help is most likely to promote the continuation of his gene pool, an individual does the best by helping his own offspring. For an individual's gene pool will continue only if there are individuals in the next generation who have genes in common with that pool. Even if the individual's siblings have children, he will still do better to help his own children, since the degree of genetic relatedness between him and his own offspring (which is one-half) will be greater than that between him and his siblings' offspring (which is one-quarter). The exception is when the sibling is an identical twin, in which case the degree of genetic relatedness between him and his twin's children will be the same as that between him and his own children.

Supposing, for the sake of argument, that the theory of kin selection is certainly applicable to human beings, observe that it was not introduced simply to explain altruism, especially parental altruism, in humans.[4] On the contrary, it was intended to explain altruism among

---

[4] See Wilson (1975), pp. 117–20. Gould (1977) writes: "Hamilton's theory [of kin selection] has had stunning success in explaining some persistent biological puzzles in the evolution of social behavior in the Hymenoptera—ants, bees, and wasps. Why has true sociality evolved independently at least eleven times in the Hymenoptera and only

species generally (cf. Bertram 1978). Put another way, the theory was in no way designed to explain the altruistic behavior of only those creatures who can engage in sophisticated computations, as well as have beliefs, about the degree of genetic relatedness of those whom they help. The importance of this observation is that it makes clear that the altruism explained by the theory is unwitting altruism and not motive altruism, and that the selfishness we get is unwitting selfishness and not motive selfishness. The theory in no way implies that parents (kin) are intentionally motivated to sacrifice for their offspring (kin) by the desire to ensure the continuation of their gene pool.

The foregoing remarks hold, mutatis mutandis, for the theory of reciprocal altruism, which (as I said) is meant to explain altruism between different species and non-kin. We are not to suppose, for instance, that in issuing a warning call, which jeopardizes its life by making its whereabouts more easily determined by a predator, a calling bird reasons to itself that it is better that it, a single calling bird, should put its life in jeopardy than that the life of its neighboring calling birds should be endangered. We are not to impute intentions of the appropriate sort to a calling bird that gives a warning call. The benefit it bestows by giving a warning call is purely an instance of unwitting altruism, which has come about as a result of natural selection. Fish that clean the gills of an entirely different species of fish constitute an example of reciprocal altruism between species (Trivers 1971). The host fish has its gills cleaned, the cleaning fish obtains a meal. At no point are we to think that the two species—through arbitration or some such thing—have worked out a mutually satisfactory arrangement for finding food and having gills cleaned. In no way is motive altruism supposed. Rather, we have unwitting altruism and unwitting selfishness operating together.

My aim thus far has been to show that when sociobiologists talk about altruism, they generally mean unwitting altruism and unwitting selfishness as opposed to motive altruism and motive selfishness. While to show this is not, I realize, to show that sociobiology under-

---

once among other insects (the termites)? Why are sterile worker castes always female in the Hymenoptera, but both male and female in termites? The answer seems to lie in the workings of kin selection within the unusual genetic system of the Hymenoptera" (p. 263). With great caution, Gould allows that the theory may be able to explain unwitting altruism among humans (p. 265).

writes motive altruism, it is very much a step in that direction. For, since neither makes reference to motives or intentions of any sort—in particular, motive selfishness—it then follows that achieving motive altruism is not a matter of going against the biological grain of motive selfishness. But, as I shall now try to show in what follows, a very persuasive case can be made for the strong claim that sociobiology underwrites motive altruism.

To begin with, let us distinguish between what a person desires to do and what as a matter of biological constitution a person is disposed to do. Suppose, for example, that as a matter of biological constitution, the crying of an infant—any infant—automatically invokes altruistic feelings within us. We are spontaneously moved to attend to the child's needs in an affectionate way. And suppose, further, that this is of tremendous evolutionary advantage, since it ensures that we will be moved to care affectionately for our offspring in spite of the physical and emotional costs of doing so. Now, none of this would seem to be an obstacle to adults' displaying motive altruism toward infants. If anything, it is possible that the biological constitution of adults enables them to better carry through with their altruistic intentions toward infants. For adults could desire to behave in a caring and affectionate way toward infants and thus be delighted that they are so constituted biologically. We can want to be, and can take delight in being, constituted in the way that we are.[5] And an act is no less altruistic simply because, given our biological constitution, we are better able to execute our altruistic intentions.

If my presentation of sociobiology and unwitting altruism is sound, then the way in which we are biologically constituted, far from being at odds with motive altruism, better enables us to realize altruistic intentions. This is quite apparent with altruism among kin and with the theory of kin selection. In general, parents care deeply for their children and delight in the fact that they do. (The example that I sketched above with regard to our reactions to crying infants obviously has a foothold in reality.) From the standpoint of evolutionary theory, the theory of kin selection tells us that it pays for us to be biologically constituted so as to be especially concerned about the well-being of our children. Again, we are in general more favorably disposed toward our kin than toward others; and the theory of kin

[5] This way of putting the point owes its inspiration to Frankfurt (1971).

selection tells us that it pays for us to be biologically constituted so as to favor our kin over others.

Let us now look at motive altruism outside of kin relationships, for it is such manifestations of altruism that are especially the concern of the moral point of view. As I have already observed, the theory of reciprocal altruism was introduced to account for various manifestations of altruism outside of kin relationships. With its obvious affinity to contract theory, the idea behind the theory of reciprocal altruism is a familiar one: when individuals frequently interact with one another they are better off cooperating to some extent than not doing so; in particular, everyone is better off with certain altruistic norms than not. For example, given how fragile infants are and how easy it is for them to get in harm's way, society is better off on balance if nearly everyone is moved to attend to the immediate needs of a crying infant, regardless of who the parents of the child are. So, the theory suggests a way of accounting for various altruistic norms among human beings. It is not supposed that individuals actually reason in this way, but only that from the standpoint of natural selection individuals are better off with respect to their gene pool's being maintained if they are disposed to comply with altruistic norms.

Now, the theory posits feelings of guilt and fear of expulsion from group membership as psychological mechanisms that have been selected for because they operate to ensure compliance with the altruistic norms of the group (Trivers 1971). It might be tempting to infer from this that the theory is therefore at odds with motive altruism as the explanation for why individuals comply with the altruistic norms of the group. However, this temptation should be resisted. Of course, if either feelings of guilt or fear of expulsion from the group is the only explanation for why a person follows an altruistic norm, then the person's compliance with the norm can hardly be said to stem from motive altruism. But the theory does not make this claim. To suppose that it does is to confuse an explanation for the way in which certain feelings may operate in our lives with how a person may be motivated to behave.

The thesis that feelings of guilt or fear of expulsion from the group operates to enhance compliance with the altruistic norms of the group does not entail that either of these psychological mechanisms is the only motive a person can have for complying with those norms. This can be easily seen by recalling a previous discussion in this section. It is obvious that the sex drive has been selected for precisely because of the importance of leaving behind progeny. Yet it hardly follows from this that it is only for the sake of leaving behind progeny that individuals are moved to satisfy this drive. Indeed, one need not give any thought at all to the idea.

Surprisingly, perhaps, support for the view that natural selection favors the compliance of human beings with altruistic norms comes from the theory of kin selection itself. The natural parent-offspring relationship among *Homo sapiens* is the longest and most complex among any species. This means that raising offspring to the point where they are able to leave behind progeny is a matter of considerable parental investment for human beings, requiring a great deal of time and energy.[6] In fact, the amount of care and attention that human offspring require is so great that humans would hardly be able to provide these things if the possibility for social cooperation among human beings did not exist. It is not just a morally good thing that human beings can live in harmony and, hence, engage in social cooperation with one another. The amount of care and attention that human offspring require necessitates that humans live this way at least to some extent.

I want to conclude this section with a very different sort of argument for the view that biology allows for genuine altruism among human beings.

It is obvious that human beings do not procreate in the most efficient of ways; enormous energy and time are spent engaging in activities that do not constitute the procreative act but only lead up to it.[7] However pleasurable the rituals (let us say) of sexual activity may be,[8] the fact is that from a strictly procreative perspective, things proceed rather inefficiently. Indeed, in a very straightforward sense, people would have a lot more time and energy (not to mention money) left to attend to other things were sexual intercourse confined strictly to the procreative act. Hence, one might very well ask: How is it that human beings have evolved so that things are not thus confined? That

[6] On the topic of parental investment outside of the human context, see Trivers (1978).

[7] Here and in what follows, I am much indebted to Wilson (1978), ch. 6. I have also profited from discussions with Andrew Manitsky.

[8] Sexual foreplay and involved preparations that are done explicitly or implicitly with sexual intercourse in mind, for example, the intimate dinner or the purchasing of garments.

is, what evolutionary advantage accrues to human beings in virtue of the rituals of sexual intercourse?

One answer that immediately recommends itself is that such rituals have an enormous bonding effect upon the involved parties, which in turn contributes to their being cooperative in the venture of child rearing (cf. Wilson 1978, p. 137 ff.). And this has an evolutionary advantage, given the length and complexities of child rearing among human beings. But with this truth, assuming it is that, we have not reached the end of the story.

The rituals of sexual intercourse primarily take place between non-kin. But if such rituals have an enormous bonding effect upon the parties involved, then what follows rather interestingly is that the capacity for altruism is more a part of our biological make-up than is often supposed. This follows from the fact that altruism (or something very much like it) flows in the wake of the formation of bonds between individuals. For the type of bond formed is one of affection, which is surely one of the fountainheads of altruistic behavior. If non-kin have the capacity for affectional bonding, for whatever reason, then altruism can be no stranger to human beings. That this capacity is evolutionarily advantageous because it increases cooperation in child rearing in no way militates against the truth of the point being made. Nor does the fact that this capacity is supervenient upon sexual behavior. For it does not follow from this that only sexual behavior can trigger this capacity.

My aim in this section has been to argue in a very general way for the view that the biological make-up of human beings is compatible with their being disposed to act in altruistic ways. To accomplish this task is not to show that all human beings will act altruistically, but only that the claims of an altruistic morality do not go entirely against the grain of our biological make-up. In the sections that follow, I hope to render this conclusion more secure by looking at a particular form of altruism, namely, love itself. I believe that a certain form of love clearly has a biological basis. That conception of love is characterized and defended in the section below.

4. Love: Transparent and Opaque

There are various kinds of love: love between friends, romantic love, familial love, and a special species of familial love, namely, parental love. Of these various types of love, parental love is perhaps the most unique. In what follows, I shall attempt to characterize the uniqueness of this love and explain what distinguishes it from other types of love. I shall do this generally by contrasting parental love with romantic love.

Romantic love is a paradigmatic instance of what I shall call opaque love.[9] It is love for a person under a certain description of that person, where the description makes reference to various attributes of the individual: the person's character, personality, style, physical features, skills, or what have you. It is love grounded in the attributes of the person. One can be married to a person about whom one knows nothing, as with prearranged marriages,[10] but not romantically in love with a person about whom one knows nothing.

With romantic love, then, the description under which the person is loved is of considerable importance. Literally, a person may be loved under one description and not another. For example, suppose that unbeknownst to John, Susan leads two rather disparate lives. By day she is a major corporate executive; by night she is a drug dealer. Not only can we easily imagine John being quite in love with Susan the corporate executive, but not Susan the drug dealer, we can easily imagine him falling out of love with Susan upon discovering that she is a drug dealer.

Of course, I do not mean to suggest that romantic love is so description-sensitive that it cannot tolerate any departures from the description under which the person is loved. That would be untenable, clearly. It is radical departures that present a problem for romantic love; and depending upon the attributes that primarily serve to ground the love, some romantic loves are more vulnerable than others to departures from the description under which the person is loved. Presumably, love grounded in physical attractiveness is more vulnerable than love grounded in intellectual talent, since intellect tends

<hr />

[9] As the term *opaque* and its counterpart *transparent* suggest, the account of opaque and transparent love developed owes some of its inspiration to work in the philosophy of language, the theory of reference in particular, between transparent and opaque reference. See, for example, Kripke (1980). In borrowing terminology, one invariably runs the risk of being misunderstood. I hope to have kept misunderstandings to a minimum.

[10] Cf. "And he [Hagar] dwelt in the wilderness of Paran: and his mother took him a wife out of the land of Egypt" (Genesis 21:21).

to weather the circumstances of life better than physical attraction. Obesity, which tends to make one less attractive, rarely curtails one's intellectual powers. And if personality and traits of character are more durable than physical attributes, then love grounded in the former is less vulnerable than love grounded in the latter.

As I have characterized it, opaque love seems to be at odds with the romantic ideal that receives its fullest expression in the traditional marriage vows. The ideal is that regardless of how each changes, the parties involved shall love one another until death separates them. As I hope to show momentarily, it is a mistake to think that opaque love is completely at odds with this ideal or, at any rate, the spirit of it. But first it will help to introduce the notion of transparent love in connection with parental love.

(It is obvious that people have children for a myriad of reasons—to make up, to prove themselves, and so on. The account of transparent love offered is not meant to address all cases of having children, but only those in which the child is desired by the parents because of the joy they hope to experience in contributing to the flourishing of a new human being.)

I regard parental love, at least at the outset, as the paradigmatic instance of transparent love. Parents display considerable love for their children from the very moment the children are born. In fact, it can be plausibly argued that such love manifests itself even sooner than that; but the issue need not concern us here. (I conclude this section with some remarks about parental love and the severely retarded and deformed.) This makes it incontrovertible that such love cannot be grounded in the usual attributes: the child's character, personality, style, physical features, skills, and so on. Whether the just-born, as I shall say, by which I mean a child no more than a few weeks old, has anything like a developed character and personality is not clear. What is clear, though, is that a just-born's character and personality are not pronounced enough at the moment of birth to make a difference in the reaction of her or his parents. These fragile creatures are not sexy-looking or coy, they do not possess a sense of presence, they are without poise, they cannot flirt, and so on. They display none of the nonverbal behavior that so often serves to explain at least the beginnings of romantic love. Any given just-born may become an intellectual giant or a symbol of physical attractiveness, but this is not known at the moment of birth. Thus, to love a just-born infant is not merely to love a bundle of unrealized potential; rather, it is to love a being the nature of whose potential is unknown to one. A just-born infant may even be without a name for awhile.

I call parental love transparent because it is grounded simply in the fact that the children in question are one's offspring. In due course, I shall slightly modify my description of the basis for transparent parental love.

Now, it may be argued that the fact that the child is one's own is surely an attribute of the child—indeed, the attribute that grounds the love that the parents have for the child; hence, the distinction between opaque and transparent love collapses, since in both cases the love is grounded by the attributes of the object of the love. This objection, I think, misses the point of the distinction.

The attribute "my child" is not a quality-denoting attribute. It does not pick out qualities that the child currently possesses or shall come to possess. The attribute indicates, and functions purely as an indicator of, the source of the child's origins, and not what the child is or shall be like. It applies equally to any child who has the same origins. Hold the origins fixed and one just-born is as good as another. It is in precisely this sense that the transparency of parental love mirrors the transparency of reference. Substitutions yield the same results.

By contrast, opaque love does not function purely as an indicator of origins. To be sure, X may very well love Y because Y is a member of the so-and-so family. But one can ask X why a person's being a member of the so-and-so family is important. And something is very much amiss if X does not have a response other than Y is a member of the family. Thus, even here romantic love turns out not to function as a pure indicator of origins. By contrast, observe that no response other than X is my child is needed to explain why a person loves X.

Parenthetically, it should be noted that as the notion of transparency is used in the theory of reference, it need not be held that no description whatsoever obtains in the case of transparent reference. If an object is being picked out at all, there has to be some description under which it is being picked out. So it is a mistake to think of transparent reference as involving no descriptions at all. Rather, the idea is that a fixed description has to suffice to pick out the object in question in all cases. Accordingly, then, the idea of transparent love is not to be understood as involving no descriptions whatsoever. Thus, without doing harm to the argument, it can be conceded that "my child" functions as a description. For the issue is whether that description suffices to ground parental love whatever else might be true. And the claim is that it does.

I have been arguing that parental love for the just-born is transparent. Children grow very rapidly. Ideally, parental love should remain transparent as the child grows. However, I have not argued that this is the case. I have not argued that once an object of someone's parental love, then always an object of that person's parental love. I want now to return to the apparent disparity between opaque love and the romantic ideal.

The traditional marriage vows suggest that romantic love that results in marriage should in effect become something rather like transparent love, in that the parties involved are supposed to love one another regardless of the changes that either might undergo. Thus, marital love is supposed to transcend, that is, not be grounded in, the attributes of the person. Instead, such love is supposed to be grounded in a deep and quintessential feature of the person. Indeed, it may be argued that unless this is the case we are quite easily replaceable by someone who just so happens to possess the very same attributes that we possess. And that, so it is argued, should not be.[11] Succinctly put, then, the claim is this: Unless marital love is grounded in some deep and quintessential feature of the person and, therefore, is not an instance of opaque love, the threat of attribute replaceability looms large. Ideally, marital love ought not to be, and is not, open to this threat. Hence, such marital love cannot be properly regarded as opaque love.

Clearly, the argument speaks to something important. There is something unsettling, if not altogether repugnant, about the idea that one's marital partner could just as easily love someone else if that person's set of attributes were identical to one's own. On the other hand, equally unsettling is the idea that marital love is as it ought to be only if one continues to love one's partner regardless of the changes that she or he undergoes. Surely, the kind of changes the person undergoes ought to make a difference. To speak in extremes, it is one thing if the person puts on a little weight; it is quite another if the person becomes an exceedingly wicked individual. Life being what it is, a change of the former type is to be expected. However, no one who gets married

---

[11] This argument is presented with great force in Kraut (1983) and Nozick (1974).

can be thought to have bargained for the latter. The objection (under consideration) to characterizing marital love as opaque love misses the mark because it loses sight of the developmental aspects of a marital relationship or it implicitly takes physical attributes to be the ground for the love throughout the marriage. People do not just get married. They get married and share their lives together. There are the joyful and painful learning experiences, the hurdles that each has gotten the other over, and the like. If all goes well, each contributes significantly to the other's flourishing. And this fact suffices to defuse the threat of attribute replaceability as an ever-present problem.

Consider the following. Suppose John and Susan get married. Five years pass and it is a good marriage. Each has contributed significantly to the other's flourishing. Having grown, they respectively now have the set alpha and beta of attributes. As it happens, there is a John* and a Susan* each having the set of attributes that, after five years of marriage, their counterparts John and Susan came to have. (Whether John* and Susan* know each other is irrelevant.) Needless to say, there could not be a more pertinent fact than that John and Susan developed with each other and not with their counterparts. It is to each other's flourishing that they contributed, with all that that involved, and not the flourishing of the counterparts. And it is to one another that each will be grateful and not someone who just so happens to have the identical set of properties. The distance they have travelled together qualitatively affects how they view and feel about each other. None of this is changed by the fact that John* and Susan* have the same attributes as their counterparts John and Susan. For Susan did not contribute to John*'s having his attributes, nor John to Susan*'s having hers.

If physical attributes are the ground of marital love, then it is much easier to see how the threat of attribute replaceability could arise, though even here it is possible to tell a story in which the threat is minimized. Something that we have an emotional investment in is not easily replaced, even by something that is indistinguishable from it, as objects of sentimental value make clear. Although a father could get his daughter, who is now a professional potter, to make him a cup just like the one she made for him twenty years ago when she was six, and which he accidentally but irreparably broke, the replacement cup cannot really take the place of the original. For the significance that the father attached to that cup was inextricably tied to the fact that it was made by his daughter when she was six. Tears of joy came to his eyes when he unwrapped the cup, which was her birthday gift to him. Another cup that looked just like it simply would not invoke the same memories, at least not in the same way. For the original cup was a token of his daughter's love as expressed at the age of six. No other cup be a token of that! These considerations shore up the points made in the preceding paragraph.

If, as a result of having flourished together, John and Susan have traits alpha and beta respectively, then the fact that there is a John* and a Susan* who have the exact same traits does not, on that account alone, pose any threat either to John or Susan. For both will have helped and been helped by each other. The depth of their sentiments will have been engaged by each other. Neither John* nor Susan* will have been anywhere in the picture. So, with romantic love it seems that the threat of replaceability would loom large in the lives of a couple only if it is allowed that a romantic relationship can be based entirely upon physical attraction and that the individuals' living and interacting together add nothing whatsoever to the relationship. But to call such a relationship an instance of romantic love is surely a misnomer.

Marital love is at its best when the involved individuals grow and flourish together. However, marital love is not always at its best, and the involved parties may part company. This is a very different phenomenon from simply being replaced by someone whose attributes are identical to one's own. After all, a couple can part company although neither party has another romantic interest on the horizon. With no difficulty, then, we can maintain that marital love is an instance of opaque love and yet do justice to the idea that the threat of attribute replaceability should not loom large in the background.

Of course, if one understands the spirit of the traditional marriage vows to be that one should remain committed to one's partner, however she or he might change, then I have hardly shed any light on the matter. On the other hand, if the spirit of these vows is that, among other things, neither party to the marriage should feel threatened by the mere fact that there are others who have similar attributes, then I believe that our understanding of these vows has been enhanced. It is undoubtedly a wonderful thing when two people love one another until death separates them. But it is unquestionably a mistake to suppose that we have genuine love only when this is the case. In particular, we need not suppose that we have genuine love only when the object of our love is irreplaceable. From the fact that it is possible that someone could replace us in a love relationship, it in no way follows that the threat of being replaced hangs over us. After all, in a similar sense of the word *possible*, it is just as possible that the one who loves us could kill us; yet we rarely see that possibility as amounting to anything like a threat of death.

Now, there is an independent reason for wanting romantic love, even in the ideal form of marital love, to be an instance of opaque love. The kind of love that is closest in character to romantic love is love between deep friends or companion friends, as I shall say (Section 9). In fact, it is notoriously difficult to distinguish the love of companion friendships from romantic love, apart from maintaining that the latter, and not the former, has a sexual component, and the expression of affection is different. Perhaps these differences are just enough to yield a difference in kind. But what must be shown is not simply that a difference in kind exists as a result of these things, but that the love of complete friendship naturally stops short of these things. In due course, I shall question this line of reasoning (Section 11).

At any rate, with both kinds of love, the love in question is an expression of choice for a person of a certain kind. Second, in both instances the ideal is that the parties involved contribute significantly to each other's flourishing. Both types of relationship give deep expression to the idea that individuals can be mirrors to the souls of each other.[12] Yet no one would maintain that two people should remain deep friends regardless of the changes that either undergoes. In particular, no one would urge the continuation of a friendship with a person who has become irredeemably wicked.[13]

The love that is characteristic of friendship is manifestly an instance of opaque love. If Aristotle is right, the relevant attributes have to do with character (*Nicomachean Ethics*, Bk. 9). The threat of attribute replaceability does not loom large on the horizon of friendships thus grounded, and this provides us with an independent reason for thinking that no such threat need be present in the marital case simply because romantic love is grounded in the attributes of the person.

[12] See Ch. 1, n. 1.

[13] No one, including Aristotle, who no doubt made this very point first. See his *Nicomachean Ethics* (Bk. 9, Sec. 3).

This holds a fortiori if the differences between the love of romance and the love of companion friendship are all but indistinguishable.

I have claimed that of the various types of love, parental love is perhaps the most unique. As one might surmise, I want to say that that has to do with its being transparent, at least at the outset. Other familial loves may also tend toward transparency; however, it is reasonable to hold that, in general, transparent love receives its fullest expression in parental love. This is because among familial relationships, sustained altruism (which is not of the heroic or saintly sort) generally receives its greatest expression in parenthood. To be sure, when their parents are along in years, children often do things for them, if not support them outright; but such behavior is often motivated to some extent by the feeling on the children's part that they have acquired a debt of gratitude to their parents. Obviously enough, the altruism that parents display toward their just-born children simply cannot be so explained.

The transparency of parental love is perhaps best approximated by love between siblings, since siblings tend to love one another because they are siblings. There is this difference, though. The altruistic acts that children perform for one another are generally not of the magnitude of the altruistic acts that parents perform for their children. Nor is sibling love an expression from the outset of a sustained commitment to the well-being and flourishing of another. The reason for this is, of course, very straight forward. Children are usually in no position to do these sorts of things. Still, it is of significance that sibling love is not initially experienced by the siblings as involving sustained support for the other, nor can it be understood in this way. It is not as if siblings are laboring under a delusion.

That some siblings are very supportive of one another goes without saying. Even so, this support is not like the support that issues from parental love. For if the siblings come to be rather like friends, then the model of friendship best explains the altruistic motives; if they do not, then the offering of support is best explained on the model of institutional obligation—the institution of the family, in this case. Neither the model of friendship nor the model of institutional obligation adequately explains the altruistic behavior of parents toward their children, especially the just-born.

I should like to conclude this section by speaking to an apparent difficulty with the account of transparent love offered. It would seem that some parents do not love their just-born child if the child is severely retarded or deformed (or both). This would seem to suggest that what grounds parental love is not simply that, as I have claimed, the child issues from her or his parents, but that the child meets certain minimal conditions of performance. I think that the matter is far more complicated than this.

To begin with, it should be observed that in no way does it follow that a disposition (or capacity) will always be realized given just the fact that it is a product of evolution. For example, according to evolutionary theory incest is strongly disfavored, since when it occurs deleterious genes are more likely to manifest themselves. However, evolutionary theory is hardly called into question simply because there have been instances of incest among the various species. Again, suppose it is true, as has been suggested, that promiscuity has been selected for even among human beings (Symons 1979, ch. 7; Trivers 1972). It hardly follows from this that human beings must be promiscuous. Perfectly compatible with this supposed truth is the existence of effectively strong norms against promiscuity. Sociobiological theory does not imply that any trait that has been selected for will actually be manifested in the lives of creatures who have the corresponding genes. In particular, the theory does not imply that human beings are completely at the mercy of their gene pool (Dawkins 1976, p. 215).

Now, our conception of a human being is inextricably tied to a conception of human flourishing, which, in turn, makes reference to the abilities of human beings. There can be no gainsaying this point, since it is in virtue of their abilities that human beings as a species are distinguishable from other species. What makes having a child one of life's richest experiences is having a direct hand in the flourishing of a human life. But this flourishing is not just a matter of any development whatsoever; rather, it makes reference to the child's developing to the point that she or he can take advantage of a great many of life's offerings. The severely retarded and deformed would seem to be especially at a disadvantage here. To invoke the notion of a plan of life here (pace Rawls 1971), the idea is that the severely retarded and deformed would seem to be at a profound disadvantage when it comes to pursuing any and every worthwhile plan of life. Without attempting to give a full account of human flourishing, we can say this much. An infant holds the promise of being able to flourish in ways that are characteristic of human beings if, at the outset, there is no reason to believe that she or he is at a profound disadvantage with respect to virtually every worthwhile plan of life. Every person who seeks to have a child very much hopes that the child will be born with the promise of flourishing.

Clearly, the notion of the promise of flourishing does not make reference to any specific talents as such. Indeed, I have given it an entirely negative characterization, namely, that there is no reason to believe that the child is at a profound disadvantage with respect to virtually every worthwhile plan of life. When a child does not meet this condition, some parents lack the psychological wherewithal to love and care for it. It would be a gross mischaracterization of the feelings of such individuals to say that their inability to love such a child stems from the fact that the child lacks some well-defined set of talents or skills, since no infant has that. Their inability to love the child stems instead from the fact that the child has no promise at all of human flourishing.

The concept of transparent love, then, does make reference to abilities in the sense that its intended object is a just-born infant who possesses the promise of human flourishing. When a child does not possess this promise and, for that reason, is not loved by her or his parents, we need not infer that parental love is not transparent, but only that, as seems reasonable, when the intended object of that love is sufficiently altered (given the conception of a human being and thus the conception of human flourishing to which we subscribe), then we will get varying results with regard to the just-born who hold no promise of flourishing. For as I have observed, a referentially transparent object is not without any description whatsoever. Transparent love makes reference to abilities only in the sense that the child should not be at a profound disadvantage when it comes to pursuing any and every worthwhile plan of life. But, needless to say, to know this about a child is in no way to know what his or her abilities and talents are. The nature of the child's potential is still unknown.

Now, to object to the idea that our conception of a human being is deeply tied to a conception of human flourishing that makes reference in some way to abilities is, I submit, to give human beings less respect than they deserve. Our conception of other living creatures, including plants, is tied to a notion of how they flourish (which is not to deny that we are sometimes egregiously wrong about these matters). And, offhand, I should think that in this regard we might accord ourselves the respect that we accord other living creatures. More convincingly, perhaps, there is our earlier point that it is precisely in virtue of abilities that human beings as a species are distinguishable from other species. Our concept of a human being refers to a creature capable of, inter alia, rational thought, speaking a natural language, possessing a culture, and acting creatively with respect to a vast array of activities. Our concept of a dog or bird or tree does not refer to a creature possessing the conjunction of these capabilities. As things now stand, we can no more talk about human beings without making reference to some abilities, however implicitly, than we can talk about cars without making reference to things with wheels. Tomorrow, we might regard a quite different-looking object as a car. But today, anything without wheels that is presented as a car either is not that at all or is very much in need of repair.

Finally, I do not deny that a defensible notion of human flourishing is notoriously difficult to articulate fully. Nor, a fortiori, do I deny that reasonable people can differ concerning such matters. In these last remarks, I have been concerned to establish only two things. One is that our concept of a human being is deeply tied to a conception of human flourishing. The other is that because this is so, we can explain why some parents do not love their severely deformed or retarded child in a way that is compatible with one of the main claims of this essay, namely, that parental love is transparent.

Now, can the uniqueness of parental love, as I have developed it, be explained by reference to our human nature? I believe so, as I attempt to show in the next section.

5. Transparent Love and Natural Selection

From the standpoint of evolutionary theory, a necessary condition for the survival of any species is that enough among each generation of the adult members of that species succeed in leaving behind progeny who, in turn, succeed in doing the same.[14] Salmon, for in-

---

[14] In *On the Origin of Species*, Charles Darwin writes: "I use the term Struggle for Existence in a large and metaphorical sense, including dependence of one being on another, and including (which is most important) not only the life of the individual, but success in leaving progeny" (ch. 3, paragraph 4).

stance, achieve this end by genetic hardwiring and mass production, as it were, spawning hundreds of thousands of eggs at a time. Salmon in no way care for their young. It is strictly a matter of instinct that the young do the right things. At the opposite end of the spectrum, there are species the adult members of which must provide their offspring with the necessary care, attention, instruction, and so on if their offspring are ever to reach adulthood and reproduce. *Homo sapiens* falls into this latter category.[15] Humans do not mass-produce; and among them, parental care may arguably be regarded as receiving its greatest expression, for the natural parent-offspring relationship among *Homo sapiens* is the longest and most complex of any species.

Among the basic needs of a human infant the need for continuous love from its parents (or parental surrogate) is said to be one of the most important, if not the most important.[16] If, as we shall see, this is indeed the case, then the fact that the human species continues to survive gives us reason enough to believe that not only do human beings have the capacity to meet this need, but that this capacity has been selected for. We can bring out the fundamental importance of parental love by looking at a crude account of Freudian child development. But first a caveat.

The crude Freudian account of child development is, of course, inspired by his writings and is not, I think, an unreasonable interpretation of his various claims on the subject.[17] However, I do not aim for

[15] Other primates fall into this category. Harlow and Mears (1979) have demonstrated that the effects of isolation upon monkeys are devastating (ch. 12, "The Hell of Loneliness"). See also Goodall (1988). She writes: "We have been repeatedly impressed by the extent to which the growing child depends on his mother. Who would have thought that a three-year old chimpanzee might die if he lost his mother?" (p. 236).

[16] Cf. Bowlby (1953). He writes: "What is believed to be essential for mental health is that an infant and young child should experience a warm, intimate, and continuous relationship with his mother (or permanent mother-substitute—one person who steadily 'mothers' him) in which both find satisfaction and enjoyment" (p. 13). Bowlby develops this line of thought in *Attachment* (1969). Bowlby's general conclusions concerning the importance of parental love are now regarded as established. See Hinde (1978) and Rutter (1978). Gregory Vlastos (1962) writes that "constancy of affection in the face of variations of merit is one of the surest tests of whether a mother loves a child."

[17] I have relied heavily upon Freud's *Civilization and Its Discontents*, ch. 5–7, especially, and his *Group Psychology and the Analysis of the Ego*. I have been much influenced by Hall (1954).

accuracy here as such. The account is intended to serve as a vehicle for bringing into sharp relief the significance of parental love. It may be thought of as a heuristic device for bringing out a point.

On a crude Freudian account of child development, fear of parental disapproval and, as a result, parental rejection is an ever-present concern in the life of the child. What gives rise to this fear is the child's realization that she is at the mercy of her parents when it comes to having her basic needs and wants, such as food, shelter, and clothing, satisfied.

From the child's perspective, at any rate, the parents have complete control over the distribution of goods that the child needs and wants. If they reject him then he is cut off from his most important source of these goods. Accordingly, the child is very much concerned to avoid parental rejection, which he deems can be accomplished by measuring up to the expectations of his parents and thus winning their approval, which often takes the form of praise. The belief is that they will continue to satisfy his basic needs and wants so long as he wins their approval often enough; otherwise they will not do so. On this view, the child's internalization of his parents' values is just a very efficient way of winning their approval, since with respect to an important range of things the child's doing what meets with their approval will be second nature to him if he has internalized their values.

Naturally, though, a child has no guarantee that he will always measure up to the expectations of his parents. And that is precisely the problem. No matter how hard a child might try, he may nonetheless fall short. His best may simply not be good enough in the eyes of his parents. And the stakes are far too high for the child to be insouciant about failing to measure up.

In view of these considerations, one can easily see why, on a crude Freudian account of child development, fear of parental rejection must loom large in the life of the child. For not only must the child perform as his parents expect, but he must in the first place discover what those expectations are. And he may fail on both accounts. In fact, it is inevitable that he will, life being what it is.

Not only can it be difficult to ascertain precisely what parents expect, but for various reasons the expectations of the parents, regarding any given activity, may change. Parents who were perfectly willing to settle for one level of excellence may not be willing to settle for that upon having seen the high level of excellence achieved by the child of another set of parents. Thus, a child could fail to measure up to the expectations of his parents not because he had misjudged their wishes from the beginning, but because their wishes had, as it were, changed en route. One does not have to postulate wicked or malicious parents to get the sort of scenario that I have just sketched. For we can all be influenced by others without realizing it. All that is needed is that the parents have been so influenced.

Needless to say, as I have developed the account, it would appear to be nothing short of a miracle that the fear of parental rejection does not totally debilitate the child. For one thing, no child is apt to be that confident about his ability to discern what is expected of him by his parents, given the child's awareness that his parents have more knowledge about the world than he has and, therefore, can interact with it more effectively than he can. For another, the child will surely fail at some point to measure up to his parents' expectations because those expectations, which he had once correctly surmised, will have changed. And this will further undermine the child's confidence in his ability to discern what is expected of him.

Now, if the child realizes that, on the one hand, being able to measure up to the expectations of his parents is crucial to his being in their good favor and therefore to his receiving from them the goods that he needs in order to survive, but that, on the other, he will often fail to measure up, then the prospect of being rejected by them would have to be a major source of concern—which is simply another way of saying that the child would have to be very much consumed by the fear of parental rejection.

However, I take it as a given that the fear of parental rejection need not be an abiding concern in the life of children. The reason for this is not that children somehow always manage to measure up to their parents' expectations. Rather, the explanation has to do with the significance of parental love. This we can get at by looking at the difference between parental love and social approval (Vlastos 1962).

In all of its forms and regardless of its source (peer, parental, or what have you), approval requires the belief that the performances in question have merit. One can sincerely approve of what a person does only if one deems her performance to have merit. Otherwise the approval is empty. Approval in all of its forms is conceptually tied to performances.

Not so for love. There is a species of love—I have called it transparent love (Section 3)—that consists of a concern for a person's wellbeing and is not tied to the person's performances. This is unconditional love not because one may never cease to have such love for an individual, but because there is no belief about that individual's behavior, performances, or what have you, that constitutes a conceptual bar to so loving that person. There is nothing a person can do, nothing a person can become, that would cause one, on conceptual grounds, to cease loving him.

These remarks show the importance of distinguishing between having the psychological wherewithal to continue loving a person and having conditions that a person must meet if one is to continue loving her or him. It is possible not to be able to continue loving a person even though one wishes that one could, just as one may wish that one were more patient. Suppose one's spouse is on a secret military assignment that will keep her away from home for three years. One may very well have no desire whatsoever not to go on loving her throughout the three years; yet it could turn out—much to one's own surprise even—that one lacks the psychological wherewithal to do so.

What I have called transparent love, or something very much like it, is thought to be one of the defining features of Christianity. And observe that while the Christian commandment to love one's enemies is regarded as exceedingly difficult,[18] doing so is not ruled out on conceptual grounds. It is not on a par with being commanded to square a circle (the logically impossible) or to leap tall buildings in a single bound (the physically impossible). Since transparent love is not tied to performances, it is compatible with disapproval. It is this distinctive feature that accounts for the significance and importance of parental love in the life of the child.

On a crude Freudian account of matters, parental acceptance is tied to parental approval. Hence, the child attaches great importance to measuring up to parents' expectations. There is, then, no conceptual space for acceptance without approval. That is why parental disapproval ineluctably portends parental rejection. But if parental love

[18] "But I say unto you, Love your enemies, bless them that curse you, do good to them that hate you" (Matthew 5:44). This form of Christian love is generally referred to as agape love. See Meilaender (1981) for an excellent discussion of the character and scope of agape love.

has the features I have claimed for it, then precisely what it offers is conceptual space for acceptance without approval—indeed, for acceptance with disapproval. Thus, when parental love is functioning optimally, it has the effect of allaying, if not precluding entirely, the child's fear of parental rejection. For the parents engender in the child the conviction that their love for him, and so acceptance of him, is not contingent upon his performances' meeting their approval. It is a good thing, then, that parents will often display a modicum of affection toward their child after having expressed disapproval of the child's behavior. For such behavior on their part serves to secure the aforementioned conviction. This is because a child could want for no greater sign that he is loved by his parents than constancy of affection on their part in the face of varied performances on his part (Vlastos 1962).

In view of these considerations, we may say that parental love engenders and sustains in the child basic psychological security, which we understand simply as a sense of worth that is in no way tied to performances. As a result of their displays of love, the child believes that his parents' acceptance of him and their desire to support him is not tied to his performances. Accordingly, the child believes that in the eyes of his parents he has worth regardless of whether his performances meet their approval. No such security is forthcoming on a crude Freudian account of child development. Naturally, I do not mean to suggest that there is nothing at all to be said for parental approval and disapproval. I shall say something about that momentarily.

Now, basic psychological security is surely one of the keys that unlocks the door to a child's flourishing. Here is why. It is through exploratory behavior that a child learns how to master her environment and so to acquire a sense of competence.[19] An extraordinary amount of what may strike an adult as merely playful behavior on the child's part is behavior through which the child is acquiring a sense of what she can accomplish in her environment. She is getting a feel for her powers, if you will. But exploratory behavior is just that—

---

[19] Here I follow Rutter (1978) and, especially, White (1963), ch. 3. See also Gruen (1988). It is worth mentioning that one of the central aims of White's work is to show that Freud's theory of the personality is inadequate—in particular, Freud's account of human motivation.

exploratory behavior. Things go wrong when one explores, and one can end up in a quite unpleasant predicament. Given that this happens to adults who have a wealth of experience to draw upon, it will obviously also happen to children, who have yet to master their own experiences. It is clear, then, that a child's willingness to engage in exploratory behavior is enhanced by the assurance that her parents will be there to offer comfort and protection when difficulties arise, that is, an assurance that the child can retreat to the protective arms of her parents in the event that things should get out of control. If, as is evident, such assurances have a deep, settling effect in the lives of adults, then a fortiori they have such an effect in the lives of children.

Now, consider the difference between a child's engaging in exploratory behavior under the constant threat of parental rejection and her doing so under the wings of transparent love as manifested through parental love. In the former case, it seems most unlikely that the child could come to feel assured that her parents would be there to offer comfort and protection when difficulties arose. If parental acceptance is always tied only to behavior that meets with their approval, what basis could the child have for this assurance? By contrast, when parental love is an instance of transparent love, then acceptance is not tied to approval; and that fact makes it possible for this assurance to be generated.

On the crude Freudian model, parental upbringing is not conducive to the child's development of basic psychological security. This is because the view has it that the child will invariably see that his worth in the eyes of his parents is tied to his measuring up to their expectations.

To sum up, then, I have tried to show the significance of parental love as an instance of transparent love. I have argued that the significance lies in the fact that such parental love engenders basic psychological security on the part of the child, and that this security, in addition to allaying or altogether precluding the fear of parental rejection, is one of the keys to the child's flourishing.

If the argument is sound, then from the standpoint of evolutionary theory we have reason to believe that the capacity for transparent love as manifested through parental love has been selected for. It will be recalled that a necessary condition for the survival of any species is that enough among each generation of adults succeed in leaving behind progeny who, in turn, succeed in doing the same. Far from playing a peripheral role in the survival of the human species, basic psychological security on the part of the child proves to be indispensable if the child is to have a chance of flourishing. For having basic psychological security is incompatible with being plagued by fear of parental rejection.

Now, as I have adumbrated, the importance of parental love notwithstanding, I do not mean to suggest that parental approval and disapproval have no place in a child's upbringing. Both play an important role in the child's motivation to adopt the values of her parents and to pursue various ends. It is through parental approval that the child comes to have a sense of how to do things properly and, more important, the conviction that she can do things properly. The child looks to her parents to understand the significance of what she does and the character of her accomplishments. It is through parental approval and disapproval that she comes to have that understanding.

On these points, there is no gainsaying Freud; and I have not tried to. Rather, I have tried to show the importance of distinguishing between parental love and parental approval. To be sure, it is a consequence of the view presented that when it comes to the psychological well-being of the child, parental love plays a role that parental approval cannot. But this is hardly to say that the latter is unimportant.

Before moving on, a final comment. I have argued that the capacity for transparent parental love has been selected for. What I have meant by the argument is that in general we have the capacity for such love in virtue of being human—not in virtue of having children. The psychological attitude of adults toward the children of others and, especially, toward the prospect of having their own children would be quite inexplicable if the capacity for parental love were triggered only by actually having (or conceiving) children. Under such a view, we could make little sense of the great joy that the very thought of having children gives to people presently without them. Further, it seems that any view that gives such weight to actually having (or conceiving) children puts males at an enormous disadvantage with regard to the capacity for transparent love, since it is females, and not men, who conceive and bear children. But there is absolutely no reason to believe that, in comparison to women, men have a diminished capacity for transparent parental love.

Now, perhaps the best and most compelling evidence that can be proffered in support of the view that the capacity for transparent parental love derives from being human is that some adults adopt children; and the love these adults have for their (adopted) children is indistinguishable from the richness and depth of love parents have for their natural children. Taken as a class, the parents of adopted children are indistinguishable from the parents of natural children when it comes to displaying love toward their children. If the capacity for transparent parental love came only in the wake of having natural offspring, or if it reached a particularly heightened form as a result of natural offspring, then there should be a discernable difference between the capacity of parents of adopted children to love their children vis-à-vis that of parents of natural children to love theirs. (This would be true even if the difference could be overcome.) None, however, is to be found.

6. Love, Morality, and Self-Interest

If there is a biological basis for transparent love, then it follows that there is a biological basis for what I called motive altruism, since love is an altruistic concept. And if there is a biological basis for motive altruism, then it follows that there is a measure of congruence between our biological make-up and altruistic morality. In fact, an even stronger claim can be made, namely, that our biological make-up is an ally of morality. This is so, at any rate, if one regards love as a natural, and thus nonmoral, sentiment. For I have argued that transparent love has a very straightforward evolutionary underpinning or, at any rate, that it is not implausible to suppose that this is so. And if any sentiment embodies motive altruism, surely love does. Together, these considerations entail that motive altruism itself has a basis in our biological make-up. If so, then it follows that the altruism that morality calls for has a biological underpinning.

Observe that in terms of our attitude toward others, morality, too, calls for a measure of transparency: Whether or not we should find ourselves attracted to others on account of their attributes, there is a minimum amount of respect owed to persons simply in virtue of their being such. A satisfactory moral theory is not formulated with reference to proper names or indexicals. If all persons have certain rights (on a rights-based theory) or are owed certain duties (on a duty-based theory), then they should be treated accordingly regardless of their attributes. Generality and universalizability are regarded as formal constraints of the right. My point here, of course, is not to deny that the proper way of treating people can ever have something to do with their attributes, but simply that the minimum amount of respect that an altruistic morality requires us to have for all people is not in any way tied to the specific attributes of persons: their skills, physical features, traits of character and personality, style, and so forth.

Fairness, an indisputable aspect of morality, nicely illustrates the transparency of morality. That we should treat others fairly clearly has nothing to do with, for example, their physical features, personality, physical or mental health, natural talents, or wealth. This is so notwithstanding the fact that what constitutes fair treatment in a specific instance may have everything to do with these things. Whether or not they both deserve punishment, the severely battered housewife of twenty years who kills her husband in a fit of blind rage should not, as a matter of fairness, be meted out the same punishment as the housewife who calculatingly murders her husband in order to obtain his wealth.

There are, to be sure, fundamentally important differences between morality and transparent love. I have not claimed otherwise. Rather, I have been concerned to draw attention to the significant truth that a characteristic kind of moral behavior, namely, behavior in the referentially transparent mode, is anchored in our biological make-up by way of parental love. We may think of parental love as the capacity to value someone without regard to that person's attributes. Morality involves this very same capacity to a significantly lesser extent. Parental love calls for a strong altruistic disposition toward another in the referentially transparent mode, and morality calls for a weak (that is, a weaker) altruistic disposition toward another in the very same mode.

Now, from the standpoint of evolution we may suppose that if human beings are endowed with the former, then they would be endowed with the latter unless it were specifically selected against. And the primary reason for thinking that the capacity for weak transparent altruism has not been selected against is that, first, social cooperation plays a preeminent role in the survival or, at any rate, the betterment of the human species, which is unmistakably the lesson to be learned from social contract theory; and, second, weak transparent altruism is essential for social cooperation.

As I noted earlier (Section 5), the natural parent-offspring relationship among human beings is the longest and most complicated among any species. Attending to the needs of the child requires considerable time and energy. Parents simply could not effectively meet the needs of the child if they had to concern themselves with protecting themselves against the exploitations of others. For such an enterprise would surely consume them. The point here is exceedingly straightforward: Being a good parent is incompatible with having to fend off constantly the attempts of others to exploit one. This is not because one could not have the genuine desire to do both, but because one would not have either the physical or psychological wherewithal to do both.

After all, being a good parent is rather like being on call twenty-four hours a day. It is not just a matter of performing a well-defined set of tasks, at designated times, both of which are known well ahead of time, thus making advance preparation possible. Such a conception of parenting cannot do justice to the nurturing role that is deeply characteristic of parenting and the spontaneity that is likewise characteristic of such a nurturing role. One might be able to feed a child on schedule and yet be able to concern oneself with constantly warding off attempts to exploit one. However, constantly protecting oneself against exploitation would surely be a formidable obstacle to one's playing a major nurturing role in the life of the child.

These considerations make it manifestly clear that if the child is to flourish in the parent-child relationship, then the parent must be able to attend to the needs of the child without having always to worry about being exploited by others. Only in a community in which a genuine spirit of cooperation prevails are worries of this sort put to rest or sufficiently abated. From an evolutionary standpoint, then, it follows that the very survival of the species is tied to human beings' having the capacity for genuine cooperation. And these considerations favor having the capacity for weak transparent altruism. Let me explain.

In what follows, I assume that persons have the capacity for genuine cooperation if and only if they have the capacity to adhere to the requirements of altruistic morality. This assumption is reasonable enough, as genuine cooperation would seem to involve fair play. For one thing, cooperation entails the willingness to do one's part when it is one's turn and to forgo benefits for the sake of others. For another, it entails that a person not depart from the rules of cooperation just because, first, he can thereby advance his interest and, second, he can do so without in any way undermining the willingness of others to continue cooperating. The claim is not that cooperation and morality amount to the same thing, but only that to have the capacity for one is to have the capacity for the other. A practice that calls for genuine co-operation need not be an instance of morality; and not all of morality is a matter of cooperation.

Now, there can be no doubt that individuals are capable of passing up a present benefit for a greater gain further down the road. This is not altruism, however, but enlightened self-interest. Much moral philosophy is aimed at showing that morality is compatible with enlightened self-interest; some even want to make the stronger claim that enlightened, self-interested individuals will, in virtue of being such, adhere to a set of moral principles.[20] I do not believe that any explanation as to why people cooperate that appeals to their self-interested motives, and only to such motives, can yield genuine altruistic behavior. Self-interest cannot be transformed into altruism; for the very idea behind self-interest is that one maximizes the satisfaction of desires that pertain to the self. Thus, if one starts only with self-interest and does not add altruism along the way, then one will end up with nothing but self-interest as an explanation for the motivations of persons. To be sure, self-interest can go quite far in getting people *merely* to behave in accordance with the precepts of an altruistic morality (cf. Gauthier 1986). Still, to behave morally only for self-interested reasons is not to value moral behavior as a good in and of itself (Thomas 1988c); nor, a fortiori, is it to have an altruistic motivation for behaving morally.

Conceptually, any arrangement by which essentially self-interested people are supposed to adhere to the principles of an altruistic morality will be inherently unstable. This is because however much each self-interested member of society may find it in her self-interest

[20] While K. Baier (1958) and Gauthier (1986) are both very explicit in their aim to found morality directly upon enlightened self-interest, it would seem that Rawls (1971) is also concerned to do so, though in a much less direct way. The parties in the original position are essentially self-interested individuals save that they have an interest in their families and descendants. Indeed, by part 3 of Rawls's work, in which he so eloquently speaks of social unions and individuals taking delight in the talents of others, one has to remind oneself that all of this interest in the good of one another sits upon a self-interested foundation. Here see A. Baier's very important discussions of trust (1986) and moral theory (1985b).

that there be an altruistic morality in place to which the members of society by and large subscribe, it will be demonstrably false that every member of society, taken individually, will always have a self-interested reason to follow the very altruistic morality that she or he wants to be in place.[21] For surely there will be windows of opportunity for wrongdoing: occasions when it will be possible for a person to substantially enhance her self-interest by acting contrary to the precepts of altruistic morality without being at all apprehended and, moreover, without in any way undermining the prevailing tendency on the part of the members of society to follow the morality. And in such instances, a person who is motivated entirely by self-interest can be given no reason not—in fact, has no reason not—to advance her self-interest by acting contrary to the precepts of the altruistic morality. Indeed, in such instances, it would be foolish for her not to act contrary to the precepts of altruistic morality in order to advance her self-interests. By definition, self-interested people will, because they have every reason to do so, avail themselves of windows of opportunity for wrongdoing when they occur. And if one supposes that such opportunities are especially likely to occur in a society in which most people are following the precepts of an altruistic morality, then it follows that a moral society gives self-interested people a reason to be immoral. Therein lies the instability having to do with self-interested people adhering to an altruistic morality. Self-interested people may wish to give the appearance of being disinterested in windows of opportunity for wrongdoing, but it would and could only be an appearance.

Significantly, this instability is owing to the absence of trust. Arguments that attempt to ground morality in self-interest have no way of anchoring trust in the lives of individuals. Such arguments can make no sense of why individuals should trust one another not to avail themselves of opportunities for wrongdoing (see Section 17).

The instability problem is not gotten around by attempting to forge the link between morality and self-interest at the level of dispositions (pace Gauthier 1986) rather than individual actions, as was the case in the preceding paragraphs. To be sure, in terms of maximizing one's self-interest, it clearly can be rational to have a certain

[21] In a word, this is Gauthier's (1970a) argument against K. Baier (1958), and my argument (Thomas 1988c) against Gauthier (1986).

disposition although one's self-interest is not maximized with every behavioral manifestation of that disposition. For example, since consuming food is generally a necessary condition for staying alive, the disposition to eat is a rational one, though obviously not all behavior that is a manifestation of that disposition is rational. A person can eat too much or the wrong sorts of foods, either of which can be inimical to his health. Accordingly, it might be thought that an argument from self-interest for adhering to an altruistic moral theory can be made along this order: for self-interested reasons persons choose to acquire an altruistic disposition. They choose to do so, one might suppose, precisely because they wish to avoid the problem owing to windows of opportunity for wrongdoing when the link between self-interest and morality is forged at the level of each individual action. For the idea is simply that in terms of maximizing self-interest, it can be rational to have an altruistic disposition even if self-interest is not maximized with every manifestation of this disposition.

Here we have to be clear about the way in which acquiring a disposition is to be conceived of as a matter of choice. Obviously, if doing so is rather like performing an action, then there is nothing to be said for the move to dispositions in the first place, since it is not clear what the difference between acquiring a disposition and performing an action would come to; and the instability problem would arise in the same sort of way. On the other hand, if acquiring a disposition is to be understood as psychologically setting oneself up to perform the actions over which the disposition ranges—that is, a choice manifested through a series of actions that binds the way in which one's future self behaves—then it would seem that persons who successfully choose to acquire an altruistic disposition thereby cease to be self-interested individuals. Hence, we no longer have the case in which self-interested individuals are adhering to the requirements of an altruistic morality. This, of course, makes the move to dispositions too successful. Given the aim of showing that self-interested people can adhere to the requirements of an altruistic morality, one does not want an argument in which the people end up not in fact being self-interested.

I have tried to show, albeit rather quickly, that self-interest cannot serve as the basis for why individuals adhere to the requirements of altruistic morality. If so, then it follows that self-interest cannot serve as the basis for genuine cooperation. But I have argued that from an evolutionary standpoint the survival of the species is tied to human beings' having the capacity for genuine cooperation because of the enormous time involvement of parental care. Hence, so is altruism. I claimed that if human beings are endowed with the capacity for a strong altruistic disposition toward another in the referentially transparent mode, then we may suppose that they are also endowed with the capacity for a weak altruistic disposition toward another in the referentially transparent mode unless it was specifically selected against. I have tried to show that there is no reason whatsoever to think that the latter would be selected against.

We may think of the motive altruism that is a consequence of parental love as being the foundation for motive altruism that extends beyond offspring. Love makes us susceptible to the weal and woe of others who are not the object of our love. That is, if X loves Y, then not only will X be moved by the weal and woe of Y, but X will to some extent be moved by the weal and woe of others. This is because in the wake of love comes the capacity for both empathy and sympathy, and these capacities are then engaged not only by those whom we love. In due course, I shall develop these themes more fully. The point to be remembered at the moment is that parental altruism gives us a foothold on extended altruism, let us say, in virtue of features about the nature of love. And it is this capacity for extended altruism that makes possible genuine cooperation. Without it, nothing that might remotely resemble genuine cooperation is possible.

As was noted (Section 2), some may object to what has been argued thus far on the grounds that biology does not constitute a firm enough foundation upon which to rest moral motivations. But as I then observed, while biology does not give us the necessity of logic, as Kant himself would have wanted, there is nothing fleeting about our biological make-up. Being contingent and subject to evolutionary pressures, our biological make-up may not be here to stay. Still, there does not exist a more reliable measure of the strengths and capacities of human beings. More significantly, who we are qua human beings cannot be defined independently of our biological make-up. It may very well be true that vis-à-vis other species, we are distinguishable by our rational nature. But that nature constitutes a biological endowment and not something we have independently of who we are or might be qua biological creatures. There are no human beings (that is, *Homo sapiens*) who are rational independent of their biological make-up.

These last remarks are helpful. Moral theories call for a measure of rationality, just as they call for a measure of altruism, in that they apply to only those creatures who can grasp the theories' content (at least to some extent), which presumably requires some rationality. However, it is just as contingent a feature of human beings that they are rational as it is that they are endowed with the capacity for motive altruism. If the former contingency is not threatening because it does not admit of any necessity, then neither should the latter, since both are equally contingent features of human beings.

Finally, there is this. What we are willing to settle for is clearly a function of what we take our options to be. To be sure, if moral reasons had the kind of motivational force that is claimed on their behalf (Section 2), then we would not need to be concerned with whether or not there was a congruence between our biological make-up and altruistic moral theories, with respect to our capacity to be altruistic. But insofar as moral reasons do not seem to have such powers, we must look elsewhere for the springs of our moral motivations. In the arguments of this chapter, I have aimed to show that the alternative to moral motivations' being grounded in the necessity of reasons is not their being grounded in desires that are ever so fleeting. For that which is contingent is not fleeting on that account alone. Our capacity for altruistic motivations, albeit contingent, constitutes a deep feature of the nature of human beings. From the moral point of view this capacity gives us something very substantial to work with.

Before moving on, there is an important objection that needs to be considered, which can be put simply as follows. History reveals that human beings have committed all sorts of evils against one another. Does this not show that it is false or, in any case, rather unreasonable to suppose that, as a matter of their biological make-up, human beings have the capacity for deep altruistic motivations? Rhetorically, one understandably asks: How can it possibly be held that the capacity for such motivations is part of the biological make-up of human beings in light of such moral atrocities as American slavery or the Holocaust?

At the outset, it should be noted that the arguments presented do not commit us to the thesis that all human beings always behave in deeply altruistic ways. Like talents and skills, moral capabilities surely need to be realized. To have a natural aptitude for, say, playing the piano, does not mean that one will play the piano well whether or not one practices, but only that as a result of practice one will more readily master the techniques and methods that make for excellent piano playing than will someone who does not have a natural aptitude for playing this instrument. One will perform much sooner with proficiency the more difficult finger movements, and so on. As a rule, in order for our natural talents to flower, other things must be in place. It is very rare that they flower under the most unfavorable circumstances. Our capacity for altruistic motivations must be viewed on the order of a natural talent—precisely on that order—so I maintain. Accordingly, one should not expect these motivations to be realized come what may, any more than one should expect a person's natural aptitude for playing the piano to be. Thus understood, behavior that is manifestly not altruistic does not show that this capacity does not come in the wake of our biological make-up, but only that it was not sufficiently realized in the lives of individuals who perform such behavior. Also pivotal to the realization of our capacity for altruism are the values that are constitutive of our self-concept; and exactly which values come to have this place in our lives depends very much upon our parental and social environments (Section 25).

This line of reasoning does not constitute a kind of philosophical sleight of hand. Consider. I have argued that human beings have the capacity for transparent love with respect to their offspring. This argument is not defeated by the reality that some parents care poorly or do not care at all for their children. It is clear or, in any case, it certainly can be true that as a species human beings have this capacity, although it is not always realized in the lives of particular individuals.

The objection may very well rest upon a confusion as to the nature of this project. I have not been concerned to show that human beings will be altruistic in their behavior simply in virtue of being human. My aim has been far more modest. I have wanted to show that being altruistic is in keeping with our biological nature because we have a deep capacity for altruism; for I have wanted to show that our acting in accordance with the requirements of an altruistic morality is not incompatible with the capacities that a deep-structured biological account of our motivational structure would reveal. So I have only been concerned to make a biological case for our having the capacity for genuine altruism, thereby providing a far less precarious foundation than self-interest, enlightened or not, for our being disposed to act in accordance with the requirements of an altruistic morality. To make this case is not to show that everyone acts altruistically all the time.

In this chapter, I have made much of the importance of parental love from a biological perspective. I have done so with an eye toward morality itself. In the next chapter the relevance of parental love to morality is taken up.

CHAPTER THREE

Parental Love: A Social Basis for Morality

That we have a morally good character is not settled by our biological make-up. Aristotle observed that we are neither good nor bad as a matter of nature (*Nicomachean Ethics* 1103a15–20). As an observation about the sort of moral character that we come to have and, therefore, the moral nature of our actions, this is surely right. While I have argued that we have a natural capacity for motive altruism, I have not claimed that this capacity is realized regardless of the circumstances of our lives. Our social development plays a decisive role in this regard, and thus in shaping the kind of moral character that we come to have. Pivotal to that development is, of course, parental upbringing. In this chapter I aim to offer an account of the contribution that parental up-bringing makes to a good moral character. Altruistic moralities require that from time to time we forgo a benefit for the sake of others. I hope to show that parental love can play a significant role in our coming to take delight in such behavior. To this end, I explore the significance of the child's coming to love his or her parents. Once again, a crude Freudian account of matters shall serve as a vehicle for developing the account offered.

7. The Freudian Moral Character

On a Freudian account of human development we are by nature quite self-centered individuals concerned to enhance our own happiness.[1] The happiness of others is only of derivative importance to us, if at all. As infants we can for awhile get away with being completely self-centered. At some point we realize that we cannot always have our wants satisfied upon command, as it were. Whereas crying once would immediately result in the infant being fed, the infant comes to learn that there are appointed times for receiving food. Whereas the infant once could relieve himself wherever he pleased, he comes to learn that there are appropriate receptacles for this sort of thing. The infant quickly learns that he has to temper the completely self-centered way in which he was initially able to attain the satisfaction of his basic urges, since that way is tolerated less and less by his parents.

What moves the child to adjust her behavior is the profound realization that her parents control the distribution of goods that satisfy some of her basic needs. This fact about the child's parents, along with their having the undisputed advantage in terms of physical strength, provides her with strong incentive to act in accordance with their wishes, and so to behave in ways that not only avoid incurring their disapproval but that actually meet with their approval. Thus, on a Freudian account the child has an incentive to act towards her parents in ways that are characteristic of altruistic behavior and to internalize the parents' personal, social, and moral values. The upshot, then, is that the child comes to temper her display of manifestly self-centered behavior in order to minimize parental disapproval and, ultimately, parental rejection. In turn, the child minimizes the risk that parents will withhold from her goods that meet her basic needs.

As the child matures, guilt feelings and conscience-ideals replace fear of parental rejection as the psychological mechanisms that operate to hold in place the child's internalization of his parents' values. So, in the last analysis, an individual's displays of behavior characteristic of both altruism and, more generally, of the moral values of

[1] Cf. Freud (1961), ch. 3, 4. My understanding of Freud owes much to Hall (1954). Something very much like the account I offer is put forth by Gilbert Harman (1977), ch. 5. He does not explicitly hold, as I do, that the Freudian personality is basically self-interested; however, I do not think that Harman's account of matters is incompatible with this view.

his society are nothing other than a repression of his natural self-centered impulses. And in a word, this the individual comes to do in order to survive. The mature Freudian individual turns out to be less manifestly self-centered in his behavior not because he is in fact a less self-centered individual, but because, starting with his interactions with parents, being less manifestly self-centered is the key to survival.

The key psychological mechanism at work is guilt. It is out of the desire to avoid feelings of guilt that the individual often does what is morally right (as determined by the standards of her society) even when it would be very much to her advantage to do what is morally wrong and, furthermore, she has every reason to believe that her morally wrong actions would go undetected. Indeed, on a Freudian account of things, guilt may be thought of as the solution to the n-person prisoner's dilemma situation. It is Freud's answer to Hobbes's Sovereign. Let me explain.

Freud and Hobbes assume that human beings are basically self-interested creatures.[2] Now, from time to time, at any rate, rational self-interest and altruistic morality conflict in at least the following sense: even if it is true that everyone would be better off were everyone to be moral rather than immoral, upon occasion it will be in the interest of some individual to act contrary to the claims of morality. This will be so on the quite plausible assumption that on some occasion a person could do so without detection or, in any case, without in any way affecting the commitment of others to continue acting morally. Should such an occasion present itself, it would be foolish for a person not to act immorally unless he is given some incentive not to do so. For Hobbes, that incentive is provided by the Sovereign. Those who act immorally are punished.

Hobbes's Sovereign is, of course, a heuristic device: there are no such creatures. It is a heuristic device that brings into sharp relief the problem of cooperation among basically self-interested creatures who have no reason to cooperate but for the fact that individuals are better able to pursue their self-interests by cooperating than by not cooperating. Such individuals have no reason to follow in every case the rules constitutive of cooperative acts. For not every such act will coincide with a person's self-interest and, moreover, in some instances

[2] My thinking here has been inspired by Roy (1976).

it will be possible for a person to better advance his self-interest by performing an act contrary to moral standards, since he will be able to do so without in any way affecting the commitment of others to act cooperatively. While this is usually because he will be able to do so without detection, this need not be the case. For instance, others may be so convinced that the person is committed to acting morally that they see the infraction as an isolated case about which they have nothing to worry. (We can assume for simplicity's sake that if a person's act would so affect the commitment of others, then it would not be in his interest to perform the act.) The problem, then, is that unless cooperation can be assured in cases of this sort, there will be no cooperation at all.

Freud's ingenious solution to this problem is feelings of guilt. Everyone can have feelings of guilt in abundance; guilt can be present at the sight of the smallest infraction and in the most secretive of circumstances; and, finally, feelings of guilt are not readily dislodged from the conscience. That is, once they are sufficiently associated with the performance of various behaviors, the psychological tie is extremely difficult to break. Since guilt feelings are unpleasant, they are to be avoided. Together, these considerations entail that a person will surely act morally if she can be made to feel sufficiently guilty for acting otherwise. So, on a Freudian view, the mature moral personality has sufficiently internalized the moral precepts of her society and is strongly motivated to avoid acting contrary to these precepts because that would cause sufficient feelings of guilt. She is thus motivated even when it would otherwise be in her interest to transgress and she could do so without detection. And it is the fear of parental rejection that sets the stage for this sort of internalization.

Now, it is a consequence of the Freudian account that I have developed that acting morally is not something a person finds intrinsically delightful. Rather, acting morally is something that a person is motivated to do because there is an external sanction attached to acting differently. The sanction is initially fear of parental rejection and, in due course, the desire to avoid feelings of guilt. The springs of moral motivation turn out to be nothing other than the avoidance of pain. Needless to say, on this account of matters altruistic morality can hardly be said to hold a natural attraction for us. Instead, it is something of a weight chained to us by certain psychological mechanisms. Take away the psychological mechanisms and we would hardly be inclined to behave in accordance with the demands of altruistic morality. Morality is not expressive of our true nature but is a device with which we must contend if we are to have any chance of living together harmoniously. And a high degree of compliance is ensured by feelings of guilt. Of course, Freud would be the first to acknowledge that most people probably would not describe their feelings in this way. Most people are not inclined to describe morality as an unwanted burden. However, in the final analysis that is what it turns out to be even if few ever recognize it as such. Or, at any rate, so it is on the Freudian account that I have constructed. A Freudian account of moral development is at odds with genuine motive altruism. I do not deny that moral development may take place in such a way as to yield a Freudian moral personality; no doubt it often does. However, it need not.

No doubt one reason why the Freudian account of the moral personality has, at least in part, seemed so appealing is that it would seem to yield the right view of the role that guilt does and should play in our lives. Given that guilt feelings are psychologically unpleasant, it is rather easy to suppose that the only role these feelings could possibly play in our lives is that of a psychological restraint in regards to morally wrong behavior. After all, no normal or psychologically healthy person would take delight in feeling guilty; we do not take intrinsic delight in experiencing feelings of guilt in the way that we do in experiencing, say, feelings of love. Thus, if feelings of guilt have any value at all, they have only instrumental value in the way just mentioned: they constitute a psychological restraint in regards to morally wrong behavior.

Freud saw what many since him have failed to see, which is that the more importance we attach to guilt's playing this kind of role in our lives, the more difficult it becomes to construe morality as the sort of thing that is, itself, intrinsically desirable. Indeed, any theory that presents morality as being attractive in its own right must accord guilt very little weight as a psychological constraint to acting contrary to morality. For given such an account of morality, there is precious little to be said for such a restraint. In this regard, it is interesting to note, as an aside, that Plato, who was as concerned as anyone to show that the just (moral) person is happier than the unjust person, made no reference to the desire to avoid feelings of guilt as an explanation for why people would be motivated to do the just or moral thing.

I have gone on at length about the tension between a Freudian account of the role of guilt in our lives and the view that morality is intrinsically desirable because I have wanted to make it very clear that we must give up anything like the former view if we are intent upon holding on to the latter. I do not want to suggest that guilt comes about in the way that Freud held that it did. Even so, he serves as a reminder that the explanation for why persons are motivated to act morally is very much related to their upbringing. Theories of reconstructed and rarified moral persons and accounts of the principles or agreements they would reach can be very illuminating (e.g., Gauthier 1986; Rawls 1971). But to show that such persons would agree to such-and-such is not to show that patterns of upbringing and, more generally, the development of the moral personality are or could be congruent with the moral theory advanced. If so, then any hope for compliance with the theory is a matter of wishful thinking. Or so it is unless one thinks that moral reasons have sufficient motivational force in and of themselves, and regardless of a person's circumstances. Because I do not think that, I believe it is of the utmost importance to show that, given reasonable assumptions about the nature of social interaction, the development of the moral personality is congruent with the demands of altruistic morality. I take the work of Freud as a reminder of the importance of attempting to accomplish this task.

A final comment is in order. I have argued (Section 1) that persons of good moral character are morally autonomous. Another difficulty with a Freudian account of the moral personality is that moral autonomy, as I have characterized it, is not attainable. Being independent in his thinking about moral matters is precisely what a person cannot be if his moral personality has developed along Freudian lines. This is because not only is a person's sense of right and wrong more or less handed down to him through the internalization of his society's moral values, but because he will be uncritically accepting of them if, indeed, the psychological mechanism of guilt is operating as it ought. For as I have argued, the very point of guilt is to ensure compliance with the moral values of society; and this it would do rather inefficiently, if at all, if persons were very much inclined to scrutinize the moral values of their society.

These observations serve to confirm the claim made earlier that being morally autonomous simply cannot be a matter of having only firm convictions (Section 1). For there are all sorts of reasons why a person can have firm convictions. On a Freudian account of matters, the psychological mechanisms of fear and guilt give rise to firm convictions, the result being a morally nonautonomous person. This is because if a person has a Freudian moral personality, then his commitment to doing what is morally right is not born of an appreciation for and understanding of what is required of him, but of a set of psychological mechanisms that operate independently of his understanding of the nature of his moral actions. Doing what is moral turns out to be more of a matter of compulsion than anything else.

On Freud's view, guilt is seated in the superego, and when the superego has developed properly, a person will be very much disinclined to act contrary to the moral values he has internalized. My remarks take this point one step further in a way that is quite consistent with the spirit of Freud's writings. I am suggesting that on a Freudian account, when the superego has developed properly, a person will be very much disinclined not only to act contrary to the moral values he has internalized but also to subject them to critical scrutiny as well. This is especially so if, as many do, the person interprets scrutinizing his values as a sign that he is simply looking for an excuse not to adhere to them. After all, it is only when we carefully examine our values that we are able to see the limits of their applicability and, therefore, that applying them can be exceedingly complicated precisely because there are hard cases.

These latter remarks bring out the authoritarian features of the acquisition of morality from a Freudian perspective. In the beginning a person's parents constitute his moral authority; parents are later replaced by the superego. Just as the child fears that it is inappropriate to question the moral values of his parents, he likewise feels that it is inappropriate to question the moral values he has internalized. In both cases, the guiding principle is that authority should not be questioned. The location of that authority is beside the point. Hence, it is irrelevant that the authority speaks through either the voice of his parents or the voice of conscience.

In view of these considerations, we are certainly justified in concluding that the Freudian moral personality is incompatible with moral autonomy. For it will be remembered that a characteristic feature of morally autonomous persons is that neither appeals to numbers nor arguments from authority suffice to settle moral matters with them. The suggestion here is not, of course, that neither parents nor the conscience plays an important role in the moral life of the morally autonomous person, but only that neither plays an authoritarian role in such a person's life. In what follows, I attempt an account of the acquisition of morality that embodies a nonauthoritarian conception of the moral personality.

8. Acquiring Altruistic Morality and Autonomy

The problem with a Freudian account of child development is that it underestimates the significance of parental love in the life of the child. More specifically, it misses the fact that parental love allays, if not precludes entirely, the fear of parental rejection. This is significant precisely because once the fear of parental rejection is eliminated or, at any rate, made negligible, then the door is open for a very different explanation as to how the child initially comes to be disposed to forgo a benefit for the sake of others, since in this regard fear no longer plays the explanatory role. And guilt can no longer be seen as the psychological mechanism that takes over where fear of parental rejection leaves off. As one might surmise, I want to say that the explanation is that the child comes to love her parents because they love her and, by their words and deeds, indicate to her that she is the sustained and manifest object of their affections.

At the outset, it must be noted that the explanation that the child is loved by her parents automatically casts a very different light upon why they provide for her. For to love someone is to take her well-being to heart, to delight in her flourishing, and so to want one's own actions to contribute to the enhancement of the person loved. One cannot love a person and be indifferent to that person's good; nor, a fortiori, can one love a person and desire, let alone seek to bring about, her or his downfall—at least not under that description. We can all be mistaken about both what a person's good is and how we can contribute to it.

Now, it will be recalled that on a Freudian view, providing for the child looks rather like a power move on the part of parents to ensure the child's compliance. The child, sensing this, comes to see that it is in her interest to comply. But if indeed parents love their child we surely have a very different explanation for why they provide for her. They delight in seeing her flourish, and in meeting her needs they contribute mightily to this. Sensing this, the child responds with love.

There can be no doubt that the assumption that parents love their child yields an account quite different from Freud's as to why parents are motivated to care for her. And the fact that children can discern the difference in how they are treated reveals the depth of their capacity to monitor human behavior. It is a capacity that manifests itself even in the absence of the child's ability to articulate the way in which she is treated by her parents.

The capacity to grasp the motivational structure of other persons is one of the deep features of our psychological make-up, and this capacity manifests itself very early on in human development. This should come as no surprise. After all, it is as children that we are most susceptible to feelings of vulnerability because so very much of what happens around us is beyond our comprehension. Children are constantly looking for assurances that the environment in which they find themselves is not a hostile one. And parents are among those who provide that assurance. Herein lies the fountainhead for the child's profound capacity to grasp the motivational structure of persons, namely, the child's need for assurances. Notwithstanding the fact that this need is great, children are not easily deceived in this regard. That is, deception cannot be sustained over a long period of time. This is because assurances must be constantly forthcoming.

At this point, I should like to introduce what we may call the principle of reciprocity: we become disposed to act favorably toward those who act favorably toward us.[3] From an evolutionary standpoint, there is a very good reason to suppose that this principle is to be invoked in the parent-child relationship. It is that unrequited love can be hard to sustain and, in any case, is emotionally unsatisfying. Being a parent would be very unsatisfying if children did not respond in kind to the love shown them. For a child's love for his parents creates a bond, which, in turn, replenishes the emotional outlay that comes with caring for a child.[4] Thus, the child's responding with love to the attention of parents renders the task of caring for the child enormously more tolerable psychologically. This, of course, is a good thing from an evolutionary standpoint.

[3] Cf. Rawls (1971): "The child comes to love the parents only if they manifestly love him" (p. 463). Rawls introduced this principle. My remarks are intended to give it a defense that is not to be found in his writings.

[4] E. O. Wilson (1978) writes: "The smile appears on the infant's face between two and four months of age and immediately triggers a more abundant share of parental love and affection" (p. 61).

Furthermore, children become adults. I have argued that, on evolutionary grounds, adults have the capacity for transparent love. Now,
since children are but the biological predecessors of adults, then we
may hold that if adults have this capacity, then children do as well,
unless, of course, there is an important biological account to the contrary. It is, to be sure, logically possible that transparent love is an
asymmetrical capacity triggered only by having offspring. But many
things are logically possible, the truth of which we have no reason
whatsoever to believe in (for example, by the year 2000 the institution
of marriage will no longer exist). There is no reason to believe that
the capacity for transparent love is triggered only by having offspring,
and I have already indicated why (Sections 5, 6). The capacity for
social cooperation is contingent upon the capacity for genuine altruism. And the biological capacity for transparent love is indeed evolution's gateway to genuine altruism. If adult members of the human
species have this capacity, then so must their children.

Now, I am not suggesting that an infant's responding lovingly to
parents constitutes a display of transparent love. That seems manifestly false. Rather, the point I wish to make is that if, in fact, all
human beings—and, therefore, all infants—are invested with the capacity for transparent love, then the principle of reciprocity is given
a very sure theoretical footing. This is so, at any rate, if one assumes
that if a being has the capacity for transparent love, then it has the
capacity for opaque love. This assumption seems reasonable enough.
If it is possible to come to love others without regard to their talents
and performances, especially on one's behalf, then surely it is possible
to come to love another on account of these things. And given that we
have the former capacity we will certainly be susceptible to feelings
of good will and affection toward those who make us the manifest
object of their affections. Putting the point this way allows for the fact
that there can be very good reasons for resisting the genuine affections of another. It may be necessary so to respond toward a person
with whom one does not wish to be romantically involved. All of this
should be apparent. Human beings have a remarkable capacity for
bonding (Section 5). The affections of others serve to trigger feelings
of bonding.

An additional reason for supposing that the principle of reciprocity is to be invoked in the parent-child relationship has to do with
the fact that the child may be a parent some day and that how to

display love and affection is not known innately but learned (Gruen 1988, pp. 7–10). It is primarily through interaction with parents that the child learns that some forms of physical touch, such as the ubiquitous kiss, constitute displays of affection and other forms, such as the pulling of hair, constitute displays of aggression. In other words, the interaction with parents gives the child an important lesson in nonverbal communication—namely, what the difference between displays of affection and displays of aggression comes to, which will never be revised but merely refined throughout the remainder of the child's life. It is a lesson upon which the child will draw when he has children of his own.

On the assumption that the principle of reciprocity is operative in the life of the child, we can say that she comes to love her parents. And once we can say this we can get an entirely different explanation for how the child initially comes to be disposed to forgo a benefit for the sake of others. To begin with, there is the simple fact that if we love someone, then we will be favorably disposed toward her and take her well-being to heart. Thus, it is impossible to love someone and, at the same time, be indifferent to whether others, including oneself, cause that person harm. It is, to be sure, quite possible to be ignorant of the fact that one is causing a person harm; but that, clearly, is a different matter entirely. We must often learn what causes harm to another. With adults, this usually pertains to learning what causes a person psychological harm, such as distress or anxiety or some other form of mental trauma; with children, this first pertains to learning what amounts to physical harm.

Accordingly, if we love someone, then the belief that we would cause that person harm (mental anguish or bodily injury) by our actions normally suffices to move us to refrain from executing the action under contemplation. Leaving aside cases in which it is supposed that no harm in the form of mental anguish would result if the action went undiscovered by the appropriate person,[5] it might still seem that this claim admits of too many exceptions to be true. There are those cases in which other intense feelings are also operative, such

---

[5] The case need not be one of infidelity. X may know that Y (parent, sibling, or friend) would be devastated if she knew of X's sexual orientation or that X no longer adhered to the religious beliefs according to which he was raised or that X is planning to marry a person whose ethnic identity differs from his.

as extreme jealousy. And there are cases in which parents who love their children nonetheless subject them to considerable physical abuse when they (the parents) are under enormous stress. Cases of this sort are paradigmatic examples of what I shall call emotionally estranged cases with respect to love. For these are cases in which other emotions are an obstacle to the proper expression of love. The thesis, then, is that in the absence of emotionally estranged cases with respect to love, the belief that our actions would cause harm (mental anguish or bodily injury) to a person we love is normally enough to move us to refrain from such actions.

This holds for children as well as adults. It is just that with children there is, as I noted earlier, the task of learning what constitutes an act of harm, a task that is complicated by the fact that children rapidly increase in both size and physical strength without fully appreciating it. Over the span of a year a playful act can become a painful one. The significance of this point, given our concerns, is that rather than fear of parental disapproval and therefore parental rejection, the child's love for his parents can serve as the primary explanation for how the child initially comes to be disposed to forgo a benefit for the sake of others.

Let me turn now to another feature of love, namely, that because we admire them we desire to be like those whom we love. From the very start, this claim needs to be qualified. To this end, it will help to distinguish between a self-in-realization and an unrealized self. Roughly, the former is one who can be understood as having various ground projects (cf. Williams 1976b), is guided by a conception of the moral good, and so on. The latter is one for whom none of these things holds true. When a self-in-realization admires another, she does so as one whose life has meaning and momentum independently of the person admired. Thus, she can have the deepest admiration for the person without adopting the goals and aims of that person. By contrast, the life of an unrealized self lacks sufficient meaning and momentum on its own to break the influence of admiration for another.

This distinction enables us to explain why, on the one hand, parents do not turn out to be like their children though they love them dearly and why, on the other, children usually very much desire to be like their parents. Generally parents are selves-in-realization, whereas children are, without exception, unrealized selves. And it is unrealized selves who are most vulnerable to the influence of their admiration for others. Furthermore, the child stands in a special social relationship to his parents, whereby he is the sustained and manifest object of the affections of his parents, two selves-in-realization.

It is in this light that one must consider the love and admiration that the child has for his parents. Social circumstances generally preclude the possibility of there being any serious competitors for these sentiments on the part of the child. Parents do not have to win their child's love in the way that we sometimes think individuals must do in cases of romantic love. Whereas one who pursues another in romantic love is generally concerned to show that she or he measures up to the romantic ideals of the person being pursued, the child does not start with, or subsequently convey to his parents, a deep conception of what loving parents should be like and which his parents then expend a great deal of energy trying to measure up to. On the contrary, it is precisely through interacting with his parents that the child comes to have a conception of how his parents should treat him, a conception that is eventually informed through his interactions with other individuals, children being foremost among them.

This reveals just how enormously important parents are in the life of the child, in that his conception of himself is so radically tied to how they treat him; for he does not bring to that interaction a prior conception of how his parents, or anyone else, should treat him. Now, to be sure, our conception of ourselves as adults can be influenced by how others treat us. It is just that as adults we bring to our social interactions some conception of ourselves. We have a conception of who we are, of what we can do, and of what we deserve and, therefore, of how others should treat us. And it is this conception that, for better or worse, is modified as a result of our interactions with others. The child brings to her interactions with parents no such conception to be altered. In view of considerations that have been advanced thus far in this section, it should be clear that, contrary to Freud, fear of parental rejection is no more necessary as the primary explanation for why the child internalizes her parents' values than it is for why the child consumes food. Her love and admiration explain much.

Bearing in mind the preceding discussion, let us look at Freud's observation that the child internalizes the values of his parents, including their moral values. It will be recalled that according to Freud, the primary explanation for this internalization is the fear of parental rejection. This follows from his picture of the personality itself, according to which the satisfaction of our own desires is the primary motivating factor in our lives. And, as it turns out, conforming to the wishes of others happens to be a means to this end. Even if it be allowed that parents genuinely love their children, this picture of the personality does not leave us with any room to say that the child is moved to respond in kind. I have, however, rejected this picture of things.

I have gone on at length to show that there is an important respect in which fear need not be a motivating factor in the life of the child. The reason for this should be straightforward enough. I want to claim that it is out of love for and admiration of the parents that the child is motivated to comply with their wishes and to adopt their values. With regard to motivations along this line, fear is the most powerful alternative explanation to the view that I am presenting. Thus, the view being advanced gains some plausibility from just the fact that the alternative explanation seems less plausible than might otherwise be supposed. Fear becomes considerably less plausible as an explanation for why the child is moved to obey his parents if the child is not weary of failing to measure up to the expectations of her parents. This weariness aside, then the only fear that remains to be allayed by love is the fear that can stem from being entirely dependent upon someone for the distribution of goods that one needs in order to survive.

Now, there would be reason to suppose that this fear cannot be allayed only if there would be reason to suppose that it is impossible for parents to win the trust and confidence of their child. To be sure, not all parents do. However, there is certainly no reason to suppose that none can. The trust and confidence of others is something that certainly is won in life; and there is no reason to suppose that the child has a special resistance to being won over by his parents with respect to trusting them to provide for him, however he might behave. On the contrary, one might suppose that it is particularly easy for parents to do this by being constant in their caring and providing for him in the face of differences in behavior on his part. This would make it impossible for the child to suppose that his being cared for is tied to whether or not he measures up to the expectations of his parents and, therefore, that his relationship with them is a precarious one.

Now, it may seem that I am painting too ideal a picture of the child's moral development. The form of the objection might be to concede that, for the reasons given, fear of parental rejection is not the explanation for why the child is motivated to comply with the wishes of his parents, but that fear of parental disapproval surely is. After all, so the objection might continue, it can hardly be denied that children are very solicitous of their parents' approval and that gratuitous disapproval can be devastating. These points, though well taken, do not tell against the account that has been offered.

First, at no point have I denied the importance of fear of parental disapproval as a motivating factor in the child's coming to obey her parents. However, it must be remembered that a person can have more than one motivation for complying with the wishes of another (Section 20). There can be a primary motivation and a secondary one. On a Freudian account of moral development the child's fear of parental disapproval and, as a result, parental rejection is regarded as the primary motivation for his initial moral development. And it is this view that I have called into question.

There can be no doubt that desire for the approval of others— parents, in the case at hand—can be a powerful motivating factor. Indeed, if we love and admire them, their approval will be of tremendous importance to us. This last point explains why the account offered can speak to the importance of parental approval in the life of the child and yet not even remotely resemble a Freudian account. On Freud's view the explanation for the desire for approval is inextricably bound up with the child's desire not to be rejected by his parents. But our account of the child's love and admiration for his parents provides us with an alternative explanation for why the child is so desirous of their approval, without in any way referring to fear of parental rejection. Thus, the account of parental love offered drives a powerful psychological wedge between being solicitous of the approval of others and being fearful of being rejected by them.

The great miracle of love lies in its power to preclude fear of vulnerability under circumstances when we are indeed most vulnerable. No other sentiment can have this effect upon a child's life.

I turn now to a very different way in which parents contribute to the moral development of their children. It will be recalled that I have distinguished between the morally anchored and the morally good. A distinguishing mark of the former is that they are morally autonomous (Section 1). In what follows, I shall explain how parents contribute to the moral autonomy of their children.

As we saw (Section 1), the morally autonomous characteristically are independent in their thinking about moral matters. Therefore, neither appeals to numbers nor arguments from authority suffice to settle moral matters with them. Another way of putting this is that because the morally autonomous are not so very solicitous of the approval of others, they have a high degree of immunity to peer pressure. Parents contribute to their child's becoming morally autonomous by engendering in their child what I have called basic psychological security (Section 5), that is, a sense of worth that is not tied to performances. Let me explain.

We are quintessentially social beings. And in virtue of being such, none of us has complete immunity to the opinions of others, especially those whom we hold in high esteem. Whether others respond favorably or unfavorably to our endeavors has an overwhelming influence upon the way we view ourselves and, indeed, whether we continue various pursuits. This point is so obvious, I trust, that to say more would be to belabor it. However, what might incline one to think otherwise is that some individuals do seem to carry on with their projects in spite of what others say against them. They seem altogether unfazed by the opinions of others. In fact, a rather venerable tradition in the history of moral philosophy has it that the truly moral person is the sort of individual who will continue in her endeavors to be just though the whole world should turn against her. While I shall argue in due course that this idea is merely a philosophical fiction (Sections 15, 16), I want to acknowledge that some people do successfully carry through with their projects in spite of having been widely discouraged. How can this be, if we are all quintessentially social beings and, on that account alone, are without complete immunity to the opinions of others?

The answer is very simple: While no one has complete immunity to the opinions of others, it is possible to have a degree of immunity. In this regard, previous successes that are indisputable in the public domain are a sine qua non. The successes need not be widely acclaimed. Almost no one need know that Jones received her degree from a quite distinguished institution; still, the fact that she did may go a long way in helping Jones to carry on her projects in the face of disapproval by others. Again, few need ever know that Smith received a note from a world-famous physicist in which she claims that Smith was the most talented student with whom she has ever worked. But assuming that the physicist has trained a number of students who have gone on to be very distinguished in their field, that note will go a long way toward enabling Smith to cope with disapproval of his ideas. No reasonable person can go on forever with widespread disapproval by those who are competent to judge the nature of his enterprises. But past successes, which may include nothing more than receiving tremendous approval from someone, can go a long way toward enabling us to endure criticism over an extended period of time. Past successes yield a measure of social immunity to the criticisms of others. Other things equal, the greater the successes, the greater the social immunity to the disapproval of others.

These remarks can be recast in more technical psychological terms. There is a positive correlation between social immunity to the disapproval of others and high self-esteem; and, in turn, there is a positive correlation between high self-esteem and performances or, at any rate, a conception of oneself as a successful person (Coopersmith 1967; James 1890). Self-esteem is to be understood as the conviction that one can interact favorably with one's environment; it constitutes a sense of worth. Thus, since being morally autonomous entails having a significant measure of immunity to the opinions of others, it follows that being morally autonomous entails having high self-esteem.

It is in light of the preceding discussion that we must look at the role that parents play in the child's becoming morally autonomous. To state the obvious, a child is not born with a history of successes that can serve as the basis for his self-esteem. Indeed, a child has no conception of success. This a child learns from his parents; and the initial basis for a child's having self-esteem is, quite naturally, parental approval. Furthermore, basic psychological security is the psychological underpinning in virtue of which parental approval has the proper significance in the life of the child. I develop these points in what follows.

Consider the case of the perfect performance child. She measures up to the wishes of her parents in every way; accordingly, parental approval is always forthcoming.[6] No parent could want for a better child. And as one might suppose, her parents are ever so proud of her. It is as if their daughter anticipates the very aims and goals they set

[6] The story of the perfect performance child is inspired by the writings of Karen Horney (1942), p. 44.

for her; and she always excels at whatever she does. She is a showcase child, if ever there was one. The problem, however, is that the child is made to feel that her very right to exist depends entirely upon measuring up to the expectations of her parents.

Of course, it never occurs to the parents that they are making their daughter feel this way; indeed, they would be deeply offended if anyone should intimate this. They see themselves as model parents. There is no meeting of the parent-teacher association that one or the other does not attend; usually both do. And it goes without saying that the daughter has no material needs that go unmet. It is just that the parents carry on so about their daughter's successes that it seems that all they do for her is something of a reward for her accomplishments. She has difficulty feeling that in the absence of her accomplishments she means anything to them; for her parents are so busy being excited by her accomplishments that they do not stop to indicate to her by their words and deeds that she is deeply important to them independent of what she can do. In a word, then, the child is lacking basic psychological security.

With the perfect performance child, we have a case in which parental approval in abundance nonetheless turns out to have the wrong significance in the life of the child. It is serving as a very poor substitute for a need in the child's life that only parental love can meet. And the most unfortunate result is that the child comes to have an untoward dependency upon the approval of her parents, since it is only in virtue of their approval of her performances that she deems her life to have any significance to them. She is eager to please her parents, not so much because she takes delight in receiving approval from those whom she loves, but because she is deeply solicitous of the only affirmation of her worth that she can get from them. Ultimately, though, their approval, however forthcoming and genuine, has to be unsatisfying, since it can never secure the conviction on the child's part that she has meaning to her parents notwithstanding her accomplishments.

As one might surmise, with the perfect performance child we have a case in which success fails to result in an individual with a high measure of immunity to the disapproval of others. On the contrary, it yields one who craves the approval of others. Furthermore, in spite of her confidence that she can interact effectively with her environment and that she can measure up to the expectations of others, she remains a deeply insecure person. The insecurity, of course, revolves not around her having an inadequate sense of her capabilities. Rather, I postulate that the explanation for this is that she is endeavoring to compensate for the failure to experience basic psychological security in the formative stages of her development.

If a child is to be an autonomous being, she must be raised so as not to crave approval from others, including her parents. And this is possible only if the child is first made to have a sense of worth that is not tied to her performances. Herein lies the way in which parental love is the key to moral autonomy. It goes without saying that parental approval does and should play a most significant role in the life of the child. But it will play the wrong role if the child is made to feel that in the absence of parental approval she has no worth to her parents. For then the child will crave her parents' approval as she endeavors to compensate for this lack in her life. Indeed, she will come to crave approval more generally; and it is this craving that stands as an obstacle to being a morally autonomous person. I do not claim that this obstacle cannot be overcome. But on that account the impediment to the moral development of the child is no less serious.

The scenario of the perfect performance child is very illuminating. It suggests—somewhat surprisingly, no doubt—that it might very well be better for a child not to always measure up to the expectations of his parents. For the gap between the child's performances and the parents' expectations allows the parents the room to make it unmistakably clear to the child that his worth to them is not tied to performances. For then there can be no question but that their shows of affection are precisely that rather than tokens of approval. As with much in life, matters are helped significantly when things are unambiguously clear. The suggestion here is that when a child does not measure up to their expectations, parents have the opportunity to make the difference between parental love and parental approval unambiguously clear. And I have argued that when this is the case the proper groundwork for the child's becoming a morally autonomous individual has been laid.

Naturally, I do not mean to suggest that the most appropriate occasion for the expression of parental love is when a child has failed to measure up to the expectations of his parents. There are no occasions that have this status. Rather, the point is that expressions of affection on occasions when the child has fallen short of his parents' aims do play a most important role in the life of the child by buttressing his conviction that he has a profoundly important worth to his parents that is not tied to his performances. It is this sense of worth that I have called basic psychological security.

One might very well ask how can parents be confident that they are, by their displays of love and affection, successfully engendering basic psychological security on the part of the child. A very good indication is the role the parents play in enabling the child to cope with the opinions of others. While at the outset, perhaps, all babies are cute creatures to be loved and adored, things change very quickly. Very early on, a child is subject to a barrage of expectations and assessments. In fact, some of a child's harshest critics in this regard can be her own peers. Though children rarely criticize with anything remotely resembling deep-seated malice, they can be exceedingly critical of one another. This is understandable, for acquiring a sense of competence is part and parcel of growing up, and the child does this by interacting with peers, who, obviously enough, constitue her comparison group. A child is constantly gauging herself by who likes her and what she can do vis-à-vis others. And then, too, there are the evaluations of other adults, such as her teachers and the parents of her playmates. So much evaluation of the child occurs; and, invariably, not all of it will be favorable.

One sign that parents are engendering basic psychological security in their child is that she is able to cope well with unfavorable criticisms from her peers and other adult figures. Being the most significant persons in a child's life, parents should constitute a haven to which she can retreat from the unfavorable opinions and criticisms of others. Parents should serve as a psychological buffer, as it were. But, needless to say, this they can hardly do if the child's significance to them is inextricably tied to her performances.

I now want to bring out another way in which basic psychological security contributes to the child's becoming a morally autonomous individual. It will be remembered that what distinguishes the morally autonomous from the morally nonautonomous is that the former do not uncritically accept the moral views to which they subscribe, whether those views prevail in society or not. It is not difficult to see how parental upbringing can incline children to engage in the critical examination of moral principles.

The first moral precepts that the child encounters are those her parents require her to follow. If the child does not so crave parental approval that she is afraid to inquire as to the soundness of the precepts that she is asked to follow, then she is very likely to ask why she is being required to act in a particular manner. To be sure, sometimes such inquiries will be born of the child's reluctance to obey her parents; other times, the inquiries will be born of genuine curiosity. In any case, parents can either be accepting or unaccepting of their child's queries about the moral principles that they require her to follow. By being accepting of the queries, parents lay the foundation for the child's becoming morally autonomous; by being unaccepting, they make the child's road to moral autonomy rocky, if not altogether unpassable. Parents are accepting when, rather than rebuking the child when she asks why she should or should not do such-and-such, they attempt to explain why they require her so to behave. Rather than seeing the child's queries as a challenge to their authority, they see them as an opportunity to enlighten the child so that she can better grasp why she should want to behave as is required of her.

Naturally, there are times when parents must insist on obedience in spite of it all. I have not supposed otherwise. However, it is one thing to insist on obedience after having attempted to explain to the child why she is being required to behave in a certain way. It is quite another to insist on automatic obedience and to make it clear that one considers requests for explanations inappropriate because in and of themselves they indicate an insufficient regard for authority. There can be no doubt that sometimes children must be made to do what they otherwise would not do and that they cannot always comprehend why they must do certain things. But there can be no surer way to thwart the development of a child as a morally autonomous being than to make it clear to her that proper behavior on her part requires silent and unquestioning acquiescence to the demands of parental authority.

The moral life is exceedingly dynamic and full of subtleties and complexities. For example, honesty is rightly regarded as a virtue. Yet many parents who firmly believe that (as their deeds make clear) would have their children believe in Santa Claus (at least for awhile). A child might very well come to notice the discrepancy here between policy and practice, especially if she has a sibling who is younger by just a few years. The child who brings this to the attention of her parents should not be coerced into silence. Rather, an explanation should be offered. Even if the child does not fully comprehend the explanation, her parents will nonetheless have communicated to her that they approve, or at least do not disapprove, of her enquiries concerning what is required of her.

Parents who engender basic psychological security in their children are rather likely to be accepting of their child's queries concerning the moral precepts that they ask her to follow. This is because such parents are, from the outset, concerned to engender in the child a sense of worth that is not tied to her measuring up to their expectations. Unquestioning obedience to their authority is not the criterion by which they measure the success of their child's moral development. What is more, the child will sense this and will be more likely to feel that she can ask her parents questions about what they require of her—and that she can do so without jeopardizing her relationship with them. Basic psychological security engenders in the child feelings of self-reliance (Bowlby 1979), and these feelings are conducive to a child's becoming morally autonomous.

To be a parent is to have the opportunity to participate ever so fully in the flourishing of another life. This chapter speaks to the unequivocal importance of parental love to a child's flourishing, including her moral flourishing. It is a characteristic feature of love generally that it contributes to our flourishing, including our moral flourishing, as I hope the pages that follow make evident.

CHAPTER FOUR

An Account of Friendship

Aristotle observed that a person would not choose to live without friends although he had all other goods (*Nicomachean Ethics* 1156a5). It is clear that Aristotle took friendship to contribute in an enormous way to an individual's flourishing, including his moral flourishing. My aim in this chapter is to offer a systematic account of this rich interpersonal relationship, thereby setting the stage for the next chapter, in which the role friendship plays in our acquiring and maintaining a good moral character will be explored. Although the account offered obviously owes its inspiration to Aristotle, my aim has not been to defend his views as such. There are various species of friendship, such as friendships of pleasure and friendships of convenience. I refer to the species of friendship discussed in this chapter as companion friendship.[1] The account of friendship I offer is both descriptive and normative.

---

[1] This taxonomy of friendships is obviously Aristotle's. What I am calling companion friendship is called perfect friendship by some and complete friendship by others. John Cooper refers to it as character-friendship. My thinking on Aristotle's account of friendship has been sharpened by John Cooper's discussion of the topic. See, for example, Cooper (1980). I have also benefited enormously from the growing contemporary discussions of friendship, including Badhwar (1985, 1987), Schoeman (1985), and Sherman (1987). I have also profited from the work of Marilyn Friedman (1988).

9. The Character of Friendship

Companion friends love each other. But surely this cannot be the distinguishing feature of friendship. For as the parent-child relationship makes abundantly clear, two people can love each other quite deeply and yet not be friends. Indeed, parents and children may not even confide in one another, whereas the idea of deep friends not confiding in one another seems almost unthinkable.

There are three salient features of companion friendships that are not characteristic of the typical parent-child relationship: (1) Companion friendships are a manifestation of a choice on the part of the parties involved. (2) Neither party to the relationship is under the authority of the other. This is not to say that they are equal in the amount of authority they have; nor, in particular, is it to say that neither has influence with the other. (I leave aside job situations when in virtue of rank or responsibilities one has authority over the other.) (3) There is an enormous bond of mutual trust between such friends. This is a bond cemented by equal self-disclosure and, for that very reason, is a sign of the very special regard that each has for the other. I shall discuss these points in turn.

In one sense this first difference requires no explanation. Children do not choose their parents, though they may make lots of other choices in connection with their parents, including sometimes the one with whom they shall live. But is it just as obvious that we do not choose our friends? Well, yes and no. On the one hand, there is clearly something to the idea that friendships are an expression of choice; no one supposes that she or he had no alternative but to be a person's friend. Yet, it is all too obvious that as a rule we do not self-consciously choose our friends in the way that we choose, say, the clothes that we wear. One does not shop for a friend in the way that one shops for an article of clothing. There is a very clear sense in which we grow into friendships; indeed, we can even be surprised that our interaction with someone has given rise to such companion friendship. It might never have occurred to us that so deep a friendship would have developed. Thus, on the other hand, there is a sense in which friendships happen to us. Do we simply have conflicting intuitions about friendship or do they reflect our feelings about different aspects of this kind of interpersonal relationship? It is the latter, so I shall argue.

As I have observed, companion friendship involves love. In fact, it parallels romantic love to a remarkable extent. Now, people are often said to fall in love. I hold that a similar phenomenon can occur with friendship. In the case of romantic love, the conversational implicature (Grice 1975) is clearly that the person about whom this is said was more or less besieged by feelings of love for so-and-so, as opposed to choosing to have those feelings. Still, no one would say that a person had no choice but to love the individual in question, notwithstanding the fact that initial feelings of love are sometimes experienced as an onslaught. To understand what happens here, some observations about social interaction are in order.

We may think of such interaction as being on a continuum with respect to being structured.[2] At one end we have maximally structured social interaction, where the interaction of the parties in question is highly governed by the social roles they occupy; at the other we have minimally structured social interaction, where how the parties interact is not primarily a function of social roles, and so where matters of propriety and protocol are least apropos, if at all. In the latter instance, morality alone is indispensable to how the parties interact. Most social interaction, of course, falls somewhere between these two extremes.

Interaction between heads of state is generally maximally structured, since it often involves highly ritualized behavior: what one says, the order in which one says it, one's posture while speaking, salutations, and so on are all rather structured. Most interactions between strangers, while not involving highly ritualized behavior, are nonetheless governed by social conventions concerning the roles of the parties involved, as between physicians and their patients, clergy and their parishioners, clerks and customers, and the like. Even behavior between associates is governed considerably by social convention. Associates are people who are not companion friends but who interact from time to time because they occasionally enjoy each other's company. It is a matter of great impropriety for associates to inquire casually about each other's personal life.

While it may be thought that interaction between immediate fam-

---

[2] On the topic of social roles, I am much indebted to Goffman (1959). The notion of a role understood here seems to be generally accepted. Robin R. Vallacher (1980) writes thus: "A role can be defined as a pattern of behavior that is prescribed (expected or demanded) in a given social relationship" (p. 23).

ily members is minimally structured, if any social interaction is, the truth of the matter is that this is rarely the case (except perhaps between siblings). For until very recently social conventions have strongly dictated what the roles and duties of wife and husband should be toward each other; and, of course, interaction between parents and children is also very much governed by convention. These remarks about social roles are developed and refined below (Section 10).

(Throughout, I shall restrict the use of family to cases in which children are being raised. This restriction would seem to accord with convention; for one can ask a [married] couple whether or when it plans to start a family. If the family is thought of as an institution, this makes sense precisely because it is in the context of having and rearing children that adults would seem to acquire new obligations that cannot be circumvented by agreement. By contrast, a romantically involved couple, whether married or not, could agree to all sorts of arrangements, so long as no moral precepts were violated. Nothing about the wisdom of what is agreed upon is implied.)

As one might surmise, I want to say that companion friendships and romantic loves are characteristically and paradigmatically minimally structured interpersonal relationships. Even matters of etiquette and protocol are often put aside. We would not know quite what to make of two such individuals who, for instance, insisted upon addressing each other formally or holding each other to the minutest detail of etiquette when they were alone together, save that this was a precious form of amusement between the two of them. Deep friendship and romantic love are the only two forms of interpersonal relationships in which the involved parties interact intensely and frequently, but yet, aside from the rules of morality, the nature of that interaction is not defined by this or that set of social rules. If there is a caveat in order here it pertains to the extent to which gender alone is thought to entail a proper conception of behavior. This is a complication that I shall not pursue here. Suffice it to say that gender behavior can and often does make a difference. Females touch and embrace to a far greater degree than males (assuming heterosexual orientation across the board); and if touch is one of the ways in which bonding takes place,[3] then female-female friendships have an important dimension that male-male friendships lack.

[3] Cf. Bowlby (1979), pp. 68–69 and 129 ff. Bowlby cites approvingly the work of Harlow and Mears on rhesus monkeys. See Harry F. Harlow and Clara Mears (1979),

We are now in a position to give a partial explanation as to why deep friendships and romantic loves seem to be a matter of choice, on the one hand, and things that happen to us, on the other. I have claimed that deep friendships and romantic loves are characteristically and paradigmatically minimally structured interpersonal relationships. Needless to say, though, we do not go about our daily activities under the assumption that we could interact in this way with any person whom we might come across. Quite the contrary, we have every reason to believe that there are very few people with whom we could interact in this way. For minimally structured interaction will be harmonious only if the parties involved are sufficiently attuned to the way in which each other views and interacts with the world. Only the most self-centered of individuals could assume that most people are so attuned to him or her.

Now, not only do we go about our daily activities under the assumption that we could not have this kind of relationship with most others, but there is surely no way of knowing that such a relationship with someone is possible except through interacting with her or him. This is not to say that we cannot exclude some people outright, but that the only measure of whether or not it is possible to have such a minimally structured relationship with someone is to see how one's interaction with that person proceeds.

Given these considerations, the surprise element of deep friendships and romantic loves can be put thus: While interacting with a person under the ubiquitous assumption that most social interaction does not give rise to minimally structured relationships, we come to have the feeling that in the instance at hand such a relationship is possible. We are surprised because we had no more reason to believe that our interaction with this person would have given rise to such feelings than we had to believe that our interaction with others would

---

who observe: "The [monkey] infant differs from the human infant in that the monkey is more mature at birth and grows more rapidly; but the basic responses relating to affection, including nursing, contact, clinging, and even visual auditory exploration, exhibit no fundamental differences in the two species" (p. 103). A few pages later they write as follows of their experiments with monkeys: "We were not surprised to discover that contact comfort was an important basic affectional or love variable, but we did not expect it to overshadow so completely the variable of nursing; indeed, the disparity is so great as to suggest that the primary function of nursing as an affectional variable is that of insuring frequent and intimate body contact of the infant with the mother" (p. 108).

have done so, assuming that all those in question are moral individuals with their share of foibles. A person may unwittingly generate this feeling in various ways: by telling a story or revealing a facet of his life that strikes a rather responsive chord in our hearts, by behaving in a way that we find particularly moving, and so on. Though we have no control over a person's doing or saying things that so move us, what we do upon experiencing such feelings is another matter entirely. That is up to us.

This is where the element of choice in friendships and romantic love comes into the picture. We can examine our feelings in light of previous ones, if experience permits this. We can more carefully examine the life of the person whose behavior generated these feelings. In particular, we can examine our feelings about his behavior in several different contexts to be sure that there was nothing peculiar about the context that initially gave rise to the feeling that we could have a minimally structured relationship with the person. It is one thing to be intrigued, fascinated, and even captivated by a person who can generate this sort of feeling in us. We are rightly or, at any rate, understandably so moved by a person who can cause us to have such feelings. However, it is another thing to lose entirely one's sense of reason and perspective on things. Falling in love undoubtedly sometimes has this effect upon people, but this is not part and parcel of what it means to fall in love or, for that matter, to fall into a deep friendship. Before moving on, I should like to mention that I am well aware of the fact that deep friendships and romantic loves are not alike in all respects. It is generally held that the latter has a sexual element, whereas the former does not. I maintain only that the two are alike with respect to, on the one hand, being an expression of choice and, on the other, being experienced as something that seems to happen to us.

I turn now to the second salient feature of companion friendships, namely, that neither party to the relationship is under the authority of the other, which is not to say that neither is much influenced by the other.[4] (It will be remembered that I leave aside job situations in which in virtue of rank or responsibilities one has authority over the other.) Understandably, friends are quite influential in the lives of one

[4] On the topic of authority, I am much indebted to Kurt Baier (1972), especially for his distinction between authority and influence.

another. We can explain the significance of this feature of friendship by looking briefly at the parent-child relationship in this regard.

Parents are thought to have justified authority over their children. The right of parents to determine the good for their children is regarded as an important part of parental authority. Understandable though this may be—since children rarely have the wherewithal to determine their own good—the fact remains that children initially experience their parents as individuals who are entitled to determine the good for their children, and thus as individuals who are entitled to make authoritative assessments of the behavior in their lives. Hence, there is the presumption that children should defer to their parents' authority. It is this fact that explains why parents and children rarely form companion friendships. Parents generally take this presumption for granted; children spend a lifetime calling it into question.

Even after a child has become an adult and has acquired a defensible vision of his own good, this presumption tends to linger on the part of his parents. Consequently, the bond of trust that is indispensable to deep friendships is rarely formed. For in examining our lives with another, it is of the utmost importance that neither party feels entitled to make authoritative assessments of the other's life or feels that she or he is owed deference. Otherwise self-examination with another is more like having another sit in judgment upon one rather than the attainment of self-understanding that it is meant to be. The absence of such authority enhances the willingness of individuals to open the window of their lives to each other, which in turn cements the bond of trust between them. These considerations speak to the importance of deep friendships' being between equals.

While it need not happen as a matter of logic, it often does happen that when two people are sufficiently unequal with respect to their stations in life, the one with the higher station is inclined to think that his utterances have more authority than those of the other. This consideration, in turn, sheds some light on why companion friendships between the young and the elderly are rather unlikely to flourish in any society in which the elderly are, in virtue of being such, accorded special honor and privilege. For the elderly will be inclined to think that their utterances have more authority than the utterances of those who are many years younger. Thus, we have an additional factor that operates against the formation of companion friendships between parents and children, namely, the disparity in age.

We come now to the third salient feature of companion friendships, which, it will be remembered, is that there is an enormous bond of mutual trust between such friends and that this bond is cemented by voluntary self-disclosure and, for that very reason, is a sign of the very special regard that each has for the other.

There is a great deal of information that anyone can obtain about us merely by watching what we do and listening to what we say as we go about performing our various social roles.[5] I shall refer to this information as public information. It constitutes the outline of our lives. It is information over which we are concerned to exercise little or no control. Or, to put the matter differently, we are either indifferent or care very little about those in whose hands the information falls. Then there is guarded information about our lives, that is, information the dissemination of which matters considerably to us.[6] This I shall variously refer to as private or intimate information. Neither private nor public information is an all-or-nothing matter. Both admit of gradations or degrees. In any event, a person who has enormous public information about our lives will normally not be able to infer much concerning the private information of our lives. One important reason for this is that our motives for doing things constitute a significant aspect of the private information of our lives. And not only are our motives not always transparent, but we can often deny motives attributed to us without incurring much suspicion as to the veracity of our claims. I shall illustrate these points in the next section.

The bond of trust between deep friends is cemented by the equal self-disclosure of intimate information.[7] Why this is so shall become clear in what follows.

[5] Erving Goffman (1963) writes: "Although an individual can stop talking, he cannot stop communication through body idiom, he must say either the right thing or the wrong thing. He cannot say nothing. Paradoxically, the way in which he can give the least amount of information about himself—though still appreciable—is to fit in and act as persons of his kind are expected to act. (The fact that information about the self can be held back in this way is one motive for maintaining the proprieties)" (ch. 3, sec. 3, p. 41).

[6] The importance that I attach to private information is shared by others: cf. Gerstein (1978), Reiman (1976), and Schoeman (1984).

[7] The literature on self-disclosure is voluminous. I am indebted to the following: Archer (1980), Cozby (1973), Jourard (1971), Rubin and Shenker (1978), and Walker and Wright (1976). For our purposes, it is particularly important to keep in mind the difference between intimate and nonintimate self-disclosure and that self-disclosure

The distinction between public and private information can be blurred in one of two ways. We can be public about virtually everything in our lives or we can be exceedingly private. While perhaps both extremes are to be avoided, what is true, surely, is that deep friendships are very nearly impossible in the former instance. This is because the extent to which a person is willing to reveal to us private information is the most significant measure we can have of that person's willingness to trust us, where the trust in question implies considerably more than that the person takes us to be of unquestionable moral character. For we can trust a person in this way and still not have a deep friendship with that person. We can think of our trust that a person has a good or minimally decent moral character as basic trust. The more confident we are of the goodness of a person's moral character, the deeper our basic trust. We have deep basic trust in some neighbors and colleagues with whom we do not have companion friendships. We may think of the trust that is characteristic of companion friendships as intimate or privileged trust.

Now, the point is that if we are public about virtually everything in our lives, then we are left with little that can serve as the basis for intimate trust. We have few, if any, resources left whereby we can convey to another that we regard him as someone in whom we can have intimate trust. And there can be no deep friendship if we cannot convey this. Against this point, it might be said that notwithstanding the fact that we are very public about our lives, we could indicate to another that we regard him as someone in whom we can have privileged trust provided that we only accepted (or solicited) advice about our lives from him. Not so, however.

For, if things go as they should, our acceptance of another's advice is contingent upon our believing that he is in the position to give us advice. While various factors determine this, one of the most important is the amount of information the person has about our lives. So, to be very public about our lives is, by the very nature of things, to put ourselves in the position to receive advice from anyone who

---

tends to be reciprocal across levels of intimacy. That is, if A conveys to B information of a certain level of intimacy, then B will either respond in kind or attempt to break off the conversation, provided that B is not simply in the business of accumulating facts about A's life. As I hope is clear, the terms *private information* and *public information* as used in the text mark different ends of the intimacy scale, with the latter being less intimate than the former.

is frequently within the sound of our voice. Accordingly, we would not have much reason to accept a friend's advice over the advice of anyone else, save that we generally thought that the friend offered sounder advice. But, then, the determining factor in our accepting his advice would not be the friendship, but rather our favorable assessment of the soundness of his advice in comparison to that of others. Consequently, our accepting the friend's advice could hardly serve as an indication of the depth of our regard for him.

This is a good point at which to note the difference between companion friends and therapists, both of whom are good listeners, at least ideally. A therapist-patient relationship is formally unidirectional in that by and large the flow of private information is supposed to be from the patient to the therapist, and not the other way around. For in virtue of her training and experience, the therapist is deemed an expert at helping people to achieve self-understanding by listening to private information about their lives (to put matters rather simply). The psychiatrist's comments, therefore, have the status of authoritative utterances. The client is motivated to reveal private information to the therapist not out of delight in sharing such information with someone whom he loves, but out of a need to achieve self-understanding; and the therapist is regarded by the patient as someone who can facilitate this end.

An upshot of the foregoing considerations is that a marked disparity in the amount of private information that two individuals possess about or self-disclose to each other is an obstacle to the flourishing of a deep friendship because it bespeaks an authority relationship between the two individuals, with the one possessing the greater amount of information being in the superior position. When there is great disparity of this sort, what we have is not a friendship but something akin to a therapist-patient (or counselor-client) relationship.

In a relationship that both parties are interested in maintaining, there is usually reciprocity with respect to self-disclosure. That is, if A self-discloses to B a piece of information of a certain degree of privacy, then B reciprocates by disclosing to A an equally private piece of information. If B fails to reciprocate, then A will usually discontinue self-disclosing information at the level of privacy at which B did not reciprocate. If, however, A should continue self-disclosing to B at a level of privacy at which B will not reciprocate, then either A has a reckless disregard for the amount of private information that he reveals about himself or A finds that he benefits in some way by self-disclosing such information to B. Usually this would be through B's comments and queries on the things told to him by A. In this case, not only is B contributing to the attainment of A's self-understanding, but B's doing so is on the order of the therapist contributing to the client's self-understanding.

It goes without saying that friends are moved to help each other. They are moved to do so out of love; each takes delight in giving to and assisting the other. However, whenever there is a marked and continued difference in the extent to which two people can contribute to each other's good, the more favorably positioned one is likely to be moved out of feelings of pity to help the less favorably positioned one. There are two implicit premises here. One, of course, is that in personal relationships we do not take delight in self-disclosing our private information when self-disclosure at that degree of privacy is not reciprocated. The explanation for this is quite simple. The failure to reciprocate usually indicates one of two things: either the person does not trust us or he does not value our perspective on his life.

The other implicit premise is that, barring a reckless disregard for revealing private information, only someone in dire need of assistance in getting a perspective on his life would continue self-disclosing private information in the absence of reciprocity. This premise is grounded in the fact that, in the absence of their meeting an important need, we value associating only with those who indicate by their words and deeds that they have a positive regard for us. Those who neither trust us nor value our opinion regarding their lives make it manifestly and painfully clear that they do not have such a regard for us. Thus, self-disclosing private information to someone who does not have a positive regard for us in these ways is belittling and constitutes a form of self-effacement; hence, we are disposed to reveal private information in such instances only when we find doing so enormously beneficial. And so, like the patient to his therapist, we self-disclose not out of delight in sharing private information about ourselves with someone whom we love, but out of the need to obtain a better perspective on our own lives.

I wish to conclude this section with two comments concerning the role of self-disclosure in friendship.[8]

First, it is a mistake to suppose that we have reciprocity of self-

---

[8] In what follows, I am grateful to Norman Care for helping me to be clearer about matters.

disclosure only when the parties in question self-disclose about the same sorts of things. The emphasis in reciprocity is upon the level of intimacy as opposed to the type of information. This is as it should be, since what is deeply revelatory about the lives of individuals may vary. For some it is their sex life; for others, their struggle to excel; and for still others, their deep commitment simply to staying alive. It is understandable that during the course of any given conversation reciprocity of self-disclosure will yield information about the same sorts of things, since conversations generally have a focus. And sometimes the point of a conversation can be none other than self-disclosure itself, as when A reveals something quite intimate to B, and then asks B to reciprocate, period. If, however, in discussing a personal problem, A discloses certain information to B, it would be very insensitive of B to attempt to match the intimacy of A's self-disclosure by revealing something related to an entirely different aspect of life. B would do better not to disclose anything. And it is obvious, I trust, that the idea behind reciprocity of self-disclosure is not that of immediate reciprocity.

The second comment I wish to make is this: It might seem that I have made so much of the importance of self-disclosure in friendship that I have lost sight of the other very important aspects of friendship. After all, so it might be noted, friends—even companion friends— help one another in quite straightforward ways. This last point is true enough. I have made much of self-disclosure, however, because I have assumed that this is the predominant way in which companion friends can and do contribute to each other's flourishing, where the emphasis here is upon the improvement of character and personality. Insofar as individuals can be understood as being self-sufficient in that they have an adequate livelihood, I have assumed that by and large companion friends are self-sufficient or, in any case, that the material help each provides the other is quite ancillary to the friendship. This assumption, far from revealing a Western bias, enables us to see more clearly how rich a friendship can be that does not turn upon material offerings.

10. Friendship: A Gloss on Aristotle

I want now to discuss explicitly a number of Aristotle's claims, as a way of completing and rounding out the account of friendship offered.

My aim here is not so much to get Aristotle right as it is to develop some insights that are his or, in any case, plausibly regarded as Aristotelian.

Aristotle observed that friendship consists in giving rather than in receiving affection (*Nicomachean Ethics* 1159a28). In this regard he likens affection between deep friends to the affection that parents have for their children. It might seem that my remarks are at odds with this conception of friendship. But not so.

There is no incompatibility between A's being motivated to give B affection simply in virtue of taking delight in doing so and A's being cognizant of the extent to which A and B each contributes to the other's good. The reason why parental affection inclines one to think otherwise is that at the outset, at least, it is taken for granted that the child does not contribute equally to the good of his parents (save in the derivative sense that they feel good on account of contributing to the child's good). By the same token, it is all too obvious that, as Aristotle observed, parents are the greatest benefactors of children (*Nicomachean Ethics* 1162a5). We are all cognizant of the nature of this asymmetrical relationship between parents and child.

Needless to say, there is a very straightforward explanation for why parents should be accepting of this asymmetrical parent-child relationship. It is that the responsibility of contributing to the good of a helpless creature is precisely what one incurs in virtue of causing the child to exist. From the very start, this explanation blocks any claim to the child's contributing equally to the good of his parents. But this explanation does not obtain between friends. Nor is there any alternative explanation as to why anyone should continuously contribute to the good of someone who lacks the wherewithal to reciprocate.

What must be added to what has already been said is the fact that friends look to each other for spiritual and emotional support, whereas the child looks to his parents for such support, and not the other way around. For the needs of adults along this line are different from those of children; the latter are in no position to provide support of this kind to adults. It is because friends look to each other for such support that things become problematic when they do not contribute equally to each other's good. For no matter how much delight A may take in giving to friend B, A will nonetheless want to be able to look to B for support. And if he cannot find it there, that will be unsettling. For it will mean that B cannot play in A's life the role that A plays in B's life and, moreover, that A wants B to play in his (A's) life. This want on A's part is natural if A and B are supposed to be companion friends.

This brings us to Aristotle's claim that self-love is the basis for friendship.[9] It comes as no surprise that we want and delight in our own flourishing. So it is very understandable that we endeavor to do those things that contribute to it. It is also understandable that we should want others to contribute to our flourishing. But it is a different thing altogether to take delight in another's having considerable influence in the manner in which our flourishing expresses itself and to be solicitous of her or his opinions concerning our projects, where in neither case is the reason for this that (a) in the absence of that person's approval we do not feel that what we do is worthwhile, (b) we are fearful of being rejected by the person if our projects do not meet with her or his approval, or (c) the person is a sycophant in whose flattery we delight.

Deep or companion friends characteristically take great delight in the fact that the other has considerable influence in the manner in which the flourishing of each expresses itself. When such a relationship holds between two people, it is very easy for self-love to serve as the basis for friendship. To begin with, each loves the other and knows that he is loved by the other out of choice, and, therefore, each experiences the other as a fully autonomous being who, out of love and choice, profoundly identifies with and so wants the flourishing of the other. And because each has a commanding perspective of the other's life, each experiences the other's remarks and observations about his life and projects not so much as a different person offering an assessment, but as a form of self-reflection.

Through choice and mutual love, then, companion friends are an integral part of each other's lives. Thus, for each to want his own flourishing is for each to want the other to flourish. It is in this sense that self-love can serve as the basis for companion friendship. Just as a person naturally desires his own flourishing, companion friends naturally desire each other's flourishing precisely because each regards the other as an integral part of his life. In this sense, the love of friendship is very much like that of parental love. A child's flourishing does not have instrumental value in the eyes of his parents, but is regarded

[9] *Nicomachean Ethics*, Bk. 9, Sec. 4. In writing this section, I have profited from A. Baier (1982).

as a good in and of itself, for the very reason that parents see the child's good as an integral part of their good. The difference is that this identification with the good of the other is reciprocated in companion friendships but not in the typical parent-child relationship.

In his discussion of friendship, Aristotle raised the question of how many companion friends we could have. His well-received answer was that we have neither the psychological wherewithal nor the time to have more than a few such friends. I have no intentions of challenging Aristotle on this point; on the contrary, I think that it may very well be difficult to have more than one companion friend. However, it is worth noting that the considerations adduced raise only practical difficulties with having many companion friendships, not in-principle difficulties. If a person had endless emotional resources and were capable of using her time most efficiently, would there be any difficulty with her having a large number of companion friends? I believe so. For as I shall try to show in what follows, there would seem to be in-principle difficulties to having more than one companion friend.

As we saw, privileged trust is the bond of companion friendships, a bond that is cemented by the self-disclosure of intimate information. So, if John and Tom are companion friends, then it follows that each has been most revealing about himself to the other—on the assumption that such information would be held in the strictest of confidence. This fact, alone, points to why a companion friendship with more than one person would present difficulties. Suppose that there is Paul, a third candidate for a companion friendship. Paul is either companion friends with both John and Tom or with only one of them, say, John. Respectively, we have a closed triangle companion friendship, in which all three are equally friends with one another, and an un-closed triangle companion friendship: John and Paul are companion friends, as are Tom and John, but not Paul and Tom. Starting with the latter, I shall argue that we have in-principle difficulties in either case.

If John and Paul were to become companion friends, then there would be one profoundly important part of John's life—namely, John's friendship with Tom as it involves intimate information concerning Tom—that John could not, without violating Tom's trust, share with Paul; and there would be another profoundly important part of John's life—namely, John's friendship with Paul as it involves intimate information concerning Paul—that John could not share with Tom without violating Paul's trust. It is understood that this is because Paul and Tom would object bitterly to such a thing. Hence, there would be an in-principle obstacle to the companion friendships between John and either Tom or Paul plumbing the depths that it should.

These difficulties are not gotten around if John, Tom, and Paul form a triangle of companion friendship, so that all are equally deep friends with one another. This is on account of what we may call the principle of the autonomy of self-disclosure. According to this principle, the more intimate a piece of information about us is, the more important it is to us that such information be revealed to others by ourselves and not by another, however confident we are that the person could present the information without in any way distorting it. The explanation for this principle has to do with what we may call the phenomenology of self-disclosure, especially of intimate information. When we reveal a piece of intimate information about ourselves, we try to gauge our listener's reaction to that information. And the more intimate the information is, the more attentive we are to the reactions of our listener. This is so whether we are disclosing the information out of the need for guidance or out of the desire to share an important part of our lives with another (something we may do for a variety of reasons, including to be supportive). In any case, our listener's reaction is important to us precisely because it indicates to us how the information we have revealed has been received. Did we lower ourselves in his eyes? Had he suspected so all along? Was the person particularly touched by the self-disclosure? Was he embarrassed? Was the self-disclosure interpreted as a sign of weakness? And so on.

Now, a person's reaction to a piece of intimate information is not composed simply of his verbal response, but his nonverbal behavior as well.[10] And there can be no substitute for witnessing a person's nonverbal response to what we have revealed. A person's assessment of how the information he disclosed was received is inextricably tied to his assessment of the listener's nonverbal behavior (Section 17).

---

[10] In addition to Goffman's work on nonverbal behavior, I have learned much from the essays in Hinde (1972). See, especially, the essays by Michael Argyle, Irënaus Eibl-Eibesfeldt, and Jonathan Miller. Nonverbal behavior has two parts: (a) body language, which includes proximity to speaking partner, appearance, posture, head nods, facial expression, gestures, and eye contact and (b) character of utterance, which includes pitch pattern, stress pattern, pausing and timing, and breathiness. See Argyle (1972), pp. 246–51. For a good, yet textbook, discussion of nonverbal behavior, see Malandro and Barker (1983).

Painful self-disclosures come readily to mind in this regard—such as revealing that a parent committed suicide or that one had been sexually abused by a parent. But the self-disclosure need not be painful, as when one shares a very personal letter written to one many years ago by a sibling. The letter may contain nothing more than some wonderful musings by the sibling as to the kind of person that one would turn out to be.

With regard to the triangle friendship under discussion, no matter how accurately John might report to Paul the verbal response of Tom, John could not display or mirror Tom's nonverbal response to the information.[11] This John could do only if he could somehow manage to reproduce Tom's nonverbal behavior so perfectly that it would be as if Paul had in fact witnessed Tom's nonverbal response to the information about Paul that John had revealed to Tom. But the problem here is that by hypothesis Paul would know that this was an act on John's part, hence Paul would not be witnessing a genuine reaction to what had been revealed about him to Tom but, instead, a flawless reproduction of a genuine reaction to what had been revealed. This is relevant because no matter how Paul might be moved by John's performance he will not be responding to Tom. Not only that, we can easily think of cases in which Paul clearly ought not to respond to John as he would respond to Tom. Suppose Paul is enraged at Tom on account of having been moved through John's flawless reproduction of Tom's response. It is all too clear that Paul should nonetheless not be angry at John.

In a word, then, being able to witness and respond to a person's initial and genuine reactions to intimate information that the person has learned about us is important to us; and we can do neither if such information is conveyed to that person by a third party. This is true no matter how close the third party is to all individuals concerned, and no matter how accurately he reports the response of the person to whom he revealed the information. What is more, if the foregoing considerations are sound, then the difficulties we encounter in the triangle companion friendship between John, Tom, and Paul are not far

---

[11] In "Language and Human Nature," Charles Taylor (1985) eloquently writes: "Expressions, by contrast, make our feelings manifest; they put us in the presence of people's feelings. Expressions make something manifest in embodying it. What expression manifests can only be manifested in expression" (p. 219).

removed from those we encounter when John and Tom are companion friends and Paul is a candidate for companion friendship with John. For in the triangle case all parties will have reasons of an in-principle sort for not revealing intimate information about one member of the triangle to the other.

Aristotle concludes his rich discussion of friendship with the observation that companion friends seek to live together.[12] His explanation here would seem to be straightforward enough: Because they take delight in each other's company and in doing things together, they want to maximize the amount of time spent together. There is, however, another significance to be attached to friends' living together in order to maximize the amount of time spent together, namely, that through doing so friends come to have a commanding perspective of each other's lives. This point can be best brought out by again looking briefly at the notion of a social role.

As I have remarked (Section 9), a great deal of social interaction involves role playing. We have role playing whenever there are well-delineated modes of behavior that are generally expected of a person, given the position he occupies in an institutional structure (for example, professor or student) or the significant social category in which he falls (for example, member of a gang or an affluent class); and the primary explanation for the person's behavior in a given situation is that he occupies an institutional position or falls into a social category of which the preceding is true. As these remarks suggest, the significance of social roles lies in the fact that they specify the appropriate forms of behavior for the individuals over whom the roles range. And the range of behavior here may include both interpersonal and noninterpersonal behavior. For instance, gender roles clearly specify how men and women should behave toward members of both genders. And just as clearly, they specify how men and women ought to behave though they should interact with no one at all.[13]

Needless to say, the idea here is not that role playing constitutes

[12] He writes: "What the erotic lover likes most is to see his beloved, and this is the sort of perception he chooses over the others, supposing that this above all is what makes him fall in love and remain in love. In the same way, surely, what friends find most choiceworthy is living together. For friendship is community and we are related to our friend as we are related to ourselves" (*Nicomachean Ethics*, 1171b30–35).

[13] See, for example, the important collection of essays in Mayo and Henley (1981).

less than genuine behavior on the part of a person. The point, rather, is that widespread social expectations substantially influence the behavioral patterns that we develop. Most social roles that we occupy can be and are played out in a variety of ways. Not only are there members of the clergy, parents, businesspeople, professors, students, and so on, of all stripes and persuasions, but people generally act these roles out differently depending on the circumstances and context. On the first day of class, for instance, a professor may out of concern to demonstrate her professional competence come across as very erudite and impersonal; afterwards, she may warm up to her students. Sometimes being a parent calls for gentleness, sometimes firmness, sometimes both. I shall refer to the way in which people act out their roles as role expression.

It is obvious, I trust, that role playing is virtually inescapable, since all of us either occupy some institutional position or fall into some significant social category. Gender-based or familial roles come quickly to mind here. Generally, we play one or both of these roles throughout our lives. In truth, the majority of us occupy a number of roles simultaneously. Someone may at once be a professor, spouse, parent, church deacon, and member of a company's board of trustees, although it is rather unlikely that she will have to play all of these roles simultaneously. Still, she may experience tension on account of the demands of these roles. Her church's position on an important social issue may be somewhat at odds with the policies of the company on whose board of trustees she sits.

We are now in a position to explain why maximizing the amount of time spent together enables friends to acquire a commanding perspective of each other's lives. As we shall see, there are two respects in which this is so.

One of them, clearly, is that maximizing the amount of time spent together enables friends to observe the behavior of each other over a wide range of the social roles that each occupies, and to do so in a variety of contexts. This, in turn, enables each to have a very informed picture of how the other expresses himself in his various roles. For it is in part through the roles that we occupy that we live our lives, since they are one of the primary vehicles through which we engage in social interaction. But, it will be remembered that at any given time we do not act out all of the social roles we occupy. Thus, a complete picture of a person is not to be had if our observations are limited to only one of the individual's social roles. Nor, a fortiori, is one to be had if we are unfamiliar with the variety of ways in which the person may express himself in that role. This is because it is primarily through role expression that traits of character and personality are revealed or that we can come to have a sense of the contours of those traits.

For instance, whether a person is insecure or ambitious is not readily revealed by the social role that she occupies, since any number of such roles are compatible with these traits. But over time, her role expressions will undoubtedly reveal the truth about her in this regard. And it is only through a person's role expressions that we can know the way in which her kindness, say, manifests itself. Obviously enough, a well-informed picture along these lines is rarely to be had at a single glance.

Now, the other reason why maximizing time spent together is indispensable to friends' coming to have a commanding perspective of each other's lives is that when they do so, the interaction between them is minimally dependent upon the social roles they occupy. Let me explain. In general, our social interaction revolves primarily around our social roles. Moreover, the nature of our interaction is generally determined by one or more of these roles. We interact as fellow employees, members of the same profession, customers and merchants, physicians and patients, lawyers and clients, parents and children, husbands and wives, and so on. Now, since social roles pertain to the ways in which people are expected to behave, this means that our behavior is significantly influenced by prevailing expectations. This point holds whether or not we act in accordance with the norms of the social roles we occupy. Our behavior may very well be designed to shock people; but this can be our aim only if we choose to act contrary to the norms of the social role in question. To flaunt a social norm is not simply to fail to do what the norm requires; it is to act contrary to the norm in a calculating and self-conscious manner, and so with an acute sense of what the norm requires. Hence, our behavior is still influenced by the prevailing expectations regarding the social role in question.

By contrast, precisely what distinguishes the interaction characteristic of companion friendships (and loves) from other forms of social interaction is that none of the social roles that friends occupy serves as the primary basis for their interaction.[14] It is not primarily because they are fellow employees or have entered into a client-lawyer relationship, or some such thing, that friends interact with each other. Rather, the raison d'être for their interaction is the delight that they take in being with each other. It follows, then, that the expectations of others as refracted through the prism of social roles minimally, if at all, influence the way in which friends interact. This last point is of great significance because it means that friends can count on each other not to evaluate them simply in terms of the prevailing expectations concerning the social roles they occupy. (The claim is not that friends do not evaluate each other.) This, in turn, contributes mightily to their having a commanding perspective of each other's lives.

It should be intuitively clear why this is so. An interaction not governed by social roles is freer in the sense that how each party reacts to the other is not substantially influenced by the expectations of others. Specifically, precisely because each can count on the other not to evaluate him simply in terms of the prevailing expectations concerning their social roles, each is able to speak freely about his roles and the ways in which he expresses himself in them. In speaking freely in this way, each makes himself most vulnerable and provides the deepest insight into his own character and personality.

To take an example, suppose Susan and Mary are companion friends and that Paul is one of Susan's Ph.D. students. It is generally assumed that the reason why Susan interacts with Paul, who is married, in such a formal manner is the same as everyone else's, namely, Paul's quite arrogant manner. But Susan confides in Mary that while she (Susan) agrees that Paul is arrogant, the real reason why she keeps her distance from him is that she finds him incredibly attractive—in fact, his arrogance is part of the attraction—and feels that she will best be able to respect his marriage if she maintains a formal relationship with him.

Here Susan is commenting on the nature of her role expression in

---

[14] I wish to record my awareness of the fact that male-female relationships generally involve considerable role playing along gender lines, in spite of the fact that the basis for the interaction is love itself. One can either suppose that male-female roles are primitive in some way or that the entrenchedness of the roles is due to other factors. I believe that the latter is the case, as should be clear from what I go on to say in the text (Section 11). See also my (1980b) discussion of sexism and racism.

her interactions with Paul. Her remarks are very revealing. For one, they reveal that Susan is able to use formality to hide sexual attraction. Not everyone can effectively use formality in this way. For another, they give tremendous insight into the kind of person she finds romantically captivating, and so what traits of character and personality are important in a potential romantic candidate. Many find arrogance very off-putting. For a third, her determination to respect Paul's marriage reveals that she is a person of principle. No one could possibly glean so much from simply observing Susan's interaction with Paul.

Susan makes herself vulnerable to Mary in the following way. By revealing to Mary that she sometimes uses a formal manner to mask her deep feelings, Susan thereby discloses that her formal behavior can be interpreted in two ways, one of which entails that she is deeply affected by the person with whom she is interacting. She thus gives Mary reason not to assume always, as otherwise it would only be reasonable to do, that her (Susan's) future formal behavior is just a matter of keeping an arrogant man in his place. To be sure, if queried, Susan can always deny that there is anything more to her behavior than this. But the point is that Mary's query has a reasonableness it would, and could, not have had but for Susan's revelatory remarks to Mary; and Susan knows this. Thus, as these observations suggest, it is possible to know something quite significant about a person's life and yet not be entitled to broach the subject with that person, if the individual has not voluntarily disclosed the relevant information.

Thus, suppose that for several nights in a row a couple forgets to pull their shades, while leaving the lights on. The result is that the neighbor (in the geographical sense only; these individuals do not interact socially) across the street can see clearly into the couple's bedroom; and she sees the couple engaging in strange sexual behavior. The neighbor has not come by that information illegally or immorally. If anyone is at fault here it is the couple, for failing to secure their privacy. Nonetheless, it would be quite inappropriate for the neighbor to offer commentary upon the couple's sexual behavior, should the neighbor and the couple become social acquaintances. Indeed, this holds even if everyone should become the closest of friends, provided that the couple really has not broached the topic with the neighbor and, as would be hard to imagine, there is no overriding moral reason for the neighbor to raise the subject with the couple.

Before bringing this section to a close, I wish to speak to two further characteristics of individuals who are companion friends.

One of the arguments of this section is that deep friends come to have a commanding perspective of each other's lives, since the interaction between them is minimally structured. This is important because it points to why such friends are able to contribute significantly to each other's self-understanding. If in general people are mirrors to one another,[15] then friends are especially so precisely because of the commanding perspective they have of each other's lives. That companion friends contribute to each other's self-understanding is a familiar enough point, which I believe is especially significant when it comes to the moral flourishing of individuals. This consideration shall be developed in the next chapter. For the moment, I want to call attention to an important character trait that individuals must possess if they are to be able to contribute masterfully to the self-understanding of another individual. This character trait is easily expressed in negative terms, namely: such a friend cannot be a sycophant. He cannot be so solicitous of the approval of his friend that he is unwilling to jeopardize the friendship by calling attention to an unnoticed failing or shortcoming on the part of his friend. It is understood, of course, that a friend does not point up a failing with all the thrill of playing a sport. Nor does he sit in waiting for a fault to manifest itself, rather like a cat might wait for a mouse to appear out of hiding. The enormous love that friends have for each other ought to preclude this sort of thing, surely.

Preserving a friendship cannot be so important to a person that he is prepared to tolerate egregious moral failings in his friend. It is difficult to be much more precise than this. After all, infallibility, moral or otherwise, eludes everyone. If there is a general principle to be followed, it is this:[16] A person should not jeopardize the good qualities of her own character on account of a friendship; nor should she tolerate a friend's indifference to his own failings. Being fallible is not as such the problem; being indifferent to one's shortcomings is.

A directly relevant issue here is the question of loyalty. Formally, loyalty differs from altruism in that the former presupposes a preexist-

---

[15] See Ch. 1, n. 1.
[16] I am inspired here by Nozick (1981), ch. 5, sec. 1, 2.

ing bond or tie. Complete strangers (Section 16) cannot be loyal to one another, though they can be relentlessly altruistic. Further, whereas altruism invariably expresses itself in the bestowal of a benefit, this is not so with loyalty. In the political arena, for instance, one mark of the loyal follower is that he does not forsake his candidate even though he is unable to improve the candidate's circumstances in the relevant respects by remaining with her. Staying with a defeated candidate does not change a past defeat into a victory, except perhaps in the extended sense of bringing about a future victory. Likewise, the loyal soldier does not desert his captain in battle, though there is no reason for the soldier to believe that staying by his captain's side, so to speak, will turn the tide in the captain's favor. On the contrary, the soldier can have every reason to believe that nothing of the sort will happen. The loyal soldier does not, upon seeing the inevitable capture of his own captain, turn to see whom he can best help next. An extraordinarily altruistic and brave soldier might do just that should he have no loyalties.

Companion friends are loyal to each other. They believe that it is important to stand by each other even when doing so will hardly serve to improve the other's lot. It is the pull of loyalty, which is part and parcel of deep friendship, that often explains why one party to the friendship will tolerate deep shortcomings on the part of the other. There is something rather unsavory about walking out on a friend just because her behavior, moral or otherwise, is not to one's liking. In fact, one may think that just as there is something quite admirable about the soldier who is loyal to the death, there is something equally admirable about the individual who remains loyal in spite of the moral depravity of his friend.

Well, to begin with, while it is very easy to be loyal to the death (in battle) without in any way jeopardizing one's moral character, it is far from clear that it is easy to be loyal to a morally depraved person without adversely affecting one's own character.[17] After all, by one's loyalty

[17] In what follows, I am guided by Marcus Tullius Cicero's remarks on friendship: "If by some chance a friend of ours possessed ambitions which, while not entirely laudable, nevertheless needed our assistance since either his life or his reputation were at stake, then we should have some justification in turning aside from the path of strict moral rectitude—short, that is to say, of doing something absolutely disgraceful, since there are limits beyond which friendship could not excusably go." See his essay "Laelius: On Friendship" in his work *On the Good Life*.

one would, at the very least, be indirectly supporting evil. Thus, to be steadfastly loyal to a morally depraved person would entail becoming somewhat inured to evil itself. And this one should never allow oneself to become. Friends should be loyal, but not blindly loyal. I believe that the principle stated earlier should guide us here: A person should not jeopardize the good qualities of her own character on account of a friendship; nor should she tolerate a friend's indifference to his own failings. Clearly, now, these two considerations are related; for we cannot be too tolerant of another's moral failings without becoming inured to moral shortcomings; and a person thus affected is one whose moral character has been adversely influenced.

I believe that this principle applies without exception to the loyalty that exists among romantic loves. There is nothing to be said for a romantic love that in the end destroys one's good character. This strengthens our earlier observation (Section 4) that romantic love should not, on that account alone, be transparent.

11. Friendship and Romantic Love

A question that naturally arises when reflecting upon both companion friendship and romantic love concerns the nature of the difference between them.[18] The answer that most quickly comes to mind is that complete romantic love includes sexual involvement, whereas the most complete friendship does not require this. I do not believe, however, that this answer is a satisfactory one. For surely the proposal cannot be that the two are alike in all respects save that romantic love involves sexual involvement and friendship does not. To be sure, sexual involvement is significant; it does make a difference. But the issue is whether it makes so profound a difference. Is it that companion friends are all but romantic lovers except for sexual involvement? If so, then what explains why they refrain from taking this further step? Or, to ask the question in a slightly different way, what explains why romantic lovers go on to take this further step?

To resort to biology here would be to make a somewhat tendentious move, since there is no in-principle reason to suppose that romantic love cannot obtain between members of the same gender.

[18] In writing this section, I am greatly indebted to Andrew Manitsky and Ira Yankwitt for much instructive conversation.

Nor is there any in-principle reason to suppose that companion friends must both be of the same gender.

I do not believe that there is a deep formal difference between friendship and romantic love, though I do want to say that any attempt to render the two indistinguishable must make sense of the fact that sexual involvement is generally taken to make the difference between them. It is indisputable that sexual involvement between romantic lovers is taken to signify union. Indeed, it is necessary to consummate a marriage. Surely, though, there is no conceptual reason why, on the one hand, sexual involvement must signify union and why, on the other hand, something else cannot signify it. In the language of convention, it is a deeply and all but universal convention that sexual involvement signifies union, though there is no formal reason why it must signify this.

Now, the fact that there is one widespread and deep convention that signifies union between individuals, namely, sexual involvement, suffices to explain why lovers cannot readily designate something else to signify union. Still, there is no conceptual bar to there being something else that signifies union.

By contrast, there is no deep and widespread convention that individuals mark their having become companion friends by engaging in a certain specified behavior. But there is no conceptual reason why this cannot be so. Thus, suppose that the widespread practice was that when two individuals took themselves to have become companion friends, they purchased two very fine glasses of crystal. It is worth noting that the attitude that the friends took toward the crystal would mirror the attitude of fidelity in romantic love. It would certainly be expected by both friends that neither would give his or her crystal glass over to day-to-day use or would allow it to be used by anyone. The expectation, certainly, would be that each would use the crystal glass only on special occasions and, preferably, with each other.

Suppose, now, that a companion friendship of the type described above (i.e., with crystal serving to mark the friendship) between A and B dissolves and A goes on to form a new companion friendship with C. A and C in turn purchase fine crystal. It is very unlikely that A will parade in front of C the crystal glass that belongs to the pair that A and B purchased. As should be obvious, what we have here is a nonsexual analogue to fidelity. Something cannot be widely and generally used and, at the same time, be an indication of something special. The mark of something special is that its use is reserved or restricted in some fashion. More generally, then, it can be said that whenever there is a widespread and deeply entrenched convention according to which a specified behavior is an expression of the fact that two individuals take themselves to have reached a deep level of intimacy, then as a rule the pair will not want either party to engage in that behavior with others. Obviously, there exists such a convention regarding romantic love—namely, sexual involvement—but there is none regarding companion friendship. However, as should now be clear, this difference does not hold as a matter of conceptual truth.

That we have a convention of this sort in connection with romantic love is no doubt due to the importance of the family as a social institution, as well as the high risk of pregnancy (and thus moral and social responsibility) that, until recently, inevitably came with sexual involvement. Technology has significantly minimized the risk that sexual involvement will lead to pregnancy. Consequently, more people have become sexually involved without supposing that their involvement is an indication of romantic love, a fact that strengthens our claim that it is not a matter of conceptual truth that sexual involvement is the mark of romantic love. For, if in a nonromantic context, an evening of sexual involvement need not be any more than that— an evening of sexual involvement—and nonromantic sexual involvement is widespread, then clearly sexual involvement is not seen as something that is reserved for romantic love. And if there is no difficulty in seeing sexual involvement as not being reserved for romantic love, then on that account alone the idea that sexual involvement is not conceptually tied to romantic love achieves greater plausibility.

At best the foregoing considerations suggest that sexual involvement, which is normally characteristic of romantic love, cannot be the distinguishing feature between companion friendship and romantic love. But this truth, assuming it is such, is compatible with there being a profound difference between romantic love and friendship. In what follows I argue in a more general way that companion friendship and romantic love is a distinction without a conceptual difference.

In passing, it was noted that touch is one of the ways in which bonding takes place (Section 9). I shall assume without argument that however rich a relationship might be, its richness is immeasurably enhanced if touching is an important aspect of it. Touching is not to be understood here simply in terms of sexuality. Much touching is important even though it has absolutely nothing to do with sexuality or, in any case, is not fueled by sexual desire. Touching can be comforting or encouraging. It can be an expression of support or love (not tied to sexual arousal). It can be an expression of togetherness. A hug or caress or affectionate squeeze of the hand can sometimes be more appropriate and effective than a verbal expression of one's love or support. Now, as noted earlier, if females touch and embrace to a far greater degree than males (assuming heterosexual orientation across the board), then female-female friendships have an important dimension that male-male friendships lack. And surely our ordinary observations bear out the truth of the antecedent as a general claim about social interaction. To a far greater extent than men, women can embrace and hold hands without readily having their heterosexual orientation called into question. There is the notion of mothering. Although the idea behind mothering may have its roots in child care, it has come to be more broadly associated with warmth, nurturance, and emotional expressiveness; and touch is central to mothering behavior. I assume, without argument, that the explanation for this difference between men and women is socialization pure and simple. It is not because women have some biological predisposition for touching one another that men happen to lack.

For the sake of convenience, let us refer to touching that is associated with mothering, encouragement, togetherness, and so forth, as nurturing touching. Although as a result of socialization such touching receives greater expression between females than it does between males, it is nonetheless only in romantic love that nurturing touching generally receives its greatest expression. Here, but not in same-gender companion friendships, we have unrestricted nurturing touching, as I shall say. The fantasizing that seems to characterize romantic love and not friendship, while it may surely be sexual, often has nurturing touching as its object: sitting on a beach arm-in-arm, watching the sunset; or walking through a field hand-in-hand on a glorious spring day; or sitting out in the sun with one's lover and caressing her or his forehead as the individual lies in one's lap. While I hardly wish to deny that these activities may escalate into something intensely sexual, the truth remains that these activities are very much enjoyed for their own sake. It seems clear that human beings delight in participating in unrestricted nurturing touching.

But now I take it that there is no compelling explanation for why nurturing touching receives its greatest expression only in romantic love save that this way has been ordained by a conception of social union between two individuals according to which the female-male union represents the very hallmark of a union between any two individuals. That is, I take it that a heterosexual conception of romantic love as this involves the flourishing of two lives together is what accounts for why nurturing touching receives its greatest expression only in romantic love. On this view full nurturing expression, as we might say, between members of the same gender is perverted. There is, however, no more reason to believe that full nurturing expression can occur only between members of the opposite gender than there is to believe that females, but not males, have a biological predisposition for touching one another. And just as there is no reason to believe that touching should be more characteristic of female-female companion friendships than male-male companion friendships (even though it is probably foolish to think that things are likely to change), there is no reason to believe that full nurturing expression should only be between members of the opposite gender (though again, it is probably foolish to think that things are likely to change).

The focus upon nurturing touching has enabled us to identify what must certainly be a deeply and extraordinarily important aspect of romantic love that is not tied to sexual involvement, which, as I have already argued, cannot bear the weight of the supposed distinction between companion friendship and romantic love. Much fantasizing has to do with nurturing touching; and a profound sense of vulnerability may very well come in the wake of this sort of touching between two parties—a sense of vulnerability that is not likely to be had in the absence of nurturing touching. So, the focus upon nurturing touching enables us to account for that "something," not tied to sexual involvement, which seems to be so much a part of romantic love. But as I have tried to show, there is no conceptual reason why the distinction between companion friendship and romantic love should be that the latter is designated the proper and only relationship for full nurturing expression.

A consideration that very much supports this conclusion is that companion friends are given to jealousy in precisely the same way as lovers. Friends make time for each other; and if one fails to do this too often, this becomes a source of concern to the other—which holds, a fortiori, if it turns out too often that it is in order to do something with another person that the other excuses herself or himself. More to the point, a person who appears to be a potential threat to a companion friendship will be a cause of concern and will generally occasion feelings of jealousy. Furthermore, not only is it the case that sometimes a friend is jealous of the other's intended spouse, believing that the friendship will be qualitatively different on account of the marriage, but also there are times when the future spouse, and in some instances the actual spouse, is jealous of the friend, believing that the friend is an obstacle to the flourishing of the marriage in the way that is desired.

Jealousy admits of two senses. One has to do with being especially desirous of an advantage that another has, particularly an advantage that another seems to have preempted one from having. The other has to do with being especially desirous of maintaining the special relationship that one has with another. Companion friends and romantic lovers are jealous in both senses, although in the preceding paragraph I have spoken only about jealousy in the second sense. Yet it is because both are jealous in the second sense that jealousy in the first occurs.

Needless to say, the point here is this: The truth that companion friends and lovers can be jealous of each other in precisely the same way would suggest that, respectively, friends and lovers play a like role in each other's lives—to such an extent that the same emotions are called into play. And if that is so, then it would seem rather arbitrary to suppose that full nurturing expression should be the exclusive domain of romantic love.

This completes our account of companion friendship. Conspicuously absent, no doubt, is a discussion of friendship and autonomy. I have assumed all along that companion friends are autonomous, and the observation that such friends are not sycophants should clearly bring this out. If there is anything particularly interesting to call attention to here, it is that there is no incompatibility between being autonomous and being greatly influenced by another. This is because there is no incompatibility between being autonomous and taking seriously the claims of another—even claims about oneself. For one can have good reasons to do just that, which is not the same thing as uncritically or blindly accepting what another says. Companion friends have especially good reasons to take seriously what each says about the other, since each knows that the other has a commanding perspective of his life and, moreover, that the other cares deeply for him. Indeed, it is precisely because friends have enormous influence with each other that they can play a substantial role in each other's moral flourishing, as I shall endeavor to show in the next chapter.

CHAPTER FIVE

Friendship: A Social Basis for Morality

I want now to illuminate the role that friendship plays in developing and maintaining a virtuous moral character. We have seen the contribution that parental upbringing makes to this end, and one might naturally suppose that friendship picks up where parental upbringing leaves off. As we shall see, this is indeed the case in many ways. The idea that social interaction is the thread from which the fabric of moral character is woven finds its greatest expression in companion friendship, so I believe. Unlike parent and child, friends participate equally and significantly in each other's flourishing—a difference that is as it should be. Because friends interact in this way, friendship contributes to our moral flowering in a way that parental love cannot. The account of friendship presented in the preceding chapter is presupposed.

12. The Acquisition of Autonomous Altruism

It will be remembered that for the purposes of this essay an altruistic conception of morality is assumed (Section 1). Hence, we are interested in how the capacity to restrict our behavior for the sake of others is acquired and sustained and, in particular, the role that friendship plays in this. Needless to say, so restricting our behavior can be seen either as a burden or as a deep expression of something that we desire to do. When it is the latter, I shall regard so restricting our behavior as a part of the virtue of self-command.

Let us begin the discussion by distinguishing between autonomous and gratitudinous altruism. ("Gratitudinous" is a neologism, but not, I hope, a barbarism.) As the term would suggest, gratitudinous altruism refers to altruistic behavior that one performs in response to having been the object of altruistic behavior on the part of another. The object of gratitudinous altruism is someone who has benefited us. It might be objected that an act of gratitudinous altruism cannot be genuinely altruistic, since, by definition, it is performed only in response to the altruistic act of another. Such an act is more obligatory than altruistic, being the mere settling of a debt of gratitude —so the objection might go. While it may be argued that the expression "debt of gratitude" is no more than a *façon de parler* and hence does not imply that a real debt is owed, let us, for the sake of argument, understand the expression to mean that a real debt is owed. The owing of a debt of gratitude is no bar to the genuinely altruistic repayment of that debt, for in general a person's having an obligation to do something hardly prevents his behavior from being altruistic. After all, it is generally acknowledged that parents have an obligation to provide and care for their children. Yet if parents do this out of love, as we think should be the case ideally, then parents are quite altruistic in providing for their children, though in making such provisions they do what they have an obligation to do.[1]

Indeed, since (on the view developed here) morality itself requires a measure of altruism, then one surely hopes that there is no conceptual difficulty with being altruistic and doing what is required of one. This point is further spoken to below.

As one would surmise, autonomous altruism differs from gratitudinous altruism in that the former is altruistic behavior that is not a response to one's having been the object of another's altruistic behavior. A person who is simply moved, beyond the call of duty, to come to the assistance of a perfect stranger displays autonomous altruism. I shall regard autonomous altruism as fully developed altruism. For although gratitudinous altruism certainly constitutes genuine

---

[1] My thinking in this and the next several paragraphs owes much to the work of Lawrence Becker (1986) and Lawrence Blum (1980).

altruism, it is nonetheless occasioned by an altruistic act of another, whereas autonomous altruism is not. And I assume that however much delight a person may take in responding to the altruism of others, a person's altruistic capacities are less than fully developed if he is incapable of being moved to help others independently of having been the object of their altruism.

As should be abundantly clear, a person's altruistic act toward another is more likely to be autonomous (rather than gratitudinous) if she was not first treated altruistically by the other person. On the other hand, there is no reason to think that a person's altruistic act toward another is formally barred from being autonomous just because the other person had treated her altruistically first. Considerations of time alone suffice to show this. If Sanchez had every intention of performing an altruistic act toward Cohen—as is evidenced by the fact that Sanchez had ordered an item for Cohen but had not gotten around to picking it up—and in the meantime Cohen performs an altruistic act toward Sanchez, the altruistic act on Sanchez's part, which now follows Cohen's is no less autonomous on that account. For Cohen's altruistic act is not a response to Sanchez's, though it does follow Sanchez's. And this is so although, as one might imagine, Sanchez's positive feelings toward Cohen are enhanced by Cohen's action.

Or, to take a different kind of example, suppose that for quite some time Jones has been wanting to do something very nice for Smith, who is struggling to make ends meet. But, as it happens, Smith is a very proud individual who in no way wants to be seen as an object of pity. Accordingly, acts of kindness are not received warmly by her. Realizing this, Jones has refrained from giving Smith a very generous gift. One day, however, just as he is pulling out of his driveway, Jones gets a flat tire. Flustered because he has no mechanical skill and could not begin to change the tire, Jones turns to Smith, who gladly changes it. Under the guise of thanking Smith for her help, Jones gives her that quite generous gift that he had been wanting to give her, the magnitude of the gift being all out of proportion to the help that he received from Smith. (We may allow that this has not been lost on Smith. It suffices that she is able to receive the gift without feeling a loss of pride.) Though it is in response to Smith's help that Jones gives the gift, in that in all likelihood Jones would not have given it but for having received some form of help from

Smith, Jones's altruistic act is autonomous nonetheless. For it was only as an expression of gratitude that Jones was able to bestow a significant kindness upon Smith. That the magnitude of the gift is out of proportion to the help that Jones received is merely a device for perspicuously making the point. There need not be this sort of disparity. A proud and fiercely independent person may greet even small kindnesses with much coolness; hence, it may be necessary to wait for a similar sort of opportunity in order to be generous toward such a person, even though one's generosity is small.

In view of these remarks, I trust that the difference between gratitudinous and autonomous altruism has been made clear enough.

Now, it goes without saying that the altruism that morality requires of us is autonomous altruism; individuals who have only the capacity for gratitudinous altruism would have constitutional difficulty living up to the demands of altruistic morality. A moment's reflection suffices to make this evident. Surely, our moral behavior should not be directed toward only those who treat us morally. Among individuals who have never encountered one another, morality does not take a holiday. So, if the claims of altruistic morality are not to be burdensome, then it is of the utmost importance that human beings have the capacity for autonomous altruism and that social interaction provides for its realization. In what follows, I shall defend the thesis that friendship is the vehicle of social interaction through which we come to have the degree of autonomous altruism that morality requires. But first a bit of conceptual ground-clearing is in order.

The very idea of an altruistic morality may appear to be nothing but a conceptual muddle. How, it may be objected, can one be required to be altruistic? I suspect that this objection takes the requirement of legal systems as the model for the requirement of morality, where with the former to be required to do something implies (crudely) that should one fail to behave as required, force can be used to ensure one's compliance (cf. K. Baier 1966). The requirements of legal systems are, by definition, coercive. The requirements of morality are not coercive. Now, if it is objected that the very idea of altruism is incompatible with any conception of requirement, then we have seen already that this view is mistaken. If parents ought to love their children, and loving a person entails treating that person altruistically (at least some of the time), then it follows that parents ought to treat their children altruistically. Although it can be questioned whether or not we have a moral ought here, such a move would be rather spurious. Parenthood embodies a certain ideal, a way in which parents ought to be—namely, that they should love their children. This ideal is a requirement of parenting in the sense that parents cannot fail to love their children and yet be good parents. The case of parenting shows that there is nothing incoherent about a conception of the good that is both a requirement and one that calls for being altruistic.

These considerations notwithstanding, the objection is not without a point. We would do well to distinguish between two levels of altruism: norm-anchored and free-floating altruism. Nothing especially deep is intended here. The former refers to altruistic behavior called for by a norm to which arguably people ought to subscribe, the altruism of parental love being a case in point; the latter, to altruistic behavior not so prescribed. The performance of free-floating altruistic behavior is optional. Although to give one's grand piano to a needy and talented piano player rather than sell it is to do what is tremendously altruistic, such an action is not norm-anchored. By contrast, many instances of familial altruism (sibling to sibling, child to parent, and, of course, parent to child) may be norm-anchored; likewise for many instances of altruism between companion friends. If because of an illness one's companion friend needs assistance that one can provide, then one ought to do so (Section 18). It is not always evident whether an act is free-floating or norm-anchored. However, my objective in these remarks has been to block the objection that one can be required to be altruistic while acknowledging that the objection is not without a point.

Let me now make good the claim that friendship is the vehicle of social interaction through which we acquire the measure of autonomous altruism that morality calls for. The lean version of the argument is as follows. As we have seen (Section 5), parental love through the principle of reciprocity contributes to the acquisition of this autonomous altruism. As a result of being an object of her parents' love the child comes to love them and thus to take their good to heart. Hence, restricting her behavior in order not to harm her parents comes to be a deep expression of something that she desires to do. Thus, we have the beginnings of altruism. But it is only the beginning. For surely the altruism on the child's part, as realized through the principle of reciprocity, is properly characterized as gratitudinous rather than autonomous altruism, as it is in direct response to being loved by them that the child comes to love his parents. For they are the natural object of the child's first expressions of love precisely because they are the catalyst of his coming to love, that is, of his realizing his capacity for love. Thus we have an explanation for the altruistic behavior of the child toward his parents.

It is no doubt natural for children to come to love their parents. But it is not out of choice that they do so. It is not just that children do not initially choose to be the object of their parents' love, for the same can be said of other loves; rather, it is in virtue of being loved by their parents that children come to realize their capacity for love, and their parents are the natural object of that awakened capacity. Needless to say, the love of friendship cannot be explained along these lines, and thus neither can the altruism that is characteristic of it. The love that friends have for each other does not, as with parental love, have as its catalyst a prior display of norm-anchored deep love on the part of either party: it cannot be said that, according to some norm, either party to a friendship ought to have loved the other prior to the friendship. Accordingly, the altruism flowing from the love of friendship is not directed toward someone who had first showered the other with altruism. Hence, the altruism of friendship is properly characterized as autonomous altruism rather than gratitudinous altruism.

It is natural for friends to love each other. But the love that friends have for each other is indeed an expression of choice (Section 9). Friends are not the natrual object of each other's love because their capacity to love was realized through their having been the object of the other's love. At the outset, friends judge each other to be worthy of their love; and their love for each other is an expression of that judgment. The love that the child has for his parents cannot initially be construed as the expression of such a judgment.

I want now to embellish the preceding argument somewhat by contrasting the way in which parents and children contribute to one another's flourishing with the way in which friends do so. I begin with a brief account of flourishing. A person is flourishing if she has a (morally acceptable) conception of the good, which is more or less as a result of her own choosing, and she masterfully realizes her conception of the good. A conception of the good should to some extent satisfy what is called the Aristotelian Principle (pace Rawls 1971, p. 426), in that it should require talent, skill, discipline, or training.

Thus, on this account not everyone can be said to have a conception of the good, such as the person who wastes her days consuming alcohol. Yet the account is not overly intellectual in that it does not entail that a person is flourishing only if his conception of the good calls for tremendous intellectual talent. This is as it should be, since there are many activities that require considerable discipline or training though they are not intellectually taxing as such. A person is not flourishing just because he spends most of his life engaging in a particular activity. Nor can every form of work in which a person might engage (in order to earn a living, for instance) count as a way of flourishing. On the other hand, a person can be flourishing though her aims do not refer to the sciences and the so-called high forms of culture. I do not claim that this account of flourishing is anything more than a first approximation; but it will suffice for the purposes of our discussion.

I turn now to the task at hand, namely, to contrast the way in which parents and children contribute to one another's flourishing with the way in which friends do so. To begin with, there is an enormous asymmetry between the extent to which parents and children contribute to one another's flourishing; the greater contribution is clearly borne by the parents. This is not by any means to belittle the way in which a child contributes to the flourishing of his parents. There can be no doubt that through raising their child, and so taking seriously his good, parents come to experience otherwise unattainable joys, to acquire insights into their personality that undoubtedly would have gone unnoticed, to be resourceful in ways that would never have occurred to them but for their child-rearing activities, and so forth. But these things notwithstanding, it would be a gross distortion of what being a child is about to claim that a child aims to have his parents develop in these ways. The child's contribution is therefore unwitting (Section 3). However much parenting may contribute to the flourishing of adults, it is not the explicit aim of the child that his parents flourish. Securing the flourishing of his parents is not one of his major, if not overriding, goals. No one supposes that this is how a good child should live, let alone in fact lives.

Just the opposite holds for good parents. The flourishing of their child should be a major, if not overriding, aim. The child's flourishing is not supposed to occur simply by accident. To be sure, there is, as with most endeavors, an element of luck in parenting as well.[2]

---

[2] On moral luck, see Nagel (1976) and Williams (1976a).

Sometimes things could not have turned out better for the child despite the fact that the parents could have done a whole lot better. All the same, even if many good things should happen to the child fortuitously, it should nonetheless be the explicit aim of her parents to secure her good. No matter how wonderful a child should turn out to be, if her parents scarcely attended to her needs or if they abused and mistreated her although they provided for her materially, then they were not good parents. Their contribution to her flourishing should not be a fortunate accident. Nor should it amount to unwitting altruism. Parents are under a moral obligation that this should not be so. We have, then, a clear asymmetry in the ways in which parents and children contribute to one another's flourishing. For with children the contribution can only be unwitting, whereas with parents the contribution morally ought not to be unwitting in large measure, but ought to flow from their endeavors to secure the good of their child.

What is more, parents constitute the backdrop against which the child comes to have a conception of his good. It is through their praise and their encouragement that the child comes to have a sense of competence. Although it may be true that the child contributes to his parents' having a greater sense of competence, what is manifestly false is that, in the first place, his parents come to have a sense of competence only through interacting with a child. Since in the absence of a sense of competence no human being can rightly be said to be flourishing, it follows that parents and children do not contribute equally to one another's flourishing, but that the former make the greater contribution. Precisely because a child does not commence life with a conception of the good already in place, to be a parent is to have the opportunity to participate as fully in another human being's flourishing as is humanly possible. No other social interaction affords one such an opportunity. In any event, the child does not participate as fully in the flourishing of the parents, since their flourishing is usually well under way by the time the child arrives.

The preceding discussion should certainly lend support to the claim that the altruism on the child's part toward his parents is best characterized as gratitudinous altruism. For, ideally at any rate, the child identifies his parents as individuals who are committed to his flourishing. It is in this light that the principle of reciprocity should be understood.

Now, at the outset I have claimed that in important respects friendship picks up where parental love leaves off. We can best see why this is so by making explicit why it is a good thing that there is the pronounced asymmetry discussed above in the contribution that parent and child make to the flourishing of each other. That is, I want to make explicit why it is a good thing that the child does not come to see her role as that of participating fully in the flourishing of her parents. The argument is very simple. If the child, being an unrealized self, is not to have the conviction that she has only instrumental value in the eyes of her parents, then it is crucial that she does not suppose it incumbent upon her to participate fully in the flourishing of her parents. Otherwise, it would be as if she were merely an extension of the will of her parents; and a child's so viewing herself is incompatible with her own flourishing. (Recall the discussion of the perfect performance child [Section 8].) In other words, a child cannot flourish if she believes that her conception of the good should always be subordinated to that of her parents, given just the fact that they are her parents. If she is to flourish, she must be encouraged to see her good as separate from theirs, and so not to identify readily with theirs. Good parents so encourage their children.

This last point brings us to friendship and enables us to begin with a very succinct characterization of the difference between it and the parent-child relationship. Above, I remarked that however much parenting may contribute to the flourishing of adults, it is not the explicit aim of the child that his parents flourish; and as I noted in the preceding paragraph, good parents encourage their child to see his good as separate from theirs. Neither of these things is true of companion friendships. Such friends equally desire and take delight in each other's flourishing; they significantly and equally participate in each other's flourishing; and, moreover, each desires and delights in the fact that the other so participates in her or his flourishing.

In view of these considerations, it might be thought that the altruism of friendship is anything but autonomous. Not so, however. Naturally, the behavioral manifestations of the love that friends have for each other move each to respond in kind. But the reason why each is moved to participate in the other's flourishing is not simply, nor primarily, that the other participates in his. Thus, in general, gratitude is not the primary explanation for why friends are moved to participate in each other's flourishing. Of course, one wants to allow for friends to be moved to perform specific acts of gratitude if one friend has been especially gracious or kind to the other. What I have meant to deny is not the occurrence of this sort of gratitude, but only the view that gratitudinous altruism is the primary explanation for why friends participate in each other's flourishing. Companion friends are committed to each other's flourishing, not to responding to each other's altruism.[3]

It might be thought to follow from the idea that the altruism of friendship is autonomous that a person can be a true friend to another only if she is indifferent to how the other responds to her. But this surmise is mistaken. One can ask whether a person is a befitting object of an act of altruism. If a person were looking to give away a grand piano, a rogue would not be a befitting object of such a gift. If another were looking to give someone a scholarship to college, a needy and talented child would be a fitting object of such a gift—not a sixty-five year old Nobel laureate. It would not be befitting to give a car to someone with many cars unless, say, the car was an antique and the recipient a collector of antique cars, or some such thing. A person who first considers whether another person is a befitting object of his would-be act of altruism is no less altruistic on that account.

In the same vein, a person can be an unfitting object of a friend's love. For the giving and caring that are characteristic of the altruism flowing from the love of friendship are of a very special and demanding kind; and a person might very well prove unfitting of such altruism, just as a person might prove unfitting of any number of acts of altruism. Perhaps a completely self-centered individual is unfitting of such altruism; perhaps an individual whose goals and objectives are completely at odds with one's own. I shall not attempt to spell out such criteria here. The point is that a person is no less capable of being a true friend because she is mindful of whether or not another

[3] These remarks are somewhat consistent with Aristotle's observation: "Nevertheless, friendship appears to consist in giving rather than in receiving affection. This is shown by the fact that mothers enjoy giving affection. . . . The giving of affection seems to constitute the proper virtue of friendship" (*Nicomachean Ethics*, 1159a30). However, contrary to what Aristotle seems to suggest, I do not think that on this score the parallel between the affection of friends and the affection of parents can be exact, due to the biological ties between parents and child, which are not severed by the fact that the child is raised at the outset by individuals who are not her parents. Biological parents do not cease to be that because they have never interacted with their children, whereas two people who never interact are not simply bad friends—they are not friends at all.

is befitting of the particular altruism of her friendship, and so is not indifferent to how the other responds to her. On the contrary, surely there is something wrong when a person gives no thought to the matter, just as there would be something wrong if a person indiscriminately walked up to anyone in the street and gave him an antique grand vase. Companion friendship is one of the most valuable things a person can offer to another. A person who indiscriminately offers that which is of value belittles himself.

A person's altruism should have a befitting object. The most befitting object of the altruism of companion friendship is undoubtedly a person who would likewise be a companion friend to one. For only someone who gives in a like manner can value the depth of giving that being a companion friend calls for. A person who is mindful of this is no less altruistic on that account.

Parenthetically, a very interesting question to ask is whether a child can ever be unfitting of his parents' love. I raise this question not to answer it, but to draw a contrast between friendship and the parent-child relationship. As I have observed, parents contribute to their child's flourishing. Arguably and ideally, in any case, it is more important to parents that their child flourish than that he value their contribution to his flourishing. This, I have just indicated, is not true of companion friends. These considerations suggest that the grounds for friendship love are more stringent than the grounds for parental love. Hence, it is easier for a person to be unfitting of companion friendship than it is for a child to be unfitting of parental love. Thus, we can agree with Aristotle that both parents and friends take delight in loving, respectively, their children and friends. The difference lies in the importance that each attaches to his or her love being valued by the object of that love.

13. Friendship and Moral Self-Examination

I have observed that more often than not, parents and children are not companion friends though they love one another dearly. One reason for this, I have said, is that parents have or have had authority over their children. In any case, it is the fact that parents and children rarely volunteer to share intimate information with one another that best indicates the absence of companion friendship between them. What this means is that, between setting a moral example and facilitating moral self-examination, the moral role that parents play in the lives of their children's moral development primarily consists of the former. Because of the level of intimate information that companion friends share with each other, it is they who best facilitate moral self-examination in each other's life.

This view of companion friendships is no doubt common enough (cf. Cooper 1980). Indeed, it is in the air, as it were. In what follows, I want to give considerable structure to this well-received view. Throughout, I am guided here by Hume's observation that the minds of individuals are mirrors to one another. I take Hume to have been making the obvious, but far from trivial, point that we learn of ourselves through social interaction: what we can cope with, are indifferent to, are (positively or negatively) moved by, and so on are all learned or most poignantly grasped through social interaction. Friends play a special role in this regard because they have a commanding perspective of each other's life as a result of their interaction and mutual self-disclosure. It is with this point firmly in mind that one should understand what I now go on to say.

To be human is to be fallible. While human fallibility manifests itself in a variety of ways, its most interesting aspect from the moral point of view lies in the fact that individuals are sometimes mistaken or at least unclear about their motivations. This is understandable, if for no other reason than that it is possible to have more than one motivation for performing an action, including a right action. If a person who finds himself in great financial need should come upon information that will most certainly lead to the arrest of a mass murderer, then he has a substantial amoral reason for doing the right thing— giving the information to the authorities—if a handsome reward is involved. Or, if a person is very envious of her colleague, then she has a substantial immoral reason for doing the right thing and thus reporting his illegal practices to their superior, if this will result in her colleague's being dismissed. Though a person should have an anchored moral character, he can nonetheless fail to be clear about his motivations in situations of this sort.

But, of course, a person with an anchored moral character aims to be clear about her motivations generally and, for that very reason, leads a life of self-examination. Not infrequently, however, self-examination requires a dialogue. For sometimes it takes the challenges of someone who has a measure of distance from one's circumstances —that person's probing and questioning—in order for one to see that one's motivations are other than one has supposed them to be either in depth or content. Obviously, because companion friends have a commanding perspective of each other's lives and, therefore, a deep grasp of how each is motivated, it is such friends who are in the best position to probe and question in this sort of way.

But there is more to the story. To be a person with an anchored moral character is not to be a moral masochist. It is not to take delight in being told that one is wrong, in having one's positive assessment of one's moral behavior challenged, in being told or reminded of one's moral foibles. A moral person recognizes the importance of being made aware of her shortcomings. But being made aware of them is not a source of delight for her. After all, we do not delight in discovering that we are morally inadequate; nor, a fortiori, do we delight in others' discovering this.

To put the latter point differently, we do not delight in the exemplification of our moral shortcomings; that is, we do not delight in the fact that our moral failings are revealed before others. This is because, first of all, it is a blow to our moral self-esteem, that is, the sense of worth that is tied to our conviction that we measure up morally. A blow to our moral self-esteem stems simply from the realization that we have failed to measure up to the moral standards to which we subscribe. Second, when others are aware of this, too, our pride is wounded as well, since not only have we fallen short in our own eyes, but we have also fallen short in the eyes of others in that they have witnessed behavior that is contrary to the image of ourselves that we are concerned to project before others. They have before them a concrete instance—something they can point to—of a moral failing on our part. It is one thing to be regarded as morally fallible simply because, after all, everyone is; it is quite another to be regarded as such because others are aware of specific events in one's life that illustrate the particular ways in which one is morally fallible. The wound to our pride consists in being uncovered in this way. For in being known for having fallen short in a certain way, one becomes an example of what one should not do, of what not to be. And being seen in this light is a different experience entirely from simply having fallen short.

Because in general we wish to appear to others as we aspire to be, it is quite disconcerting when our lives can be held up to others as an example of the way in which a person may fall short of the aspiration in question. The morally anchored person is not the exception here. The exemplification of our moral shortcomings forces our hand, as it were, in that whether we like it or not our life (or some aspect of it) can be used by others as illustration of the way in which a person may fall short of leading a morally virtuous life. And the pain that comes from the realization that we can be seen by others in this way is quite different from the pain that comes from the mere realization that one's moral behavior has been unsatisfactory in this or that respect.

But if it is true that companion friends are rather like another self, then moral self-examination between such friends clearly minimizes the extent to which having one's moral failings uncovered (by the friend) is a blow to our pride. Obviously, the idea that a companion friend is something akin to another self is meant to have a great deal of explanatory power here. But, of course, nothing much is explained if one merely pushes the point that a companion friend is akin to another self. Indeed, things can quickly become trivial. If enough is made of the idea that a companion friend is another self, then the reason why having one's moral failings discovered by one's friend is not a blow to one's pride is identical to the reason why it is not that when one's failings are discovered only by oneself. But the explanation can only be pushed so far. A companion friend is not a pale shadow of who one is; she or he is a different person entirely.

The primary reason why having one's moral failings uncovered by one's companion friend does not constitute a blow to one's moral pride is not just that companion friends love each other, although the love is most certainly relevant. For as parent-child loves demonstrably show, that two individuals love each other hardly entails that each regards the other as another self. The primary reason, instead, is that a companion friend has a commanding perspective of one's life and, therefore, of the motivational structure of one's behavior. Not only that, it is a perspective that one has invited the individual to have. Recall our earlier discussion concerning having information about a person's life (Section 10). One may know all sorts of things about a person and yet not be entitled to discuss them with that individual. A distinctive feature of companion friends is precisely that they invite one another to plumb the depth of their lives. Accordingly, they can ask questions and raise issues about each other's lives that would be extremely out of place for anyone else. This means that companion friends have a deep grasp of each other's strengths and weaknesses. Specifically, companion friends have, in virtue of being such, a composite moral picture of each other. They know a great many of the moral issues to which each is particularly alive, which each finds perplexing; by and large they know where and why each departs from prevailing opinion, and so on. It is in light of the fact that companion friends have, and invite each other to have, a composite moral picture of each other that moral self-examination between them is to be viewed.

It is one thing to be morally exposed before someone who has no sense of one's weaknesses and limitations and thus has no life-context in which to place a significant moral failing on one's part; it is entirely another to be exposed before an individual whom one has invited to have a composite moral picture of one's life. Whereas in the former instance, the esteem in which one is held is immediately jeopardized, this is not so in the latter instance. This is because in the first instance one is so baldly exposed, by which I mean the person is without an understanding of one's moral character whereby she can grasp how one's failing is compatible with the good opinion that she has of one. Again, it is one thing to know that a person is not morally perfect, and yet another to have a firm grasp as to why a person with a virtuous moral character is prone to some moral failings and not others. A person who has a composite moral picture of one has this understanding. In conjunction with their deep love for each other, it is precisely because companion friends have a composite moral picture of each other that their good opinion of each other is not readily jeopardized when their moral failings are revealed to or discovered by each other. For a variety of reasons—deep fears, past hurts, impatience, weakness of will, ambitions, unacknowledged anger, and so on—a person with a virtuous moral character may be susceptible to various kinds of inappropriate moral behavior. To have a composite moral picture of someone is to have much insight into the way in which factors such as these bear upon that person's life—which, in turn, is to have a life-context in which to place significant moral failings.

If a caveat is in order here it is that in general the moral failings of companion friends must not be transgressions against each other. The reason for this is straightforward enough. To be wronged by a loved one is especially painful because in addition to whatever resentment we might feel, there is the further pain owing to the realization that the person's love for us was not sufficient to stay his hand. And it is safe to say that when a person's failing has caused us moral pain, we are not likely to be much inclined to facilitate his moral self-examination in a way that enhances his moral flourishing.

I have claimed that an anchored moral person leads a life of self-examination and that such examination sometimes requires a dialogue. It should now be clear why a companion friend facilitates moral self-examination. Not only does the person often have a desirable distance from one's circumstances, but he has a sufficiently deep grasp of one's moral character that he can see how various moral failings are nonetheless compatible with one's having a virtuous moral character. Because of that, the good opinion a companion friend has of one's moral character is not readily jeopardized by one's moral failings. Loss of pride is thus held at a minimum, if it is at all experienced, when engaging in self-examination with a companion friend. It is in this sense that, in the role of moral self-examination, a companion friend is rather like another self.

Without a doubt, these considerations underscore the importance of self-disclosure between companion friends. When such friends disclose information out of love and in the absence of any behavior that immediately calls into question the high opinion that each has of the other, they thereby underwrite the bond of friendship between them.

Before moving on, an obvious qualification is in order. Although to have a composite picture of a person's moral character is to have insight into many of the ways in which the individual may fail to measure up morally, there is no reason to think, nor have I suggested, that such a picture gives one insight into any and every way in which a person might fail in this regard. A person's moral failing may be so egregious and at odds with his composite moral picture that he calls into question the good opinion that even his companion friend has of his moral character. One's moral pride can be on the line even among companion friends—though on the view I have advanced, this should not happen too often.

Once again the importance of self-disclosure among companion friends is brought out. For it is in virtue of self-disclosure that they come to have a composite moral picture of each other; and it is because they have such a picture that behavior that might otherwise jeopardize the good opinion that each has of the other fails to do so. Moreover, there is this. When deep trust is involved, the description under which we trust a person is of the utmost importance, as it is precisely because a person has revealed himself to us in a particular way that we are moved or disposed to trust him. Thus, we do not want, at least not too often in fundamentally important ways, to be mistaken about the conception of the character and personality under which we deeply trust a person. Nor do we want to feel that we have been misled in this regard. Accordingly, a companion friend who gives us no sense of his moral weaknesses leaves himself open to the charge of having misled us when without warning, as it were, he does a significant moral wrong.

I want now to look at the way in which companion friendship contributes to a person's having a virtuous moral character from a completely different direction. Love can be forgiving. Love can be understanding. It can also be demanding. Because companion friends want each other to flourish in all respects, including morally, they are morally demanding of each other. This means, needless to say, that they are not so solicitous of each other's esteem that they are unwilling to criticize. Companion friends are not sycophants. One might wish to resist this line of thought on the grounds that companion friends are accepting of each other for what each is. After all, so it might be argued, since such friends have a commanding perspective of each other's life and, therefore, a composite picture of each other's moral character, it then follows that each is accepting of the other's imperfections and loves the other in spite of them.

The line of thought just presented rests upon a confusion. Of course, I do not mean to suggest that on account of having a commanding perspective of each other's life companion friends are constantly pointing out each other's flaws in the name of perfecting one another's moral character. Indeed, pointing out each other's flaws is hardly something that they delight in doing, even as they delight in contributing to each other's moral perfection. But from none of this does it follow that each is accepting of the other's moral shortcomings, if what this means is that neither desires nor is concerned to achieve the moral perfection of the other. One can be accepting of a person in two distinct ways. One may understand how that person has come to be the way she is, and hence why it is difficult for her to change, if that is in order. Or, one can be accepting of a person in the sense that at the very outset one is prepared to interact with her given her present state of character, when it is understood that any expectations that the person should change for the better are out of order. Here the character of the person is good enough given one's purposes. Respectively, we have understanding-acceptance and as-is-acceptance, let us say. While acceptance in this latter sense is suitable for some forms of social interaction, it will not do for companion friendships. In a job situation, for instance, a person can be hired primarily for the purpose of giving her professional name to the institution in question, and at the very outset her otherwise undesirable qualities are overlooked. Even among friendships of utility, there can be as-is-acceptance. Susan is an extremely savvy politician; Mary is an extraordinarily successful businesswoman. Both recognize this in each other and agree to work together for the purpose of ridding their city of pornography. The attainment of this end is the primary reason why they interact. Improving each other's moral character, as such, is just not one of their concerns. As-is-acceptance has its place in social interaction. Companion friendship, though, is not one of them. To repeat, the former speaks to a willingness at the very outset to accept a set of character flaws. Acceptance of the flaws or traits (to put it more neutrally) is part of the agreement under which the interaction takes place. I leave aside situations in which on moral grounds one comes to believe that the initial agreement should not be binding upon one.

No doubt what fuels the idea that companion friends accept each other as is, are the considerations that character flaws can be so deep as to be ineliminable and that one does not jettison a companion friend just because of an ineliminable character flaw. Well, in truth that should surely depend on what the flaw is. But setting this consideration aside, the sort of acceptance just described is not the same as as-is-acceptance, which is rather like a commitment at the outset to not attempting to improve upon a person's character. After having tried to do so, to come to the realization that a person's character cannot be improved upon in a certain way and to love the person in spite of that is hardly the same thing as a commitment at the outset to not attempting to improve upon the person's character. This is understanding-acceptance rather than as-is-acceptance.

Having said this, I wish to acknowledge that in some instances understanding-acceptance has overtones of as-is-acceptance with respect to flaws of a certain kind. The profound inability to trust that stems from rape or an abused childhood comes readily to mind here. In the case of rape, if the rapist were a member of another ethnic group, the victim might very well harbor initial suspicions and hostilities toward members of that ethnic group that would otherwise be altogether inexcusable but for the rape experience. A companion friend to this individual might be accepting of this character flaw at the outset in the sense that the friend sees from the very start that this is the sort of flaw that one might understandably have under the circumstances and realizes that, because of the circumstances that gave rise to it, the flaw is not one that is easily eradicated. Observe, though, that what we have here is not simply an understanding of how a given character flaw came about, but something tantamount to an excuse for its existence. When a character flaw is excusable, understanding-acceptance can shade into as-is-acceptance, provided that the flaw is not beyond the pale of moral tolerability. For, to begin with, part of what the understanding entails in this case is that there exists an acceptable explanation for why the flaw in question might prove to be ineradicable. Even so, we do not have full-fledged as-is-acceptance, since it is not maintained from the outset that no attempt should be made to eradicate the flaw in question.

Whatever else is true, we want those whom we love to flourish. We want them to realize their potential to the fullest, or at least as much as possible given the circumstances of their life. Thus, insofar as being morally virtuous constitutes a form of moral flourishing, we want those whom we love to realize themselves in this way as well. In general, there is no incompatibility in loving a person and being demanding of him; and there is no reason to suppose that morality is an exception in this regard. The parent-child relationship clearly bears out the truth of this point. Parents who love their children, far from being indifferent to their children's flourishing, are very encouraging and supportive of their development. This includes, among other things, holding them up to high standards of excellence. Parental love does not wallow in mediocrity. There is nothing about the love of friendship that necessitates a shift in this regard.

Parental love reveals the way in which it is possible for individuals to both love and be demanding of one another. Ideally, at any rate, the child is held up to high standards of excellence not in a threatening way, but in a way that both gives her confidence that she has the wherewithal to measure up and inspires her do so. The confidence is generated by the belief that her parents display in her ability to do well. The inspiration is born of the delight that comes with measuring up to the expectations of and, therefore, pleasing individuals whom she loves (namely, her parents) and who love her.

In a similar fashion friendships can generate confidence and be inspirational with respect to attaining moral excellence. An adult can wonder whether he has the wherewithal to achieve certain moral standards. Or, an adult can certainly be blind to the fact that there is a morally superior way of accomplishing this or that end. Through his own life, a companion friend may reveal that things are otherwise. For the realization or acceptance that there is a morally superior way of doing things can come about as a result of seeing one whom we admire proceed in that way. And companion friends also take pleasure in measuring up to the expectations of each other, and thus can be moved to attempt what each agrees to be morally superior behavior because, among other things, doing so would please the other.

Having others be demanding of us is obviously problematic in a variety of ways, two of which come readily to mind. For one thing, people can, their good intentions notwithstanding, be demanding of us in ways that are incompatible with our conception of the good or, in particular, can fail to grasp the significance that the attainment of a goal has in our life. For another, some people who are demanding of others are full of excuses when it comes to being demanding of themselves. Such individuals need not be mistaken about the other's conception of the good.

To digress momentarily, the first kind of difficulty is not to be confused with a difficulty of a rather different sort, namely, that of correctly grasping a person's conception of the good but believing that it should be jettisoned on rational or, especially, moral grounds. Provided that we respect the integrity and judgment of a person who raises it, a concern of this sort must be taken seriously, though understandably it is not welcomed. One might be tempted to add that this holds regardless of the person who raises such a concern, given that the proviso is met. However, this is less than obvious; for it would seem that there are considerations of privacy that must be balanced against the moral gravity of the concern being raised. One's companion friend is no doubt entitled to press the issue of disclosure about one's children by a previous marriage to one's spouse-to-be; the clerk who knows of this information through handling one's files should not even raise the issue, let alone press it. The same is true if, at the age of sixty, one is about to deplete one's life's savings in order to embark upon a new venture, notwithstanding familial obligations.

However, we need not concern ourselves with the propriety of questioning the morality or rationality of a person's conception of the good, since our concern is with companion friends' being demanding of each other; and it is clear that such friends can question each other in this regard. And the issue that occasioned our digression need not concern us either, since it is reasonable to assume that companion friends do have a clear conception of each other's good. Obviously, I do not mean to suggest that companion friends can never be mistaken about various aspects of each other's good. The point, instead, is that with companion friends mistakes of this sort are infrequent.

This leaves us, then, with the second difficulty, namely, that some people are demanding of others and not of themselves. One of the interesting features of our psychological make-up is that whether we feel that others are entitled to be demanding of us is, in general, not so much a function of the correctness of their remarks as of the character of their lives and the nature of their experiences. We believe—and with good reason—that a person does not have the appropriate vantage point from which to be demanding unless she has measured up, given similar circumstances, and so can truly appreciate the wherewithal this takes and the psychological toll it exacts. Without that vantage point, a demanding person lacks the appropriate sensitivity to and understanding of the circumstances of our lives. The person is in no position to know that he is not being too demanding. The moral of the story, clearly, is that people who are demanding of others should be equally demanding of themselves, which brings us specifically to companion friendships.

It is rare for two people to become companion friends when they are from quite disparate economic, social, or educational backgrounds. The reason for this is quite simple. People who differ significantly along these lines often have quite different concerns, priorities, and vulnerabilities and, therefore, attach very different weights to things. Moreover, they rarely travel in the same circles, to use a familiar expression; and this makes it extremely awkward for either to participate in the other's flourishing. Indeed, it can make it difficult even to identify with the other's flourishing. Companion friends have a commanding perspective of each other's lives. Hence, deep trust and spontaneity of interaction are characteristic of such friendships. The lives of people from different economic, social, and educational backgrounds rarely provide a context for such interaction to occur between them. This, to be sure, is just so much common sense.

However, it is just as rare, I maintain, for two people to become companion friends when there is a significant disparity in the quality of their moral character, even though both should have an acceptable moral character. Let us assume for the sake of discussion that companion friends are no more demanding of others, and so of each other, than they are entitled to be, given their experiences and the quality of their moral life. If so, then we have at least a partial explanation for why companion friendships tend to be between equals—that is, individuals whose moral characters are equally good. Suppose Smith and Jones are companion friends. Smith is a morally superb person, constantly doing things for others that are above and beyond the call of duty. Jones, though a morally decent person, is by no means a saint, in that he is not much inclined to do things that are above and beyond the call of duty. By our assumption that friends are no more demanding of others than they are entitled to be, given their experiences and the quality of their moral life, it follows that Jones will rarely be entitled to be demanding of Smith, whereas Smith will constantly be entitled to be demanding of Jones. Indeed, in comparison to Jones's shortcomings, Smith's will pale. Thus, the very disparity between the quality of their moral characters will itself put a strain on their relationship. This is so, at any rate, in the absence of a rapid evolution for the morally better on the part of Jones or a deterioration toward the morally worse on the part of Smith.

This conclusion might seem counterintuitive, given the view that the morally anchored person aspires to do what is right and so, for that very reason, is always desirous of improving his moral character. It is tempting to think that the companion friendship between Smith and Jones would fall just short of the ideal, namely, a friendship in which both are saints; and, furthermore, that the friendship would flourish because Smith would readily contribute to the betterment of Jones's moral character precisely because in virtue of their companion friendship Jones would have before him in the life of Smith a vivid illustration and a commanding perspective of a saintly life. But this temptation should be resisted, for the inequity here will reverberate in harmful ways throughout the friendship. For one, as a consequence of this inequity, Smith and Jones do not contribute equally to each other's moral flourishing: to a significant extent, Smith will serve as a moral yardstick for Jones, but not the other way around. And, for another, this is certain to have an adverse effect upon Jones's moral self-esteem (Section 22), occasioning in him considerable shame or, at any rate, feelings of inadequacy. The first consideration casts doubt upon whether the relationship between Smith and Jones actually constitutes a companion friendship in the first place. Rather, it may be that Jones has his own personal leader.

But if denying here that we have a companion friendship seems too stipulative, the second consideration speaks to the psychological difficulty inherent in a companion friendship between individuals of quite unequal moral character. There is both the pain that comes with feeling inadequate vis-à-vis a loved one and the pain that comes with the realization that one cannot much contribute to that person's moral flourishing—at least not to the extent that he magisterially contributes to one's own. The parent-child relationship is perhaps the only relationship between personal loves in which inequality of moral character does not have an adverse affect upon the self-esteem of the party with the less developed or refined moral character. After all, a good parent-child relationship is, given the very nature of things, unidirectional in this regard, since it is through his parents that the child first comes to have a sense of right and wrong.

14. Moral Sensibilities

As it seems Aristotle would claim, doing what is morally right is a matter of doing the right thing to the right person in the right way and at the right time (*Nicomachean Ethics* 1109a25). I shall call this Aristotle's dictum of practical action. In what follows, I aim to bring out the relevance of companion friendship to the realization of this dictum.

Because of what I have called the problem of moral opacity (Section 1), there is nothing remotely resembling a decision procedure for ascertaining what is the morally right thing to do. Whether it is a matter of applying a moral principle or exercising a virtue such as honesty or kindness, there is no decision procedure for determining the exact circumstances (or description) under which the principle is to be applied or the virtue exercised. Even if we should allow, as is surely not the case, that morality simply is a matter of universalizing the description under which one is acting (Hare 1963), there is still the matter of properly stating that description; and there is no decision procedure for doing this. As we saw, analogous remarks hold for the virtues. Being moral calls for having moral sensibilities: first, a proper grasp of a person's circumstances, including the individual's emotional state; and second, a proper grasp of what remarks or forms of nonverbal behavior (Section 17) are appropriate under the circumstances and, of course, the wherewithal to act accordingly. There are, for instance, any number of ways in which one might contribute to a person's doing the right thing in the future in the light of a recent past shortcoming, not all of which will be equally effective on any given occasion. Sometimes what a person most needs is to have it pointed out to him in quite plain language that he has not done what he could and ought to have done. Sometimes just the opposite is true, and what a person most needs is not so much to be reminded that he has failed, but to be told that he has it within him to do better. Oftentimes more good is achieved by encouraging than by criticizing; and there are many ways to encourage a person. Whereas a sincere and heartfelt communication of one's confidence in a person may suffice in one instance, a physical gesture may be in order in another. And just what sort of physical gesture will be appropriate—for instance, a strong embrace versus a gentle hand on the shoulder—will surely depend upon a number of things, including the nature of the relationship and social norms concerning touch. Everyone knows that there are times when a few encouraging remarks expressed in a note can mean everything. And there are times when circumstances permit no more than an encouraging smile.

In the preceding paragraph, I have focused primarily upon the matter of doing the right thing in the right way to the same person. It goes without saying, of course, that Aristotle's dictum of practical action also implies that what counts as the right thing to do may vary with the intended object of one's action. How one should respond to a deep embarrassment owing to an indiscreet remark depends on the nature of the person who uttered the remark. Was it an adult or a child? Was it a jealous member of one's profession who is deeply envious of one, or was it a dear friend? Was it a person of shallow character known for his indiscretions or a very sanctimonious individual? And so on. I shall not comment upon each difference, except to say that each difference here is meant to bring different motives, as expressed in different personalities and characters, to bear upon the indiscretion. What counts as the right response is certainly a function of these things. With a child, one usually assumes the most innocent motives or, in any case, that the child is not fully accountable for his indiscretion. The person of shallow character should perhaps be ignored, whereas a long conversation may be in order if the indiscretion was committed by one's dearest friend.

My remarks thus far have been confined to doing the right thing, where that is a function of the person who is the object of one's actions, where a difference in this regard reflects a difference in personality and character. I have not touched upon the issue of timing. But I take it to be obvious that this, too, is of the utmost importance whether we are criticizing or encouraging a person, or whatever. However wrong a person might be in not having spoken up on one's behalf, the time to bring this to her attention is not in the middle of her presidential acceptance speech. Nor is that the time to press through the crowd in order to give her an encouraging embrace or kiss on the cheek. If she is to be encouraged during her speech, surely an encouraging smile will have to do.

Before speaking to the relevance of companion friendship to Aristotle's dictum of practical action in the light of these remarks, one final observation is in order. Just how we should act in a given situation is invariably a function of what our affective response should be to the person given the circumstances. Sometimes the appropriate affective response should be hurt, sometimes it should be anger born of resentment or indignation, sometimes it should be sheer indifference. And our assessment of what the appropriate response should be is subject to revision. I shall expand upon these remarks in the discussion that follows.

The relevance of companion friendship to Aristotle's dictum of practical action is this. Love constitutes the most fertile ground for acquiring the moral sensibilities that are necessary if one is to measure up to this dictum. The reason for this, quite succinctly, is that in matters of love a person's flourishing (moral and otherwise) takes priority over holding her or him accountable for not measuring up morally. And the reality is that not every moral failing on a person's part need be an indication that he is failing to flourish and that he has lowered his moral aspirations. The claim here, obviously, is not that holding a person accountable has no place at all in matters of love, but only that it is less important than contributing to a person's flourishing. It is certainly possible that one can err in the wrong direction by not holding a person accountable far too often or, in a specific instance, by not doing so when one clearly should. All the same, as important as it is for parents to correct and reprimand their child and, in some cases, to punish her or him outright for unacceptable behavior, none of this is to be done at the expense of the child's flourishing. Hence, none of these things should result in the child's feeling unloved by her or his parents or in some way inadequate on account of their actions. In a good parent-child relationship, the parents have struck the proper balance in not following the path of strict moral rectitude in their endeavor to contribute to their child's moral flourishing. Without their following this path, the child acquires a firm sense of right and wrong and learns to accept the idea that he is accountable for his actions. In the absence of considerable moral sensibility on the parents' part, which their love for the child gives rise to, the realization of this state of affairs is simply not possible.

In companion friendship, of course, friends do not come together with the aim of instilling in each other a firm sense of morality. Even so, because of their love for each other they are deeply committed to each other's flourishing—moral and otherwise—a commitment that takes priority over holding each other accountable for failing to measure up morally. Accordingly, through their interactions they seek to enhance rather than stifle each other's moral flourishing. In a good parent-child relationship, we have an emotionally unfashioned self (the child) interacting with and being shaped by emotionally fashioned selves (the parents). An emotionally fashioned self is an individual whose well-developed (if perhaps unarticulated) self-concept bears in large measure the mark of his emotions' having been profoundly engaged by experience and searching cognitive assessments (or, as is sometimes the case, the determination to avoid such assessments). By putting the point in terms of a well-developed self-concept, we avoid the obviously unacceptable implication that children do not have emotionally deep experiences. Ideally, at any rate, the moral sensibilities of parents toward the child reflect this asymmetry. With a companion friendship, two emotionally fashioned individuals interact with each other, and this calls for some moral sensibilities that the parent-child relationship does not call for.

To state the obvious, companion friends, unlike parents, have to be sensitive to deep fears, anxieties, biases, and (most important, perhaps) a conception of the good life to which the friend subscribes—all of which were well in place before they met the person. And while some conceptions of the good life are so morally horrendous that they can be dismissed out of hand, most cannot. Indeed, what may be objectionable is not so much a person's conception of the good life, but the way in which he pursues it or what he mistakenly thinks it commits him to in terms of views about others. Although easy to draw in the abstract, communicating to a person this difference in one's judgment takes tremendous care. This is because social interaction is dynamic: a person's thoughts and feelings do not stand frozen in time as one speaks to or otherwise interacts with her or him. It is well known that people often react to what they have anticipated one will say rather than what one actually says or meant to say. And of enormous importance, of course, is that companion friends are autonomous individuals, neither of whom has authority over the other. Thus neither is entitled to deference from the other with respect to the assessments that each offers of the other's actions. For reasons such as these, companion friendships call for moral sensibilities that the parent-child relationship does not require. One does not speak to, advise, or criticize an autonomous individual in the person of one's companion friend in the same way that one does one's own child.

It is perhaps easy to surmise what I take to be the significance of these remarks with respect to living in accordance with the precepts of an altruistic morality. In a word, the significance is that the moral sensibilities that a flourishing companion friendship realizes enhance the quality of our moral interaction with others. This the moral sensibilities that the parent-child relationship realizes cannot do, at least not to nearly the same extent—and for precisely the reasons mentioned in the preceding paragraph. The principles of morality apply primarily to fully responsible moral individuals. For the most part, these are adults with emotionally fashioned selves, as I shall assume that there is a direct correlation between being a fully responsible moral individual and an emotionally fashioned self. This assumption seems reasonable enough given human life and development as we know it. So, companion friendships, by realizing the moral sensibilities that enhance the moral interaction of the friends, realize the moral sensibilities that enhance their moral interaction with other emotionally fashioned selves and thus, by our assumption, other fully responsible moral individuals. We obviously do not have the familiarity with the lives of others that we have with the lives of our companion friends; indeed, most members of society are complete strangers to us (Section 16). Nor do we have the emotional attachment to others that we have to our companion friends. But companion friends do not constitute one species of human beings and everyone else, another. Accordingly, the sensitivities that companion friendship gives rise to put one in good stead for social interaction generally. If nothing else, one is made more alive to the ways in which experiences and events can bear upon the lives of individuals.

One may wonder why reflection upon our own experiences does not yield the same results in terms of moral sensibilities. The answer, quite simply, is that the moral liabilities that come with taking another's experiences seriously do not come with taking our own experiences seriously. In failing to assess our own experiences correctly or to respond to our own concerns in the appropriate way, we do not immediately invite the question of whether or not the failure was motivated by objectionable motives with respect to another. To be sure, the issue of whether we have self-love can sometimes be pressed (Section 18); but not even the absence of self-love warrants the assumption of objectionable motives with respect to another. By contrast, when we fail in these ways with regard to another, the very fact that objectionable motives can often be an explanation for such failures constitutes reason enough to examine our motives briefly, if only to make certain that motives of this sort are not operative. Our own pain can get in the way of our correctly understanding another's circumstances, either because it distorts our grasp of the circumstances of others or because it gives rise to objectionable motives with respect to others. Our own pain is much less likely to have this effect in our own life.

In short, because of the moral liabilities that come with taking another person's experiences seriously, we have a reason that we cannot have when considering our own experiences to proceed with great care and caution, and to be sure that our motives are pure—a reason that holds a fortiori when the person is a companion friend. When we proceed in this way to grasp the moral experiences of another, especially a companion friend, our moral sensibilities cannot help but be awakened.

The argument thus far has been that companion friendships enhance our moral sensibilities because of the endeavors of companion friends to take each other seriously. There is another way in which they do so that is in keeping with the view that reflection upon one's own experiences does not enhance our moral sensibilities, at least not to nearly the same extent. I alluded to it when I remarked earlier that just how we should act in a given situation is invariably a function of what our affective response should be.

Because companion friends have a commanding perspective of each other's lives, they can often play a significant role in getting each other to be clearer about the nature of an experience and, therefore, about what their affective responses should be to that experience. This is perhaps most apparent in connection with unfortunate experiences that do not pertain to matters between them and, therefore, when judgments about each other are not at stake and each is free to help the other understand without the suspicion of ulterior motives. A person can overreact: his anger can be all out of proportion to the wrong that he has suffered. Or, he may be mistaken about what has given rise to his hurt: the hurt may have more to do with wounded pride than with an actual wrong he has suffered. A person can mislocate the source of her moral pain: what deeply pained the judge was not so much her colleague's racist slur, but the fact that the slur came from a person whom she had trusted. Or, a person can simply fail to appreciate the extent to which she was wronged: as the lawyer worked through the horrendous experience with her companion friend it became all too apparent that the male colleague was hoping to turn the only two women in the firm against each other in order to weaken their professional clout in the firm, thereby making it easier for him to become a partner in spite of his rampant sexism. Neither the pain of sexism nor that of racism is to be belittled. Still, the fact that a person's pain is due more to having had her trust betrayed by a colleague than to his racist slur makes a tremendous difference in how she should respond to the individual in question. And she should respond in yet a different way if she was not just betrayed but, in addition, manipulated for professional gain. I trust that there is no need to comment here.

It is because companion friends can, and often do, contribute mightily to each other's coming to have a proper grasp of her or his circumstances that they can play a pivotal role in each other's coming to have the correct affective response to her or his situation. The relevance of this consideration to Aristotle's dictum of practical action is simply this: a person is more likely to be successful in the endeavor to do the right thing in the right way, and so on, if her or his affective response to a situation is as it should be.

It is beyond question, then, that companion friendships play a vital role in the realization of our moral sensibilities. More to the point, it is beyond question that they play such a role in our maintaining a virtuous moral character. I have claimed that social interaction is the thread from which the fabric of moral character is woven. I should like to think that the arguments of this chapter countenance the truth of this claim. In the next chapter, I hope to continue speaking to the truth of this claim as I endeavor to show the role that our beliefs about how others should treat us can play in our sustaining a virtuous moral character.

CHAPTER SIX

Character and Society

We are profoundly influenced by the social institutions among which
we live. In particular, the effectiveness with which persons can lead
a moral life is so influenced. If so much seems obvious, note immediately that this conception of the morally virtuous person—call it the
social conception—is at odds with the Platonic conception, which has
two parts essentially. Its central tenet is that a morally virtuous person is one who would continue to lead a morally virtuous life, and
so maintain a morally virtuous disposition, no matter how immorally
all the world should treat him. He would continue to lead a moral
life regardless of the level of immorality that should prevail in the
society in which he lives. An all-important consequence of the central
tenet is that a morally virtuous person is one whose moral disposition
never stands in need of reinforcement. Specifically, his maintaining
a morally virtuous disposition is not contingent upon being treated
morally by others. The idea here is straightforward enough: in no
way should it turn out to be on account of the positive reinforcement
that results from actually being treated morally by others that the
morally virtuous person maintains her morally virtuous disposition.
I shall argue that the Platonic conception—the central tenet and its
consequence—must be rejected as unsound or, in any case, as indefensible on the grounds that it is wedded to an unrealistic picture of
the psychological wherewithal of persons. However, in an important
respect I hope to stay true to the spirit of the Platonic conception.

There is surely something right about the Platonic view that a morally virtuous person is one whose morally virtuous disposition is not sustained by the benefits derived from being treated morally by others. I believe that it is possible to do justice to this idea even as we reject both the central tenet and its consequence. As stated, at any rate, the Platonic conception ignores the role that a person's beliefs—and nothing other than a person's beliefs—about how others would treat her can play in reinforcing her morally virtuous disposition. And this, as I hope to show, is a mistake.

15. The Psychology of the Platonic Conception

There can be no doubt that the idea that a morally virtuous person would continue to maintain a morally virtuous disposition, and so lead a moral life, no matter how immorally all the world should treat him strikes a responsive chord in our hearts. After all, such a person would seem to constitute a moral ideal. For we would have nothing but the highest moral admiration for a person who would continue to lead a morally virtuous life though all the world should treat him wrongly. However, notwithstanding the affinity that we may have for the Platonic conception of the morally virtuous person, this conception must be rejected because its central tenet commits us to an unrealistic picture of the psychological wherewithal of persons. Specifically, it fails to acknowledge that there are sentiments that can weaken, if not undermine entirely, a person's morally virtuous disposition—sentiments that are natural for a person to experience given that she has self-respect.[1]

If human beings were constitutionally unable to experience anger, rancor, and resentment, then it might very well be possible for a person to continue acting justly though all the world should treat him un-

---

[1] In his provocative essay "Values and Purposes" (1981), Stocker suggests that it would be difficult for most of us to live a good life without friendship and friendly acts. The arguments of this section may be seen as taking this idea one step further: it would be difficult to live a morally good life without some morally good people around us, some people who would treat us morally in their interactions with us. Since friendships and friendly acts are altruistic in their content, and morality is as well, so I have assumed, then these considerations together bespeak the extent to which living a morally good life is contingent upon the altruism of others.

justly. For the wrongful treatment would not then trigger any feelings that would undermine or weaken his resolve to treat others rightly, as the aforementioned sentiments are clearly capable of doing. Obviously, however, human beings are not constituted in this way. They are susceptible to these emotions, and this, in part, is tied to the fact that human beings are capable of self-respect.

A person has self-respect if she believes that others should have the proper moral regard for her—that others should treat her as the requirements of morality dictate—and, what is more, if she desires to be treated in this way.[2] This belief and desire are not a peripheral part of who she is; instead, they are constitutive of the way in which she conceives of herself. Thus, the self-respecting person is hardly indifferent to being treated wrongly by others. On the contrary, such treatment is a source of deep displeasure, owing to her not having been treated in the way that she believes she should be treated and desires to be treated.

This is not to say that a person with self-respect will never tolerate being treated wrongly and that she will always protest such treatment. For there can be morally acceptable reasons that are not self-regarding for putting up with being treated wrongly by others. For example, a poorly educated person who has a family to support may have to acquiesce to wrongful treatment by his employer in order to keep his job. And if he really has self-respect, then it is not for his sake but the sake of his children that he does not object to being treated wrongly by his employer—unless, of course, in protesting he would run the risk of losing his life. Then in this latter instance we have a morally acceptable self-regarding reason why a person with self-respect may tolerate being treated wrongly. A person with self-respect may have to tolerate being treated wrongly, but she is never accepting of such treatment as a matter of course.

Thus understood, it can come as no surprise that a person is liable to feelings of resentment on account of having self-respect. We may define resentment as the feeling of displeasure that is grounded in the following: (i) the belief that one has been wronged, (ii) the annoyance that comes with having the deep desire not to be wronged frustrated by another, and (iii) the additional affront that one experiences when the wrong either goes unacknowledged or is something

2 I follow the seminal works of Boxill (1984) and Hill (1973, 1982).

that the person takes delight in having done.[3] Since resentment constitutes a feeling of displeasure, it goes without saying that this sentiment is not something that a normal person desires to experience for its own sake. It is also clear that resentment is quintessentially a moral attitude (Strawson 1962). Creatures and things that are incapable of moral agency, and so cannot perform morally wrong acts, cannot be the object of resentment, though they can be the object of many other sentiments, including anger and envy. Given the account of resentment and self-respect offered, it is clear that an indisputable sign that a person has self-respect is that she is capable of experiencing resentment. To be sure, resentment is sometimes experienced as a result of imagined wrongs. But this truth, far from militating against what has been said, serves only to confirm it further, since the moral wrong, whether real or imaginary, is tied to the belief that others have failed to treat one as one believes morality requires that they should.

Needless to say, I do not want to suggest that a person has self-respect only if she experiences resentment whenever she is wronged. It is certainly possible for a person to overlook a wrong when, for instance, the wrong done exacts only a negligible toll upon her, or it was committed under rather extenuating circumstances, or it unexpectedly yields a benefit instead of the intended harm. Suppose that the man who has wronged one by seriously vandalizing one's car had just suffered a traumatic experience—he was gang raped. The proper appreciation of this fact should certainly incline one to be understanding rather than resentful of the person. Or, to take a quite different example, suppose that if Smith had not been tested for possible skull fractures he would not have found out that he had a malignant brain tumor that needed to be removed immediately; and, further, that he would not have gone in for such tests had he not received a blow over the head from the masked burglar in whose way he was standing and whose identity he later learns. In view of these considerations, it is quite understandable that Smith might not feel much resentment toward the burglar. Still, no self-respecting person can be indifferent to routine wrongful treatment at the hands of others; hence, none is disposed to overlook such treatment as a matter of course.

---

[3] I am indebted to Adam Smith here. In *The Theory of Moral Sentiments* he writes: "What chiefly enrages us against the man who injures or insults us, is the little account which he seems to make of us, the unreasonable preference which he gives to himself above us, and that absurd self-love, by which he seems to imagine, that other people may be sacrificed at any time, to his conveniency or humour" (II.iii.5).

Offhand, it might seem that the truly superior moral person would be above it all, and so would not experience resentment on account of being treated wrongly. This quite elevated ideal requires a perception of one's wrongdoers that is rarely available. If one holds that it is not possible for them to grasp the nature of their wrongful deeds, then it is perhaps possible not to experience resentment toward them, as ignorance of this kind may serve to defeat accountability. But not so if one believes that they clearly understand what they are doing.

With continuous wrongful treatment, resentment builds up. One resents having been wronged on this occasion, one resents having been wronged on that occasion, and one resents having been wronged on both this and that occasion, and so on. And it is built-up resentment that invariably gives rise to the concomitant feelings of rancor and anger. Together these sentiments serve to undermine a person's resolve to treat rightly those who continually wrong him, because these sentiments result either in his no longer seeing those who wrong him as fitting objects of moral treatment or, in any case, in his becoming indifferent to the fact that they are. For a person's ability to judge others favorably is adversely affected when they are the object of his intense bitterness and anger. He is more likely to magnify their shortcomings and to downplay their losses and harms. And thus even if he realizes that they deserve to be treated morally by everyone, including himself, this judgment is not likely to have much motivating force with him precisely because he is inclined to downplay their losses and harms. If all the world were to treat a self-respecting person immorally, there would be no one to whom he could turn for moral refuge, as it were. There would be no buffer against an immoral world, nothing to temper the harshness of reality. Everyone would be the object of his resentment, anger, and bitterness. Indeed, the evilness of the whole would be greater than the sum of its parts. For it is not just that everyone would be treating him immorally, but they would do so with impunity, and so justice itself would go unanswered, which would add insult to injury. Given such an environment and the negative sentiments that he would be forever experiencing, there is no reason to think that a person could find it within himself to go on acting morally. It is not clear what in his moral soul could be tapped to give rise to moral behavior.

It will not do simply to insist that if a person truly had a morally virtuous disposition, then he would not act immorally, at least not with any regularity, no matter how immorally he was treated by however many. For one has to make sense of this idea in terms of human psychology as understood in the context of human flourishing; and it would not seem that this can be done. This is why it will not do to suppose that the truly moral person would simply rise above it all. For one has to tell a story that would make sense of his not experiencing resentment and the concomitant sentiments of anger and bitterness. But there is none to be told on this front—at least not for the person who has any vestiges of self-respect. And if none is to be told here, then there can be no basis for holding that the moral person would simply rise above it all.

I have argued that the central tenet of the Platonic conception of the morally virtuous person—namely, that such a person could maintain a morally virtuous disposition no matter how immorally all the world should treat him—must be rejected as unsound. Our earlier discussion of the precept that ought implies can (Section 2) speaks to the scope of the argument.

It is, to be sure, logically possible that a person should have self-respect and yet not feel resentment though all the world should treat him immorally. There would appear to be no conceptual impossibility here, as the story of Christ is not deemed to be incoherent on precisely this account. The issue, however, is not about what is logically possible or even remotely possible, given the psychological make-up of human beings, but rather what can be reasonably expected given this psychology. The argument advanced here is to be understood in terms of reasonable expectations (K. Baier 1984). The claim is that it cannot be reasonably expected that self-respecting individuals will not experience resentment when subject to continuous wrongdoing. It cannot be reasonably expected because we have no way of articulating the psychological make-up of persons according to which we can make sense of their not feeling resentment under such circumstances. That is, we cannot extract from any such reasonable account of persons a set of premises that would support the view that persons are not extremely liable to feelings of resentment in the face of continuous wrongful treatment. Everything we know suggests that it would be inexplicable if a person were not.

Most interestingly, then, it is in virtue of having self-respect that a person would not go on living a morally virtuous life if all the world should treat her immorally. For it is precisely because she has the view that others should treat her rightly and the deep desire to be so treated that a person is unquestionably susceptible to resentment and, in turn, both bitterness and anger when she is continually the object of wrongful treatment, since the desire to be treated rightly is frustrated by wrongful treatment. An advocate of the Platonic conception cannot really be thought to subscribe to a conception of the morally virtuous person as one who is lacking in self-respect. After all, one wants the right explanation for why a person maintains a morally virtuous disposition no matter how immorally all the world should treat him; and that one cannot have if one starts with a person who does not become resentful over being treated wrongly by others, and, what is more, the very reason for this is that he lacks self-respect. This is because often enough the explanation for why he does not feel resentment is that he mistakenly takes morality to be less demanding of others on his behalf than he should.

Given a realistic picture of the psychological wherewithal of persons who have self-respect, it is clear that we must reject the view that the morally virtuous person is one who is immune to the negative feelings that develop on account of sustained immoral treatment. Any self-respecting person will experience resentment if continually subjected to wrongful treatment; thus, given such treatment, any such person is liable to feelings that would weaken, if not destroy entirely, his morally virtuous disposition. These considerations bring out exactly why we would have nothing but the highest moral admiration for a self-respecting person who nonetheless managed to continue leading a morally virtuous life though all the world should treat her wrongly. What would be most impressive morally about such a person would not be simply that she did not experience resentment, but that she had self-respect and yet did not experience resentment. After all, a person who believes that she deserves to be treated in whatever way anyone treats her will also not experience resentment. But this neither surprises us nor elicits our admiration.

16. Beliefs and Moral Reinforcement

The upshot of the preceding discussion is that a person cannot be expected to maintain a morally virtuous disposition no matter how immorally all the world should treat him. Before drawing any conclusions as to what this means in terms of being a morally virtuous person, we would do well to consider straightaway the role that a person's beliefs about how another would treat him can play in reinforcing his favorable disposition toward that other individual. I shall refer to beliefs that a person has about how she would be treated were such-and-such to occur, when the belief is not based upon her actually having been treated that way in the past, as projected counterfactual beliefs. These are to be contrasted with exemplified counterfactual beliefs, which are beliefs that a person has about how she would be treated were such-and-such to occur that are based upon her actually having been treated that way. Questions concerning the individuation of act types obviously arise here: when are two act types the same; when do they differ? But I shall not offer an account of these matters. It seems clear that Jones's lending Smith money on different occasions constitutes the same act type, although the amount lent varies from one time to the next; whereas lending Smith money and visiting him at the hospital just as clearly constitute two distinct act types. I shall assume that our commonsense intuitions about these matters suffice for our purposes.

There can be no doubt that projected counterfactual beliefs play a significant role in our lives. They tend to reinforce the favorable or unfavorable disposition that we already have toward another person, or they tend to give rise to a favorable or unfavorable disposition, or they tend to weaken that disposition. Let me illustrate. Suppose the Johnson-Smiths learn from their next-door neighbor, Jones, that he would be willing to care for their child if they should die before the child reaches adulthood, and they believe this to be a sincere gesture of good will on Jones's part, devoid of any ulterior motives. Broadly speaking, then: If already they have a favorable disposition toward him this newly acquired projected counterfactual belief will certainly reinforce it; if they are neutral in their feelings toward him, this newly acquired belief will serve to give rise to a favorable one; and if they have had a somewhat unfavorable disposition toward him, this new belief will serve to weaken it, if not dissipate it entirely. By contrast, if their newly acquired projected counterfactual belief about Jones is that if they should die before their child reaches adulthood, Jones would attempt to swindle her out of her inheritance, it is obvious that if they have been favorably disposed toward Jones they will very quickly come to be less so, and that, in general, this newly acquired belief will result in their being more negatively disposed toward Jones than they have otherwise been.

Just how any given newly acquired projected counterfactual belief about a person will affect us is a function of a constellation of factors, including the character of our previous interactions with the person, our present desires, our existing beliefs and dispositions, and so on. Thus, if the Johnson-Smiths believe that Jones is always in the business of cleverly manipulating others to serve his ends, then the projected counterfactual belief that he would take care of their child if they should die before the child reaches adulthood is not likely to contribute to their having a positive disposition toward him, as they will interpret Jones's offer as not so much a willingness to put himself out on their behalf as a desire to position himself so that he could steal the child's inheritance. But this observation hardly militates against the point that has been made about the role projected counterfactual beliefs play in our lives with respect to the disposition that we have toward a person. It merely speaks to the obvious, namely, that precisely what role a given projected counterfactual belief plays in our lives is a function of various factors. But surely no one would have thought otherwise.

I have remarked that to believe that someone would treat one in a certain way is not necessarily to have actually been treated in that way. The preceding remarks underscore this point. If the Johnson-Smiths believe that Jones would care for their child if they should die before she reaches adulthood, this is surely not because he has already done so. This belief is not based upon a trial run of sorts! Quite the contrary, they very much hope that Jones will never have to do any such thing. Hence, a projected counterfactual belief can play a significant role in reinforcing our disposition toward a person although we very much hope that the person never has to do the good that we believe he would do. Most significantly, in this instance it is the thought that counts for almost everything.

Consider another example of a projected counterfactual belief giving rise to or reinforcing a person's favorable disposition toward another. Ms. Sanchez, who is an excellent stockbroker, was chosen over four men for an appointment to the board of a major corporation. Sanchez happens to know Mr. Oppenheim, who sits on the board. She admires his skill and efficiency. She thinks he is an excellent, fair-minded corporate vice-president and rightly imagines that he voted for her appointment to the board. Now she learns—having stumbled upon a scribbled note penned by Oppenheim to the board's chairman —that had the board, which had been utterly resistant to the idea of a woman board member, not chosen her over the four men, Oppenheim would have resigned from the company entirely. While, as I said, Sanchez had always considered Oppenheim to be fair minded, it never occurred to her that he was prepared to go so far for the cause of gender equality. And there is no thought in anyone's mind of there being an ulterior motive on Oppenheim's part, since it is widely known that he is a homosexual. Now, I take it to be manifestly obvious that however favorably disposed Sanchez had been toward Oppenheim and however highly she might have thought of him, the projected counterfactual belief that Oppenheim would have resigned had she not been appointed to the board substantially reinforces her favorable disposition and positive opinion of him, although it turns out that he never did resign.

In the context of friendships and loves, projected counterfactual beliefs play a major role in our lives, as there are many things that we believe our friends would do for us that they never have had to do and, we hope, never will. It goes without saying, of course, that projected counterfactual beliefs have some basis in past treatment. No doubt many projected counterfactual beliefs are anchored in exemplified counterfactual beliefs. It is because Jones has done this and that for the Johnson-Smiths when they were in need, and it is because they believe that he would do such things again, that the Johnson-Smiths are able to hold fast to the projected counterfactual belief that Jones would take care of their child if they should die before she reaches adulthood. It is not always easy to distinguish projected counterfactual beliefs from exemplified counterfactual beliefs, but this is true of many valuable distinctions. Also, the question of whether one is justified in one's belief can arise in either case. But I have not, nor would I want to, claim epistemic certainty on their behalf.

I want now to bring the preceding discussion to bear upon the issue of maintaining a morally virtuous disposition. I shall do this by presenting a three-staged argument that, for ease of reference, I shall refer to as the thesis from neutral treatment. To begin, observe that strictly speaking the propositions "X treats Y morally" and "X treats Y immorally" are contrary propositions rather than contradictory propositions, as both can be false: X neither treats Y morally nor immorally.

Any inclination to doubt the soundness of these remarks is probably because conversational implicature (Grice 1975) often licenses us to infer that X treated Y immorally (wrongly) from the claim that X did not treat Y morally (rightly). The implicit premise is that X did interact with Y in a way that allows for a moral evaluation of X's actions; hence, if X did not treat Y rightly, then it follows that X treated Y wrongly. But sometimes this premise is not to be invoked, as when a person contends that X could not possibly have had anything to do with the moral harm that Y suffered at the hands of Z, since X was out of the country and, in any case, has never seen or heard of Z. The speaker here is hardly suggesting that in being out of the country and not knowing of Z that X did the right thing with respect to Y, but only that X's being out of the country and not knowing of Z precludes the possibility that X could have attempted to wrong Y by hiring Z, because these factors preclude the possibility that X could have treated Y rightly or wrongly via Z. It is possible even to know a person and yet with respect to a specific matter not treat her or him either rightly or wrongly. The teacher who gives a student a lower grade for the course than she deserves has wronged her, but in this regard no one else (for example, her classmates) has treated her either rightly or wrongly.

So, imagine that there are three people, Lupeter, Smith, and Doe, none of whom has encountered the others and, furthermore, knows anything about the others. It is not just that all three are strangers, but their paths have never crossed at all; indeed, none has been in any way touched by the actions of the others. Given this much, it follows that none of these individuals has been treated either morally or immorally by either of the others. Now, suppose that each knows that they will all be brought together a year from now, and Lupeter has the following projected counterfactual beliefs: Were she and Smith to in any way interact with one another Smith would be disposed to treat her morally. Were she and Doe to in any way interact with one another Doe would be disposed to treat her immorally. Assuming that Lupeter is a morally virtuous person and, therefore, has a morally virtuous disposition, I take it to be incontrovertible that Lupeter's projected counterfactual belief about Smith reinforces her disposition to treat Smith morally, whereas nothing of the sort is true of her projected counterfactual belief about Doe. This is not to say that Lupeter will treat Doe immorally, but only that her treating him morally receives no reinforcement from her projected counterfactual belief about Doe. Lupeter's projected counterfactual belief about Smith reinforces her morally virtuous disposition in the very same way that a person's favorable disposition can be reinforced by projected counterfactual beliefs in other instances. Now, it will be remembered that, by hypothesis, Lupeter has never encountered Smith or Doe; thus, the fact that Lupeter's projected counterfactual belief about Smith reinforces her disposition to treat him morally cannot be explained by reference to her having benefited from Smith's moral treatment of her, since Smith has not yet had the opportunity to treat Lupeter either morally or immorally.

With this argument in mind, let us move to the second stage of the argument. As with the first stage, we assume in both instances that Lupeter has not in any way interacted with anyone. In the first, not only does Lupeter believe that Smith would treat her morally were she and Smith to have any interactions with one another, but she believes more generally that this is true of everyone. In the second, not only does Lupeter believe that Doe would treat her immorally were she and Doe to have any interactions with one another, but she believes more generally that this is true of everyone. Assume in both instances that Lupeter has not in any way interacted with anyone. Needless to say, if Lupeter's projected counterfactual belief that Smith would treat her morally reinforces her morally virtuous disposition, then surely the more general belief that everyone would treat her morally will reinforce this disposition. Likewise, if Lupeter's projected counterfactual belief that Doe would treat her immorally does not serve to reinforce her morally virtuous disposition, then surely the more general belief that everyone would treat her immorally will not reinforce this disposition.

This completes the first two stages of the thesis from neutral treatment. I have tried to show that nothing more than a person's beliefs about how others would treat her can play a significant role in reinforcing her morally virtuous disposition. Specifically, I have tried to show that, without actually benefiting from the moral behavior of another, it is possible for a person's morally virtuous disposition to be reinforced by his beliefs about how others would treat him. It might be objected, though, that the second stage of the argument fails because the assumption that Lupeter has not in any way interacted with anyone is patently unrealistic, since no one goes through life without interacting with someone or the other. True enough, but the argument does not fail because of the assumption. For the point of the argument, clearly, is that if Lupeter's projected counterfactual belief that one person, say Smith, would treat her morally would reinforce her morally virtuous disposition, then her projected counterfactual belief that everyone would so treat her would most certainly do so; whereas if her projected counterfactual belief that one person, say Doe, would not treat her morally would not reinforce her morally virtuous disposition, then her projected counterfactual belief that no one would so treat her would certainly not do so. This point is not defeated by the truth that no one goes through life without interacting with some person or the other—no more than the claim that a person would believe in God though all the world should call her a fool is defeated by pointing out that all the world has yet to do so. Furthermore, while it is true enough that everyone interacts with someone or the other, it hardly follows from this, of course, that everyone interacts with everyone. The fact of the matter is that each of us interacts with only a very, very small portion of the Earth's population and, most significantly, even the population of the society in which we live. This truth is not to be obscured by the fact that in any given society, there are a handful of people who are so powerful and influential that their actions can affect at once the lives of many with whom they do not interact. Leaders of countries, especially influential countries, come quickly to mind here, and so perhaps do the heads of especially large corporations. And upon occasions individuals from other walks of life may have an enormous impact upon society, as perhaps one might say was true of Martin Luther King, Jr. But needless to say, most people are not so powerful and influential as to be able to affect the lives of many at once. These last two considerations bring us to the third, and final, stage of the thesis from neutral treatment.

To begin with, let us distinguish between familiar and complete strangers. A familiar stranger is a person with whom we have no interactions but whom we recognize and, through observation, identify with a specific piece of behavior or pattern of social interaction. The person whom we recognize as often catching the eight o'clock subway train on weekday mornings is a familiar stranger, as is the person whom we recognize as a patron of a particular deli. The letter carrier who generally serves a particular neighborhood can be a familiar stranger, as can the sanitation worker who does the same.

Familiar strangers are either public figures (people whose lives have public prominence) or people about whom we have formed tentative judgments of character, not so much through our interactions with them as through our observations of their mode of self-presentation in the contexts that we regularly encounter them. A complete stranger, by contrast, is an individual about whom no judgments of character have been made on the basis of having interacted with or regularly observed her or him in the past; hence, a complete stranger cannot be a familiar stranger. Unfortunately, this characterization of a complete stranger is somewhat idealistic. I must leave aside cases in which an uncharitable character assessment of a complete stranger is made because the person's ethnicity is regarded as her or his most salient feature. Alas, it would seem that this state of affairs is possible even in a moderately moral society.

In any case, as I have explicated the notions of familiar and complete strangers, I take it to be indisputable that most members of all but the smallest societies—whether moderately moral or not—are complete strangers to one another. If so, then there is no difficulty whatsoever with the members of society having projected counterfactual beliefs with respect to whether or not complete strangers will treat them morally or immorally. In a moderately moral society, the projected counterfactual belief will take the form of a presumption: A moderately moral society will be conducive to (or favor [Section 20]) all of its members' having the strong presumptive belief that were they to encounter or interact in any way with a complete stranger (in their society), the stranger would treat them morally. By contrast, a society that is not moderately (or at least sufficiently) moral will not be conducive to all of its members' having this strong presumption. Indeed, such a society may be conducive to its members' having the strong presumptive belief that were they to encounter or interact in any way with a complete stranger (in their society), they should not expect that the stranger would treat them morally. Drawing, now, upon the first two stages of the argument from neutral treatment, we can see that if a morally virtuous person lives in a moderately moral society, then her morally virtuous disposition will receive reinforcement from the presumptive projected counterfactual belief that she will have that complete strangers would treat her morally were she to interact with them; whereas if such a person were to live in a society in which she cannot expect that complete strangers would treat her morally, then her morally virtuous disposition will not receive any reinforcement from the corresponding presumptive projected counterfactual belief that a society such as this would be conducive to her having—namely, that she should not expect a complete stranger to treat her morally.

This completes the thesis from neutral treatment. I have tried to show that nothing more than a person's beliefs—projected counterfactual beliefs, I have called them—about how others would treat her can play a significant role in reinforcing her morally virtuous disposition. Specifically, I have tried to show that, without actually benefiting from the moral treatment of another owing to interaction with that person, it is possible for a person's morally virtuous disposition to be reinforced by her beliefs about how others would treat her. It might have been tempting to think that in a moderately moral society people would have only exemplified rather than projected counterfactual beliefs to the effect that they would be treated morally by other members of society. But not so. For it is not a peculiar feature of a moral society that everyone interacts with one another. On the contrary, in all but the smallest societies, moral or not, most people are not even familiar strangers to one another, but are instead complete strangers.

Recall now the Platonic conception of the morally virtuous person. Its central tenet is that a morally virtuous person is one who would continue to lead a morally virtuous life, and so maintain a morally virtuous disposition, no matter how immorally all the world should treat him. And its consequence is that a morally virtuous person is one whose moral disposition never stands in need of reinforcement. As was mentioned in the introductory remarks of this chapter, what this consequence is specifically meant to capture is the idea that in no way should it turn out to be on account of the positive reinforcement that results from actually being treated morally by others that the morally virtuous person maintains her morally virtuous disposition. Of course, if a person were to maintain a morally virtuous disposition despite being treated immorally by all the world, then it would certainly be true that his maintaining a morally virtuous disposition would not be tied to the positive reinforcement that results from actually being treated morally by others. But from this it has been fallaciously reasoned, on the one hand, that unless a person should maintain a morally virtuous disposition though all the world should treat him immorally, then his maintaining a morally virtuous disposition must be tied to the positive reinforcement that results from actually being treated morally by others. On the other hand, it has been mistakenly held that it is not possible for a person's morally virtuous disposition to receive positive reinforcement on account of others' having a morally virtuous disposition unless that positive reinforcement results from actually being treated morally by others. I shall say a word about these in turn.

As to the first point, observe that at no time in the thesis from neutral treatment was it supposed that a person had a morally virtuous disposition only if she were to maintain that disposition though all the world should treat her immorally. Indeed, it is perfectly compatible with all that was said that she would not do so. The argument was simply that a person's morally virtuous disposition was reinforced by her projected counterfactual belief that others would treat her morally should she interact with them; and this belief was not made contingent upon the person's actually having been treated morally in the past by these very same individuals, as the belief could be about complete strangers rather than someone with whom there has been past interaction. Although I have not argued this, I believe that our projected counterfactual beliefs about how others would treat us are such a determining factor in how we are motivated to act that in the absence of the projected counterfactual belief that most others would treat him morally, it is most unlikely that a person would be able to maintain a morally virtuous disposition. (The situation I am imagining here is not one in which the person has the projected counterfactual belief that others would treat him immorally instead of morally, but simply one in which he has no such beliefs whatsoever about how others would treat him.) Even so, from none of this would it follow that the positive reinforcement that the person's morally virtuous disposition receives is contingent upon his actually being treated morally by others. The positive reinforcement would still turn only upon what he believes and not how he is treated.

As I have said, the second piece of fallacious reasoning has it that it is not possible for a person's morally virtuous disposition to receive positive reinforcement on account of others' having a morally virtuous disposition unless that positive reinforcement results from actually being treated morally by others. Alas, this line of thought simply underestimates the role that can be played by our beliefs about how those with whom we have had no interaction would treat us. Our projected counterfactual beliefs play a fundamentally important role in our lives, as the cases of loves and friendships show. This is clear to everyone. I have merely noted the fact that projected counterfactual beliefs can likewise play a very positive role in terms of reinforcing our moral disposition.

One reason (given that one has rejected the Platonic conception of the morally virtuous person) why it is easy to overlook this fact is that it seems rather incontrovertible that our acquiring a morally virtuous disposition is very much tied to how others, especially our parents, treat us. But it is one thing to acquire a morally virtuous disposition and another thing to maintain it. The conditions for doing one need not be the same as the conditions for doing the other. I have argued that being the object of loving parents, at the very outset of our lives, is indispensable to our coming to have a moral disposition. I have not claimed, and it would surely be a mistake to do so, that continuing to have such parents is indispensable to maintaining a morally virtuous disposition. After all, parents often die quite some time before their adult children; but clearly it would be wildly implausible to suppose that given the very nature of things an adult child's chances of maintaining a morally virtuous disposition are adversely affected simply by the loss of her parents. If an adult child's parents should become rather immoral, we have absolutely no reason to think that on that account alone it is just a matter of time before the adult child becomes immoral as well. There is no incompatibility whatsoever, then, in claiming that being treated morally by our parents, say, is indispensable to our coming to have a moral disposition but not to our maintaining one. In this regard, a morally virtuous disposition is not unlike other capacities—the capacity to speak a natural language, for example. Being around competent speakers of a natural language is a prerequisite for acquiring the ability to speak one, but not, it would seem, for maintaining that ability.

An obvious, but far from trivial, truth is that human beings are social creatures—a truth that clearly speaks to the indispensability of social interaction to human flourishing. The arguments of this section, if sound, give further expression to this truth. For the very extent to which we are social beings is revealed by the reality that nothing more than our beliefs about how others would treat us can bear significantly upon our flourishing, our moral flourishing in particular. We need not interact with specific others in order to be influenced by them. One could not want for better evidence of our sociability than this. As I have said, that we are influenced by our beliefs about others is not new. I have merely noted its significance in connection with leading a moral life. Quite surprisingly, then, the Platonic conception of the morally virtuous person must be rejected as unsatisfactory precisely because it embodies a view of persons that, in the end, denies their sociability. A person who could lead a morally virtuous life no matter how wrongly he was treated by others and regardless of his beliefs about how others would treat him would not be a social creature—at least not as we understand this concept. Still, the Platonic view speaks to what is of the utmost importance to our conception of the morally virtuous person, namely, that she is one for whom maintaining her morally virtuous disposition is not contingent upon the benefits that come with being treated morally by others. By noting the importance that nothing more than our beliefs about how others would treat us can play in our lives, I believe that we have been able to salvage this aspect of the Platonic conception of the morally virtuous person.

17. The Importance of Basic Trust

The arguments of the preceding section underscore the importance of what I have called basic trust (Section 9).[4] I should like now to develop this notion more fully. I begin with some obvious and general remarks about trust.

Trust can be reasonable or unreasonable. It is reasonable if it is justifiably based upon a positive assessment of a person's character as to the way in which she will behave given the item(s) with which she has been entrusted: one's life, money, the care of one's children, a secret, or whatever. Otherwise it is not. The schema for trust is as follows:[5] Person X trusts person Y to act in a certain way with respect to a set of things (situations or objects) F, where F is valued by X. Instead of persons, one might very well talk about creatures

[4] As developed in the text, the notion of basic trust owes its inspiration to Fuller (1964, ch. 3) and Hart (1961, ch. 4). Fuller speaks of the internal morality law and Hart of the internal aspect of legal rules. I find the importance of basic trust to be implicit in their remarks, especially Fuller's. See, in particular, his "The Problem of the Grudge Informer" (1964, appendix).

[5] My views on trust generally owe much to A. Baier (1986). What follows in the text are some minor refinements to her very sensitive account of this concept.

capable of desires, second-order beliefs, and second-order intentions; for perhaps animals are capable of trust. I shall not press this point, though, as I am not concerned to determine the range of creatures capable of trusting and being trusted. If X trusts Y with respect to F, then X makes himself vulnerable to Y with respect to F in that if, contrary to X's expectations, Y should fail to act in the appropriate manner with respect to F, then X has good reason to believe that he will be worse off in some important respect, and Y knows this. Further, X believes that either implicitly or explicitly Y is accepting of the fact that he is being trusted by X. Specifically, then, X trusts Y only if X has succeeded in communicating to Y that he (X) is hereby making himself vulnerable to Y and if X believes that Y is accepting of the fact that X is trusting him (Y) and, therefore, that Y is prepared to treat him (X) in the appropriate manner. If X tells Y something very confidential, but because of the way that X conveys the information Y believes that X is joking, and thinks no more of the story, then X's attempt to trust Y in this instance was abortive.

These observations about trust reflect the reality that we do not trust a person whom we regard as not being trustworthy. We may, of course, be quite mistaken about whether or not a person is trustworthy. As I have intimated, trust does not require a conversation; nonverbal behavior can and often does suffice. It is obvious, for example, that we can indicate to others whether we trust them by where we stand in relation to them in, say, a subway station. And we can easily get an instance of abortive trust in a fairly empty subway station late at night. Suppose it is midnight, and Susan Smith mistakenly thinks that the person with the long, flowing hair sitting on the bench in the station is a woman. So Smith sits at the other end of the bench, whereupon she realizes that the person is a man, and she immediately moves. Smith was prepared to trust the person qua female, not qua male.

It will be recalled that I distinguished between intimate and basic trust, with each being at opposite ends of the continuum of trust (Section 9). Among strangers, especially complete strangers (Section 16), there can be only basic trust. This, essentially, is the trust that others will treat one in accordance with the precepts of morality. Now, when it comes to basic trust between complete strangers, nothing is more important than the individual's mode of self-presentation as this falls under the prevailing norms regarding the appearances of morally decent people. A person's mode of self-presentation ranges over his nonverbal behavior: his gait, his manner of dress, his speech patterns, his countenance, and so on.[6] A person's mode of self-presentation is interpreted in light of the prevailing norms regarding the appearances of the morally decent person (that is, those who are basically trustworthy), which can differ according to gender and ethnicity; and depending on the circumstances some aspects of nonverbal behavior play a more salient role in our assessment of a stranger than others. In a nearly empty subway station at midnight appearances count almost more than anything; accordingly, a disheveled and tattered-looking woman is viewed as more basically trustworthy than an equally disheveled and tattered-looking man, a well-dressed man more than a disheveled and tattered-looking man, and, in some instances, a white man more than a black man, given that their attire is the same. On an isolated street at night, gait and gender are especially important when an assessment is being made from afar, given prevailing norms regarding women and men, as well as those regarding how a morally decent person carries herself or himself. By contrast, the appearance of a disheveled person does not much concern us when we encounter her or him amongst a throng of businesspeople in broad daylight.

It goes without saying that prevailing norms regarding the appearances of the morally decent can be extraordinarily complex and subtle. Being immaculately or even expensively dressed is not enough. Both the businessman and the street pimp may satisfy these criteria, though clearly the prevailing norms concerning the morally decent favor the former: an immaculately dressed pimp is not the first thing that comes to mind when one envisions a morally decent person. One need not be immaculately dressed at all if the image that one projects is that of a disheveled professor (a stereotype more in place for men than women).

Now, trust is not simply a matter of being able to predict another's behavior, for one can do that quite well without trusting a person. If X puts everything in his house under lock and key, then he can predict with confidence that upon visiting him Y is not likely to steal

---

[6] In addition to the references mentioned in the preceding chapter, see also Trivers (1971), especially the section entitled "The Psychological System Underlying Human Reciprocal Altruism" (pp. 211–23), in which it is assumed throughout the discussion that human beings have a rich capacity to monitor one another's behavior.

anything, but X clearly does not trust Y. The appropriate belief in connection with trust is not that a person cannot act contrary to one's expectations, but that out of respect for one she will not, although she is free to do otherwise.

Likewise, it is important not to confuse relying or depending upon a person with trusting him. One can do the former without doing the latter, but not conversely. There are many respects in which one can rely upon a person if one is able to predict how she or he will behave. Commuters may rely upon the 8:30 train to be on time every morning; yet they do not trust the driver of the train, upon whom they may have never laid eyes. In view of what has been said, the reason why we do not have trust here should be clear. There has been no communication (verbal or nonverbal) whatsoever between the commuters and the driver of the train. Even if they are making themselves vulnerable to the driver, she is hardly aware of this. Furthermore, her arriving in the station promptly at 8:30 each morning is not tied to their expectations. She is reliable because she is under orders to maintain a certain schedule, and her concern to do this is quite independent of the commuters. Of course, a story can be told that places trust in the picture. Perhaps the train driver is dating a certain passenger. The point is, however, that relying or depending upon a person is distinguishable from trusting a person.

Consider a different scenario. Suppose that an excellent drugstore, located in the shopping district of a major city, is known for being open twenty-four hours a day all year round. People from all parts of the city come there at all hours of the day and night. We can imagine that this store is heavily relied upon by many members of the city to be open twenty-four hours a day. Some put off their drugstore shopping until night precisely because the store is open twenty-four hours a day. Everybody knows somebody who has shown up at the drugstore at 3:00 A.M. for some reason or the other: to pick up some wine, to have a prescription filled, to satisfy an appetite for peanuts, to make a sleepless night go by faster, and so on. Observe, though, that as much as everyone relies upon the store to be open twenty-four hours a day, there is no trust involved here at all. This is so although the owner is well aware of the fact that people from all over the city depend upon her to keep the store open twenty-four hours a day.

It can turn out that one has to rely upon someone whom one does not trust. Suppose an individual is lost in a foreign country on a harsh wintry night, and she does not speak the language. An utterly inebriated person approaches her for some coins. He, of course, immediately recognizes that she is a foreigner. She manages to convey to him that she is lost by pointing to a piece of paper containing the name of the street to which she wishes to return. He gestures for her to follow him. She can either follow him or continue floundering in her present desolate surroundings, in which case she will surely come to suffer from exposure to the elements. Full of anxiety and with halting steps, she nervously follows him, praying for her safety. She hardly trusts him, although she is allowing herself to rely upon him to get her to familiar surroundings.

Trust is also to be distinguished from being able to count on a person. The idea here is that the person has the kind of personality or talent or vision or skill that makes it likely he will be able to bring about a desired result under the circumstances in question. It may be that the fans of a team can almost always count on a certain very talented player to turn the game around. There is no trust involved here, though. For their counting on the player has nothing whatsoever to do with their making themselves vulnerable with respect to some good of theirs on account of his having indicated to them that they would suffer no harm or loss if they did so; rather, it merely reflects their desire to see the team win and their belief that the player will very likely contribute to the realization of this end in spite of the team's present predicament. There is no interaction between the fans and this player as a result of which the fans can be said to have trusted him. To be sure, those who have placed bets in favor of the team have a reason to want the player to succeed that those who did not place bets do not have. It goes without saying, however, that merely having a reason to want a player to turn a game around hardly constitutes trusting the player. Besides, those fans who placed bets did not make themselves vulnerable to the player, however vulnerable they might have made themselves financially. Of course, there is no exclusivity here: one can both trust and count on the very same person. Suppose this very talented player had said to some friends (who will be watching the game): "Trust me! There is no way our team can lose the game. For the last six months we have been practicing a brilliant play for me, which we are going to employ today. If I had ten thousand dollars, I would not hesitate to bet every last penny on our winning." Those who are moved by his remarks to bet on the team's winning are not only counting on this very talented player to come through, but are trusting him to do so, as they have made themselves vulnerable on account of what they have presumed to be his nonrhetorical remarks. The client who is the father of the lawyer representing him trusts the lawyer, whom he is counting on to win the case for him. He trusts her by revealing information to her about himself that no parent would ever want his children to know. He is counting on her in that he is hoping that the legal skills and ingenuity that have made her famous for never having lost a case will yield a court victory for him as well.

These remarks highlight the reality that to trust another is to voluntarily make oneself vulnerable with respect to some good, having been led to believe by the other's actions toward one that no loss or harm will come to one as a result. This is not a characteristic feature of depending, relying, or counting upon a person. If, when it comes to basic trust, this seems to be an overstatement of things, I suspect that this is because of the extent to which the basic trust we have in others is taken for granted.

Consider the importance of basic trust with respect to the belief that others are not inclined to kill us. Every day most of us walk through life without even the thought of wearing a bulletproof vest. It is not as if most of us own such an item, consider wearing it, and then decide against it. Most of us do not even own one—and this is not because we have not gotten around to making the purchase. The explanation for this is quite simple. Most of us go about our daily activities without expecting a complete stranger to attempt to kill us. This is because in general our basic trust is that most members of society will not (even attempt to) kill us. It is not simply that we predict that most will not out of fear of legal punishment, say; for we do not hold that most would be tempted to kill us if only they thought they could get away with doing so. On the contrary, we think that most people have no desire whatsoever to kill others. If we thought otherwise, we would live very differently, even if we were ever so confident that every murderer would be apprehended and punished to the fullest extent of the law. We would be on our guard at every turn. If we had to consider any and every stranger as a potential murderer, walking down the street would be a veritable nightmare. It is not clear that any place, save home (if that), could be considered safe. There is every reason to believe that we would find life psychologically unbearable on account of the anxiety and fear of being summarily killed.

Rarely do we come home and give thanks because we have made it through yet another day with no attempt having been made on our lives. Far from showing that we do not have basic trust when it comes to complete strangers' not killing us, what this shows is just how much we take that trust for granted. It is certainly true that there are fewer places in the world that are thought to be as safe as they were in days gone by. All the same, there are relatively few places in the world where everyone must view a complete stranger as her or his potential murderer.

It is worth repeating that when it comes to our life we would not even for a moment have basic trust in others if we thought that the only reason no attempt was made on our life is that everyone who might want to kill us is very much afraid of the legal consequences of doing so. True enough, one hopes that this thought suffices to stay the hands of anyone who contemplates the idea; but the point, needless to say, is that one does not suppose that it is this thought that explains why no attempt has been made on one's life. Rather, one very much hopes that no attempt was made because, in the first place, no one had the inclination to take one's life—and not just because, say, it was a bad day for murdering, but because, in virtue of being morally decent, no individual who could have killed one gave any thought to the idea.

With regard to life, it is clear that a society in which it was impossible for any individual to have some form of basic trust in any other individual would be psychologically unbearable, as such a society would be tantamount to a Hobbesean state of nature. There is good reason to believe that a state of nature is inimical to our flourishing because, if nothing else, it cannot afford individuals the peace of mind necessary to attend adequately both to their own well-being and the well-being of their loved ones, their offspring especially (Section 3). More significantly, though, having basic trust that others have no desire to kill them is indispensable to the flourishing of human beings precisely because they have a sense of themselves as existing over time. They think of themselves in terms of the future. A world completely without basic trust with regard to life would make the future so precarious as to make life not worth living. A world completely without basic trust would be psychologically intolerable because it would be incompatible with human beings' living as such.

Life is so important that it is natural to focus upon the significance of basic trust in regards to it. But consider the significance of basic trust in terms of having the truth told to one. Of course, murder is a far worse moral offense than knowingly saying what is false. Still, a world in which we had to suspect everyone of lying to us would be a very difficult world to get along in, and would surely take a psychological toll. Suppose a lie would greet the simplest request for information: What time is it? Which train was that? How does one get to so-and-so's office? What time does the flight depart? Does the fruit dish contain any refined sugar? (A very serious question for a diabetic.) Under these circumstances, life as we know it would scarcely be tolerable. We need information in order to be able to lead our lives, and it is not at all obvious how we could get on were the simplest requests for information greeted with a lie or, in any case, if we had to treat nearly every such response as if it were a lie. And, once again, it is important to see that the reason why we are not lied to at every turn is not that in each instance the individual considers the matter and then decides against it. The reason, quite simply, is that the individual has no desire to lie to us.

While I think that the importance of basic trust can be seen in other areas of our lives, I shall not attempt to make the case here. Basic trust is clearly of such paramount importance in the two very fundamental areas of our lives just discussed that there is no need to consider the matter further. The significance of basic trust in our lives reveals just how important our beliefs about the psychological attitude of others toward us is to our living well. For our basic trust is anchored in the belief that those trusted have no desire to harm us —not just that they will not harm us. After all, one can predict that a person will not harm one—the person is handcuffed and bound, say —without ever having any reason to trust the individual. Accordingly, it is not enough that we can predict that most people will not take our lives; trust in this matter is absolutely essential to our psychological well-being. Attempts to found morality upon self-interest fail to grasp the importance of trust in our lives (see Section 6).

Now, given the importance of basic trust in our lives and the extent to which our nonverbal behavior and mode of self-presentation indicate to others that they can have basic trust in us, one would naturally expect it to be the case that human beings are excellent monitors of social behavior. And so it is. This is borne out by the simple observation that even among our most intimate acquaintances—lovers and companion friends—our interpretation and grasp of what is said to us is inextricably tied to their nonverbal behavior. When a person says "I love you" to someone, what the intended hearer hears is tied to her or his assessment of the concomitant nonverbal behavior; and this the speaker knows all too well. There are norms of nonverbal communication. One is that sincerity is rarely communicated by laughing and giggling as one speaks; and a person who wishes to appear sincere is apt not to speak in this way. Another is that there is reason to doubt the veracity of a person's remarks if he averts his gaze too often and is constantly twitching; and a person who wishes his words to be believed is apt not to speak in this way. The judgment that a dear friend is coping well with a significant setback or loss is not based simply upon his saying that he is when asked, but, among other things, his facial expressions and the tone of his voice. If even among friends and lovers—people who have a commanding perspective of one another's lives—nonverbal behavior is of enormous importance, then, a fortiori, it is important among complete strangers.

Mastery of the skills of nonverbal behavior is an essential feature of being a person. And such mastery means not only that one has considerable facility in grasping the significance of nonverbal behavior among others, but that one's own nonverbal behavior is sufficiently cued to the prevailing norms of nonverbal communication.

As perhaps an important aside, it is worth mentioning that social interaction among humans is so tied to the nonverbal behavior that is characteristic of human beings, which in turn is tied to the affective capacities of human beings, that it is not at all obvious that human beings could successfully interact with other rational creatures who differ radically in either their emotional constitution or anatomical structure. Consider the science fiction view of the purely rational creature devoid of any affective capacities—for example, the Vulcans of the science fiction story *Star Trek*. Such creatures cannot express sorrow or remorse or sadness or joy or elation. But the expression of these sentiments is a characteristic feature of nonverbal behavior among human beings. Some of the deepest expressions of social interaction between human beings cannot be understood in the absence of the affective sentiments. The communication of sincerity itself—such as sincerely saying, "I am sorry"—revolves around these sentiments. We would not know how to assess the sincerity of a rational creature constitutionally incapable of the affective sentiments who uttered these words. To be sure, the creature might be constitutionally incapable of prevaricating, as Vulcans are said to be. But how could humans be convinced of that? Certainly not by being told that this is so.

Part of the genius of good science fiction, surely, is that it distances us from reality without ever flaunting this fact. *Star Trek* did that masterfully. The behavior of Medical Officer McCoy was masterfully employed as a vehicle to portray Mr. Spock as a rational creature constitutionally incapable of the affective sentiments. Thus, McCoy invariably becomes enraged whenever Mr. Spock suggests that the only reasonable thing to do is wait in regards to the perilous situation that James T. Kirk, captain of the USS Enterprise, is in. McCoy becomes enraged although he somehow realizes that there is nothing that Spock can do; for McCoy never accuses Spock of failing to take a reasonable course of action that is open to him. The problem that McCoy has with Mr. Spock is this: even when there is absolutely nothing that Spock can do, he nonetheless ought to become emotionally distraught over the fact that there is nothing that he can do. It is the interplay between the roles of Spock and McCoy that so masterfully serves to convey the impression that Spock is constitutionally incapable of the affective sentiments.

I have used the science fiction story of *Star Trek* to illustrate in a rather intuitive way the extent to which social interaction among human beings is tied to the nonverbal behavior that is characteristic of human beings, which in turn is tied to the affective capacities of human beings.[7] This is precisely what one would expect among creatures in whose flourishing trust plays an indisputably major role. For just as a person cannot hope to convince that she is sincere in her remarks simply by saying that she is, a person can no more hope to convince that she is trustworthy, even in terms of basic trust, simply by saying that she is. Insofar as they are reasonable, judgments of sincerity and trust are tied to assessments of nonverbal behavior.

Now, if basic trust is important to the flourishing of human beings, then so must beliefs about how others would be disposed to treat one. The second section of this chapter spoke to this point. And if beliefs

[7] The argument is more fully developed in Thomas (1983a, 1987b).

of this sort are important to the flourishing of human beings, then the Platonic conception of the morally virtuous person is not likely to be true. The first section of this chapter spoke to this point. In light of the discussions of this chapter, questions concerning the emotional structure of the moral person naturally arise. I take up many of these questions in the following chapter.

CHAPTER SEVEN

Living Well

To live well is the hope of every reasonable person, and being happy is very much a part of living well. Happiness here is to be understood as a kind of self-contentment, a measure of inner satisfaction, which can be sustained regardless of the many vicissitudes of life. Living well, thus understood, is of such importance that a most powerful consideration in favor of any activity is that it is believed to contribute more substantially to our living well than the alternatives available to us. In this regard the Platonic view that every moral person is, in virtue of being such, happier than any and every immoral person strikes a most responsive chord in our hearts. For one hopes that if any walk of life is in virtue of its very nature conducive to happiness and, therefore, to living well, then it is the moral life. I shall not, however, attempt to defend this very elevated Platonic view, since it seems implausible that every person of good moral character is, in virtue of being such, happier than every person of bad moral character. Lowering my sights, I shall instead defend the view that an individual with a morally good character is, in virtue of being such, significantly favored over a person without a good moral character to be happy and thus to live well. As I hope to show, one of the fruits of leading a moral life is self-knowledge with respect to leading a moral life: the moral person is favored over the immoral person to have such knowledge, at least when it comes to interpersonal relationships.

The aim here is to secure the view that there is a substantial connection between living well and living morally, whether or not it can be established that every person of good moral character is, in virtue of being such, happier than everyone without a good moral character. I do not believe that in the end the Platonic thesis can be established, though I shall not argue the case. But if it is possible to have a substantial connection between living well and living morally without embracing the Platonic thesis, that is a matter of considerable importance in and of itself. As we shall see, indispensable to the happiness that contributes to our living well is psychic harmony. A person is in a state of psychic harmony when his feelings are operating in his life as they should—that is, when they can serve as a reliable indicator of the attitudes and beliefs that a person has toward those with whom he interacts. I will examine the role of our feelings in this regard. Throughout, the class of feelings under discussion are the natural sentiments. I begin, however, with a discussion of self-love, as I believe that a brief look at this concept will prove very useful as we proceed.

18. Self-Love

Proper self-love has two dimensions. One pertains to flourishing and interpersonal equity primarily in friendships and loves, the other to self-respect. I shall refer to the former as the personal-flowering dimension of self-love. A person who has a full measure of self-love has the proper regard for himself along both of these dimensions. Thus, on the account offered, self-respect is a species of self-love. I begin with a discussion of the personal-flowering dimension of self-love. As we shall see, it is possible that a person could lack self-respect though he is concerned to flower personally; and it is possible that a person could have self-respect and not be concerned to flower personally.

A person who has the proper regard for herself in terms of personal flowering is, to be sure, concerned to flourish: to realize her talents and to pursue a conception of the good that is rewarding and, to a considerable extent, self-sustaining. But she also realizes the importance of engaging in activities that give her some respite from the cares of life, and she is able to reward herself for notable or sustained endeavors. Although a person concerned with personal flowering does not prefer any interests of hers, however small, to the interests of others, it is nonetheless the case that in relationships of friendship (or love), a person with the proper self-regard that is characteristic of personal flowering maintains a sense of equity. Thus, although she very much behaves in all the altruistic and affectionate ways that a friend should, she is not indifferent to whether the friend behaves in a like manner toward her. She feels slighted if the friend does not so behave when the occasion clearly calls for an altruistic or affectionate act on the friend's part. And if, often enough, the friend is not forthcoming in this way, she begins to wonder about the quality of the friendship.

As I have characterized it, not all aspects of personal flowering can be understood as having a moral dimension. Perhaps this seems obvious enough when it comes to a person's realizing his talents. It is rarely thought, at least nowadays, that a person has a moral obligation to do this.[1] On the other hand, it may seem just as obvious that in friendships (and loves) proper self-regard, as it expresses itself in a sense of equity, must surely be understood as a moral requirement. Well, not as often as one might think.

Now, to be sure, friends can wrong each other morally, as when one betrays the trust of the other. Deceit among friends and lovers whose relationship is volatile can be vicious. Still, it goes without saying that much of the give-and-take of friendship cannot be understood in terms of moral claims that each has against the other. For it is important to friends that their behavior toward each other is motivated primarily out of love. A sick person does not expect his friend to be motivated to visit him on account of a moral duty to visit the sick, but rather on account of the tremendous affection between them (Blum 1980). If the friend does not visit him, this hurts not because the friend has failed him morally, but because the failure to visit is taken as strong evidence that the friend has less affection for him (the sick person) than he had been inclined to believe. After all, we need not imagine that the person is on his deathbed or that the visit is for the

---

[1] Kant, of course, believed otherwise, thinking that it could be shown via the categorical imperative that persons have an obligation to flourish. For an excellent discussion of Kant's views here, see Nell (1975), pp. 88–89. I do not claim here that there are no self-regarding duties at all. Thomas Hill, Jr. (1973), suggests in his influential paper that perhaps persons have a duty to have self-respect, that is, a duty not to be servile. See Section 4. For a very recent discussion of these matters, see Andre (1987). K. Baier (1958) argues that there can be no duties to the self, pp. 226–28.

purpose of bringing him something that he desperately needs. Nor need we imagine that the person is in the hospital or at home alone. The person may have simply broken his leg, which was set that day, and is home recuperating with his loving parents and siblings and not in need of anything.

Often enough, the sick person just wants his friend to visit him; he does not need the friend to do so. He wants the friend to visit precisely because there is great comfort in feeling the concern of one's friends when one is so situated. He rightly feels that the friend ought to visit, but this is not a moral ought. It is rather the ought of conditions: when certain conditions obtain, certain other events—specifically, behavior—should obtain. In the case at hand, the conditions are to be specified, roughly, as follows: If there is mutual affection between A and B and A is sick, then B's affection for A should move B to appreciate that B's visiting A would greatly comfort A.[2] In our example, the sick person's believing this, and feeling slighted if his friend does not visit him, counts as his (the sick person's) having the proper regard for himself. Moral obligations, duties, and rights are not the issue here.

So, as I have tried to show, to have the proper regard for oneself in terms of personal flowering is to have a concern for the self and one's interactions with others, especially one's friends and loved ones, which, in many significant instances, does not admit of a moral rendering.

With self-respect, however, things are different. The attitude of proper self-regard characteristic of self-respect is quintessentially a moral one. A person has the proper regard for herself from the moral point of view if she believes that in virtue of her humanity she is as deserving as any other person of full moral status and, therefore, that she should be treated accordingly. Thus, she believes that there are appropriate ways for others to behave toward her quite independent of their having any affection for her. This gives us a sharp difference between the proper regard for the self that is characteristic of personal flowering and that which is characteristic of self-respect. The former pertains to the ways in which it is appropriate for individuals to behave toward one another when their interactions are due primarily to

[2] For this way of putting things, I am much indebted to Wertheimer (1972), pp. 89–102.

their being the object of one another's affection. The latter, by contrast, pertains to the ways in which it is appropriate for individuals to behave toward one another simply in virtue of the fact that each individual has full moral status and, therefore, when the interaction is not due to affection.

The other difference is that strictly speaking the attitude of proper regard for oneself that is characteristic of self-respect does not require that one be concerned to realize one's talents. It is true, of course, that persons are better able to realize their talents when they are treated in the morally appropriate way by others—that is, as human beings deserving of full moral status. But the desire to be so treated does not entail the desire to realize one's talents. We can imagine a vagabond who is quite adamant about being treated in the morally appropriate way but who has no interest whatsoever in developing any of his talents. This may be unusual and even unfortunate. That such a situation could come about may even be indicative of deep injustices in the basic structure of society; I do not suppose otherwise. Still, we can imagine a case of this sort. Thus, it seems possible to have self-respect and yet not have a full measure of self-love.

Offhand, the foregoing considerations might seem inconsistent with the claim that self-respect is the moral expression of self-love. But not so. Love for the self is not an all-or-nothing matter. A person can certainly care enough about himself that he would not want others to wrong him and yet not care enough to develop his own talents. The desire not to be wronged, that is, the desire to be treated in the morally appropriate ways by those with whom we interact, is more basic than the desire to flourish in that if one is to have any chance of flourishing at all, one must not be wronged by others, at least not too often and not too harshly. Thus, the desire not to be wronged by others is the most minimal attitude of positive regard that a self-respecting individual can have toward herself or himself. We do not have the conceptual machinery to make sense of a self-respecting person who lacks this desire but nonetheless desires to flourish, save that the individual has a profound misunderstanding of the way of the world. Lest there be any misunderstanding, let me explicitly state here that it is not because she desires to flourish that a person with minimal positive regard for herself desires not to be wronged by others, as this makes not being so treated by others merely of instrumental value. Rather, it is because she views not being treated wrongly by others as a good in and of itself, and not a good only because it is for the sake of some other good.

I have maintained that not all aspects of personal flowering can be understood as having a moral dimension. Our discussion of self-respect, however, makes it clear that sometimes personal flowering can have a moral dimension, since being treated in the morally proper way by others is a condition of our personal flowering. It might be tempting to think that any individual concerned with personal flowering has self-respect. But the temptation should be resisted, for it is quite possible that a person could be very much concerned to flourish and yet not have self-respect.

One might, for instance, understand the life of Booker T. Washington in this way. Born a slave, Washington went on to found Tuskegee Institute, a very distinguished black institution, with the aim of contributing to the betterment and flourishing of black people. Even so, various individuals fully aware of his accomplishments have considered Washington to be an Uncle Tom, a black person who as a matter of principle adopts a very self-deprecatory posture around whites. What has inclined many to think this is that, at least on the face of things, Washington seemed to have held the view that blacks must be economically successful in order to prove themselves worthy of morally proper treatment, which, in turn, made him appear to be too accepting of the status quo.[3] If Washington actually believed that on account of the dark pigmentation of their skin blacks had to prove themselves worthy of proper moral treatment, then it would seem that he was very much lacking in self-respect, since the pigmentation of a person's skin should have no bearing whatsoever on whether or not she or he is deserving of such treatment. Presumably a person of Washington's talents and intellectual abilities should have realized this.

---

[3] Washington's "Atlanta Exposition Address" (Washington, 1901) is very much the culprit here. Rather than calling for equality in that famous speech, which was heard by many (white) dignitaries, Washington seems extraordinarily accommodating:

"—No race can prosper till it learns that there is as much dignity in tilling a field as in writing a poem. It is at the bottom of life we [blacks] must begin, and not at the top."

"—In all things that are purely social we can be as separate as the fingers, yet be one as the hand in all things essential to mutual progress."

"—It is important and right that all privileges of the law be ours [blacks'], but it is vastly more important that we be prepared for exercising these privileges."

Whether Washington actually held this view is a matter that need not concern us. It suffices for our purposes that Washington's views on this issue have been open to dispute, and remain so.[4] This shows that there is no conceptual bar to a person's being concerned to flourish and yet his not having self-respect because he does not believe that in virtue of his humanity he is deserving of proper moral treatment.

Our discussion of Washington underscores the importance of distinguishing between personal flowering and self-respect in the way that I have done. In addition to making it manifestly clear that not all aspects of personal flowering have a moral dimension, our discussion of Washington reveals that an individual's commitment to flourishing may count against his having self-respect precisely because the commitment is fueled by the individual's mistaken belief that in the absence of his flourishing he is not deserving of morally proper treatment from others. If, indeed, Washington held this belief, it may be due to the unfortunate reality that in the absence of phenomenal flourishing on their part, blacks during Washington's time had little chance of being treated in the morally proper way. Since our beliefs about what we are deserving of are very much influenced by the ways in which we are treated—and, in particular, the conception of us conveyed by the basic structure of society—it is not implausible that a correct assessment of reality was transformed into a mistaken view about the conditions under which black people were rightly deserving of proper moral treatment. If so, then the fact that Washington held this mistaken belief may very well be excusable.

Self-love refers to two dimensions along which individuals should have the proper regard for themselves. Neither dimension is egoistic as a matter of necessity. With the self-respect dimension of self-love this is perhaps a conceptual point. Every human being rightly believes that he is as deserving as any other human being of full moral status; and to believe this is in no way to be committed to giving ontological priority to one's own interests and preferences. As for the personal-flowering aspect of self-love, while there is no getting around the fact that it is compatible with egoism, we have seen that a nonegoistic conception of personal flowering is possible; for neither the desire to realize one's talents nor the desire to be treated equitably entails always

[4] For a charitable way of reading Washington's views as expressed in his "Atlanta Exposition Address," see Boxill (1976).

preferring one's interests, however small, to the interests of others. On the contrary, both desires are compatible with taking considerable delight in the flourishing of others. Indeed, the love that persons have for others is at its best when persons realize both dimensions of self-love in their lives. For then their attachment to their loved ones is not born of insecurities, the need for praise, and the like. This, I trust, is clear from our discussion of friendship.

I should like to conclude this section with the very important observation that it is in virtue of being loved by others, especially our parents, that we come to have self-love. This consideration obviously lends enormous support to the view that self-love, even the personal-flowering aspect of it, need not amount to an egoistic conception of the self. Nothing is more obvious than that loving another is not just a matter of being concerned to satisfy her desires, as the case of good parents demonstrably shows. Necessarily, to love another is to view some activities and modes of social interaction as being good for her and others as being bad for her. Thus, at the very minimum, to love a person is necessarily to subscribe to a conception of the good for that person. Through parental love, the child participates in the conception of the good that her parents have for her. In so doing, she comes to have the very idea that some activities and modes of social interaction are good for her and others are bad. Without this idea, there could be no self-love. And without self-love, a person does not go on to live as well as she might.

I take love to be more basic than self-love, not only because it is love that gives rise to self-love, but also because it is in virtue of having the capacity to love that we are liable to experiencing the other sentiments, with the possible exception of anger. I turn to these matters in the following section.

19. The Natural Sentiments

Love is a natural sentiment because the capacity to love comes in the wake of being human. That is, it is a characteristic feature of the psychological make-up of human beings. When the capacity to love is manifested in our lives, there are other emotions that we are naturally prone to experience. These include resentment, indignation, guilt, shame, remorse, sorrow, and anger. For to love another is to identify in a most profound way with that individual's good—to delight in his flourishing. Love for another is utterly incompatible with either indifference to the individual's well-being or delight in his being harmed by the actions of others, including oneself. Thus, it matters dearly to us whether or not the actions of others—as well as our own actions —toward a loved one contribute to the individual's flourishing. If not —if our actions or the actions of others harm our loved one—that is a source of great concern to us, and even more so when the harm can be attributed to deliberate intent. It is because love for another entails identifying with that person's good in these ways that the other sentiments follow in the wake of our having love for someone.

We become angry at those who deliberately harm a loved one. We feel guilty when we do. We feel sorrow when we have accidently harmed a loved one, and we feel remorse when, whether accidentally or not, we have caused her irreparable harm. These feelings are not optional but inescapable given that we love another. Resentment comes into the picture if we allow for the idea of self-love. If we love ourselves enough, then as with love for others, we cannot be indifferent or delighted when others harm us. To have a full measure of self-love is not just to believe that others should treat one properly, but also to believe that one's own flourishing is important; it is to take an interest in one's living well. It is not to be narcissistic; it is not to be given to glorying in one's own triumphs or to wallowing in one's own sense of importance. Nor, in particular, is it to believe that one's own well-being has a prior claim to the attention of others. Having a commitment to one's own flourishing is hardly the same thing as either desiring others not to flourish or being indifferent to their doing so. I take it to be more than obvious that in the wake of love the other natural sentiments that I have mentioned follow. So I shall not belabor the point.

However, there is a difference between love and the other sentiments I have mentioned. Feelings of love give us delight in and of themselves. Such feelings are intrinsically desirable. During moments when feelings of love are especially salient our spirits are buoyed. What is more, through love, pain and disappointments are often numbed. It is generally acknowledged that in virtue of the realized capacity to love, life itself is just that much richer. Indeed, for this very reason some have regarded it as a mistake to characterize the egoist as one who has no love for others (cf. Kalin 1970). By contrast, nothing of the sort is thought to be true of the sentiments that I have mentioned as following in the wake of love. Even in those instances when we believe (rightly, say) that we ought to feel guilty and are relieved that we do, the relief is not properly characterized as a delight. Feeling guilty is not thought to be desirable in and of itself. Nor is feeling angry, or resentful, or sorrowful, and so on. Accordingly, it might be tempting to think that these other sentiments, which I shall simply refer to as the negative ones, are sentiments we could just as well do without, that being liable to them is simply a matter of having to take the bad with the good, namely, the capacity to love.

This view is quite mistaken. For although there is certainly no reason to believe that the negative sentiments can be shown to be intrinsically desirable, it turns out that they have enormous auxiliary value in our lives and, therefore, that being liable to them is not just a matter of having to take the bad with the good (cf. de Sousa 1987, p. 178, ch. 12). The negative sentiments play an indispensable role in the moral evaluations that we make of both ourselves and others in the course of social interaction. To illustrate this point, I shall discuss three of the negative sentiments: resentment, guilt, and sorrow in the form of grief. I shall take up the latter two first. (As a way of characterizing the role of the negative sentiments in our lives, I have chosen the word *auxiliary* rather than *instrumental* because the latter has connotations of replaceability that I wish to avoid, as I do not believe that there is something that can stand in for guilt or resentment or grief.)

Guilt and grief come most readily to mind as sentiments that sometimes seem to do more harm than good, not so much because they motivate us to do things that, in our more reflective moments, we would deem harmful to ourselves and so would not do, but because they sometimes seem to destroy our desire or will to do anything at all (as in the case of a person who is extremely grief stricken) or they render us so very unaccepting of ourselves (as in the case of the person who is extremely guilt ridden). In general, the other negative sentiments that I have mentioned are not perceived to have as deleterious an effect upon our lives. According to the Freudian conception of guilt, this sentiment has enormous instrumental value because our desire to avoid feelings of guilt is at least partly the reason we adhere to the moral precepts of our society. This way of accounting for the importance of guilt in our lives is not, for reasons I shall spell out below, a very satisfactory one. I shall attempt another approach.

Guilt, of course, is conceptually tied to the belief that one's behavior was inappropriate, where behavior here is to be widely construed to include thoughts or desires, as when a person feels guilt for merely having the desire to do what she or he takes to be morally wrong. From a moral standpoint, the Freudian explanation for the importance of guilt in our lives is *theoretically* unsatisfactory for several reasons. First, the explanation for why the moral person is motivated to do what is morally right cannot be simply that he desires to avoid feeling guilty. For, by hypothesis, he is one for whom the belief (along with the concomitant desire) that something is morally right is, in general, sufficient to motivate him to do it. And for precisely this reason, he is, in general, motivated to make amends (when possible) for his wrongdoings, careful not to commit the same wrongs again, and so on. Second, whether or not it is worth refraining from performing an act in order to avoid feelings of guilt must surely depend on what is at stake. Third, and finally, there is the simple fact that guilt feelings often diminish with time; indeed, if we do what is morally wrong often enough, then we will most likely cease to feel at all guilty about our wrongdoings.[5]

To see the importance of guilt in the life of a morally decent person, let us start with an incontestable truth about a person of good moral character. Such a person does not always treat others, including those who are close to him, as he should. Sometimes he does not speak on the behalf of others when he should, sometimes he violates their trust, sometimes he is insensitive to their needs and desires. One can think of many other examples. For the most part, it is not so much that the person of good moral character deliberately sets out to do these things (though this is sometimes the case) as it is that his resolve is weakened by such factors as temptation and duress. While it would certainly be wonderful if everyone always acted morally, it is clear that moral perfection cannot be reasonably expected of anyone. The most that can be expected is that the principles of morality are among the deepest values of a person's life, and so have considerable motivational force. It is in this light that we can appreciate the significance of guilt and shame as well.

---

[5] In Immanuel Kant's *Lectures on Ethics* we find, "Conscience accompanying the act [a morally wrong or inappropriate one] is gradually weakened by usage, so that in the long run man becomes as used to his vices as to tobacco smoke." See the first sentence of the last paragraph in the section entitled "Conscience."

Typically, one feels guilty when one believes that one has done something morally wrong, and to believe this is to believe that one has failed to live up to the moral standards to which one subscribes. Thus, feelings of guilt stand as a very firm indicator that a person has not lowered his moral aspirations, that the principles of morality remain among the very deep values of his life. Needless to say, when a person of good moral character has done something wrong, the realization that he has not lowered his moral aspirations is hardly insignificant; for barring self-deception, which I shall speak to at the end of this section, a person's feeling guilty when he has wronged another is firm evidence that he is not indifferent to the wrong that another has suffered at his hand. In this regard, feelings of guilt can even occasion relief precisely because experiencing them reminds the person that he still has a conscience. A person who merely experiences relief on this account is not to be confused with one who gloats over the discovery that the moral harm he caused is less than he had thought. Finally, it goes without saying that when we see another experiencing guilt over the wrong that he has done, we regard that as fairly strong evidence that the individual is not indifferent to his wrongdoing.

Let me turn now to sorrow, focusing upon grief, which is its most heightened form. This sentiment is conceptually tied to the belief that one has suffered (what one considers to be) a significant or tragic loss; unlike guilt, it does not, except incidentally, make reference to beliefs about one's behavior. Typically, considerable grief is experienced upon learning of the loss of a loved one. And if a person believes that he could have prevented the death of a loved one had he acted in a certain way, then the person usually experiences more grief than he might have otherwise. For instance, suppose that a parent allows his six-year-old daughter to take her first airplane flight by herself. The flight is only an hour, air travel is quite safe, and her grandparents will be waiting for her when she reaches her destination. The father plans to join the daughter a week later. But, alas, she never reaches her destination; she dies as a result of a midair collision. It is quite likely that the father's realization that his daughter would not have died if she had made the trip with him a week later will serve only to deepen his grief. It would be a mistake to hold that the deepened grief here must really be a matter of the father's blaming himself or feeling guilty for the death of his daughter. The belief that the life of a loved one would have been saved had we acted differently does not entail that we view our not having done so as reflecting negatively upon us in some way.

Now, in view of the fact that grief constitutes a form of intense mental suffering, what reason is there to think that grieving the loss of a loved one plays a positive role in our lives? Is it not more reasonable to hold that having this capacity to grieve is more like being a victim of double jeopardy? For one is already made worse off on account of having lost a loved one; and in grieving that very loss, one is made worse off yet again. As a response here, it will not do to remark that we are better off giving vent to our feelings of grief than suppressing them. For we cannot suppress what we do not have; and from the fact that we are better off giving vent to feelings of grief if we have them, it in no way follows that we are better off on account of having such feelings. And the issue before us is whether or not this is so. Offhand, these considerations would incline one to think not. It does not even seem that this capacity is instrumentally valuable in just the way that guilt is.

Consider, then, the following. In years to come, what is one of the best forms of evidence that the father could have that, up until the very time of his daughter's death, he loved her? No doubt it seems natural to say that the memories of his having strong feelings of affection toward her and of the many things that he did on her behalf should be evidence enough of this. But not so, as surprising as this may seem. Grief is a significantly better form of evidence. The best reason for thinking that memories of the sort just mentioned are not enough in the case at hand is that, with our loved ones and friends who are among the living, we do not, and are not content to, rely upon memories as evidence that we love them and take delight in being loved by them. Indeed, interpersonal relationships based upon love are far too dynamic for memories to suffice in this regard. We are constantly evaluating our past interactions in light of our subsequent ones. Our belief that, in the past, we have treated our friends and loved ones with affection is sustained, in large part, by the fact that they do not through their words and deeds give us reason to believe that we have hurt them or let them down in some way. Accordingly, their subsequent behavior displays the warmth and affection toward us to which we have been accustomed. After all, it is very easy to hurt and offend unwittingly. Not only that, the vicissitudes of life take their toll upon all of us, as a result of which our conduct toward our friends and loved ones is not always as it should be. And in such instances, we often look to them for confirmation that this is the explanation for such behavior, rather than that ignoble motives, proper, have gotten the better of us.

Similarly, it is of tremendous importance to us that, just as warmth and affection were characteristic of our past behavior toward our friends and loved ones, the same is characteristic of our subsequent behavior toward them. The ongoing closeness of a relationship is not judged simply by past memories of the warmth and affection displayed by the relevant parties. Of unquestionable importance is what present and future displays along this line are like, relative to what the past displays have been like. This is not to suggest that a scorecard is kept. The point is simply that, when it comes to assessing interpersonal relationships, key to our assessments is the subsequent behavior of the relevant persons, not merely our memories.

Needless to say, the relevance of the above considerations to the significance of grief is that the death of a loved one makes impossible the assessment of our past behavior in light of the loved one's future behavior. Death brings to a halt the reassurances of our love for another that come through subsequent behavior. In this regard, I maintain that grief stands as a monumental reassurance of our love for someone. And monumental it must be, since no other reassurance will be forthcoming. Grief is conceptually tied to the belief that one has suffered a great loss; and it is impossible to grieve the loss of someone about whom one cares nothing. Grief is a most profound expression of the realization that death forever closes the avenue of social intercourse and the rewards that come with it. Understood in this way, then, we need no longer suppose that having the capacity for grief is just a matter of having to take the bad with the good. It has enormous auxiliary value in our lives because it steps in where the opportunity for further social intercourse leaves off.

I maintain that the ordinary person understands grief in precisely this way, though his articulation is not likely to be as full. After all, we take the extent of a person's grief over the loss of a loved one as a measure of the depth of his love for that person. This is so even when it is obvious that during the deceased's lifetime the surviving party had treated him in rather objectionable ways, as we believe that people can be incapable of or, at any rate, have considerable difficulty showing their love, as with emotionally estranged love (Section 8).

Grief is an extreme form of sorrow. But, of course, sorrow does not always take the form of grief, even in regard to those whom we love; nor is it the case that we experience sorrow only in connection with those whom we love. Sorrow reflects the desire that a person not have suffered a given harm or loss. And in view of the fact that we identify more closely with the interests of our friends and loved ones than those of our associates, it stands to reason that the range of things with respect to which we feel sorrow is wider in the case of the former than the latter (associates). Anyone might momentarily feel a degree of sorrow upon learning that a family has just lost its house in a flood. But only the friends and loved ones of a person can be expected to experience any degree of sorrow upon learning, say, that he was not admitted to the medical school of his choice or that he did not get the salary increase that he was very much expecting. Thus, the experiencing of sorrow in connection with undesirable but nontragic events that happen in the lives of others constitutes very strong evidence that we identify with their interests and care for them.

Sorrow, I have said, reflects the desire that a person not have suffered a given harm or loss. It is important to put the point this way because there is a difference between causing or intending to cause a person harm and taking delight in a person's having been harmed. One can do the latter without doing the former. Thus, sometimes the issue is not whether so-and-so harmed or intended to harm a person, as it may be manifestly clear that she did not, but whether she takes delight in his having been harmed, a matter that is hardly settled one way or the other by the reality that she neither harmed nor intended to harm him. If, for example, a wife trips and spills scalding water on her husband, it may be all too obvious to him that she did not intend to cause him harm, as it may very well be that he saw that she was about to step on one of their children's skates and he even tried to warn her. Still, if she should not display any sorrow for the harm that she has done to him, albeit inadvertently (as he realizes), this will surely cause him great concern; for her displaying no sorrow whatsoever immediately invites the thought that she took delight in his having been harmed, although she did not intend to harm him. Her immediate display of sorrow for the harm that she accidently caused him precludes this interpretation.

In general, when anyone displays sorrow for a harm that we have suffered, she thereby precludes the interpretation on our part that she takes delight in our having suffered the harm in question. This is so, at any rate, unless we have reason to suspect that the display of sorrow is not genuine. If the person is a loved one, then it is important to us that she display sorrow, since we expect our loved ones, and not strangers, to identify with our good. And if a stranger accidentally causes harm, her displaying sorrow is important to us because with a stranger there is not, as with a loved one, the background assumption that the person takes no delight in having caused us harm. In the case of a loved one, the background assumption is there, but it cannot be taken for granted. That is why displays of sorrow are important even when loved ones cause accidental harm. Social interaction even between loved ones is too dynamic, as we saw in our discussion of grief, for the background assumption of love to be taken for granted in the face of a serious accidental harm.

Naturally, other factors can bear upon whether or not the person's display of sorrow precludes the interpretation that she took delight in our having suffered a harm. These factors include information that one might have about the person and one's judgment that the person's display of sorrow is sincere, a judgment that is understandably influenced but not entirely determined by the information that one has about the person. If one knows that a person is profoundly jealous of one's professional success, this is very likely to influence one's assessment, at least initially, of his reaction to one's professional misfortune. It may very well turn out that despite his jealousy, the person is truly sorry about one's misfortune. But one will have to be convinced of this if one believes that the person is profoundly jealous of one. Numerous refinements are possible here, but I think that the general picture is clear enough. The sentiment of sorrow is of enormous auxiliary value in our lives.

I should like now to move on to the sentiment of resentment. It will be recalled (Section 18) that resentment is grounded in the following: (i) the belief that one has been wronged, (ii) the annoyance that comes with having the deep desire not to be wronged, frustrated by another, and (iii) the additional affront that one experiences when the wrong goes unacknowledged or the person takes delight in having done it. As I remarked at the beginning of this section, it is in virtue of having proper self-love that a person is liable to feelings of resentment. As our discussion in the previous section makes clear, this claim is compatible with the earlier claim (Section 18) that our susceptibility to resentment is tied to our having self-respect; for as we have seen, self-respect is a species of self-love.

Given the account just presented, the significance of resentment in our lives should be readily grasped. Feelings of resentment are as clear an indication as we could want that we have a measure of love for ourselves, that we are not indifferent to what happens to us at the hands of others. On the assumption that we should care about ourselves, to have confirmation of this from time to time is important precisely because it cannot be taken for granted that we do care about ourselves. Not only can it happen that the parent-child relationship may be such that a child grows up to be substantially lacking in self-love, but unjust social institutions can result in persons' having considerable self-hatred. What is more, self-hatred of an inordinate amount is possible even as an individual leads a life that by the economic and social standards of society must be judged as successful, as the person may believe that it is only in virtue of his successes that he deserves to be treated in a morally appropriate way by others.

Again, an Uncle Tom is presumably a case in point. Here, too, it would seem that Booker T. Washington could be rightly accused of self-hatred if he believed that on account of the dark pigmentation of his skin, he had to prove himself worthy of morally proper treatment, since the pigmentation of a person's skin should have no bearing whatsoever on whether or not she or he is deserving of such treatment. What is more, given Washington's accomplishments and intellectual abilities, self-hatred seems all the more plausible as an explanation for his holding this view, if indeed he did. After all, few people, black or white, go on to establish academic institutions.

As I have already indicated, whether or not Washington actually held this view is a matter that we need not settle. The point is that there is no conceptual bar to a person's suffering from self-hatred despite her or his clear and considerable talents and intellectual abilities. It is ironic, surely, that very capable people who suffer from self-hatred are often able to hide their self-hatred from themselves by overcompensating. They appear to earn the proper moral respect of others by accomplishing much and they lose sight of or fail to appreciate the fact that they have accomplished more than they should have to in order to be so respected, since accomplishments should not be necessary in the first place.

Self-hatred is compatible with tremendous achievements. The

usual indices of success are no proof that a person has sufficient regard for himself. This, I believe, further speaks to the importance of
resentment with respect to whether or not a person has sufficient regard for himself. As I have said, feelings of resentment owing to a
person's belief that he has been wronged are as reliable an indicator as
a person could want that he has sufficient self-regard. Most interestingly, it is irrelevant that a person should occasionally be mistaken in
his belief that he has been wronged. After all, it is not the actual event
of being wronged that indicates to a person that he has proper regard
for himself, but his feeling resentful in light of the belief that such an
event took place. And one wants to allow that a person could be ever
so justified in believing that he had been wronged (and so in feeling
resentment) and yet be quite mistaken. A person who is mistaken too
often is presumably paranoid. But I shall not attempt to speak to the
role that feelings of resentment play in the life of the paranoid person.

If I have correctly identified the importance of feelings of resentment in our lives, then we have yet another instance in which a negative sentiment has considerable auxiliary value in our lives. There is
much more to be said for our being liable to having such feelings than
simply that we must take the good (the capacity for love, including
self-love) with the bad.

Focusing upon guilt, sorrow (grief), and resentment, I have en-
deavored to show that the negative sentiments play a very major role
in our lives because our experiencing them is indispensable to the
moral evaluations that we make of both ourselves and others in the
course of social interaction. The view favored here is at odds with
the idealized conception, often expressed in science fiction, of the
human being as a purely rational creature totally devoid of any feelings. There can be no doubt that sometimes feelings do get in the way
of clear thought. And if this were the only role the negative sentiments played in our lives, then we would surely have every reason
to want to be rid of them. But I have tried to show that they play an
indispensable, albeit solely auxiliary, role. Much of moral interaction
as we now understand it is supervenient upon our capacity for the
negative sentiments.

This is seen by the simple observation that although a person can
say "I am sorry," we are likely to remain rather unconvinced in the
case of nonnegligible harm that he has caused us unless we think that
he is sincere; and we will not believe that if we do not satisfy our-

selves given his nonverbal behavior that he actually does feel sorrow for what he did. The utterance alone is not enough precisely because it can be produced at will, whereas feelings of sorrow cannot be, which is not to say that we have no control whatsoever over whether or not we experience a certain sentiment (Solomon 1977). What we can and cannot do at will is a matter to be settled by theories of action, the mind, and cognitive psychology. I shall not attempt to do so here. However, it seems safe enough to assume that a person cannot experience the sentiments at will in the way that an unimpaired person can raise her free hand at will, in contradistinction to a person whose affliction makes raising his free hand a matter of some effort.

It is certainly possible for a person to do things that are likely to result in his experiencing this or that sentiment. One can probably bring it about that one experiences sorrow by thinking about the bad things that have happened to oneself or one's loved ones, playing sad music, and so on. One can probably bring it about that one experiences anger by thinking about the ways that one has been wronged, kicking one's desk, and so forth. Again, one can perhaps bring it about that one feels love for someone by doing things for and with that person that are characteristic of having feelings of love for that individual. None of this amounts to being able to experience any of these sentiments at will, though.

Needless to say, it is because the sentiments cannot be experienced at will that they play an indispensable and invaluable role in the moral evaluations that we make of both ourselves and others in the course of social interaction. Necessarily, motives and beliefs are relevant to our moral evaluations of ourselves and others. And the feelings a person displays constitute the best guidepost that we have, albeit a defeasible one, to what his motives and beliefs are. For our experiencing any particular negative sentiment is a function of the beliefs that we have.

20. Psychic Harmony Realized

As is well known, Plato advanced a view that can be summarized as follows: (i) The soul has three parts: reason, spirit, and appetite; (ii) a person has a just soul or morally anchored character, as I shall say, if and only if each of its parts is functioning properly; and (iii) it is only in the soul of persons of morally anchored character that the spirited part of the soul is an ally of reason. If Plato is right, then having a morally good character is indispensable to living well because it is only in virtue of having such a morally anchored character that a person is able to rely upon his feelings in his interactions with others. Specifically, a morally bad person cannot rely upon his feelings. One has psychic harmony if and only if one is able to rely upon one's feelings in this way.

To see that Plato can be plausibly understood in this way, observe that by implication (iii) gives us: (iv) it is not the case that for the morally bad person the spirited part of the soul is an ally of reason, which can be understood in several ways. For the morally bad person: (iv-a) the spirited part of the soul is never an ally of reason; (iv-b) sometimes the spirited part of the soul is an ally of reason, sometimes it is not, and the morally bad person does not, at least not often enough, know which is the case; or (iv-c) sometimes the spirited part of the soul is an ally of reason and sometimes it is not, and the morally bad person can always discern which is the case. I take (iv-b) to be the correct reading of (iv), since on this reading the morally bad person is clearly at a disadvantage when it comes to whether or not he should regard his feelings as being in the service of reason. On the (iv-a) reading, it is obvious that the morally bad person should ignore his feelings entirely; for it is impossible that he should come out the worse for doing so, since on this reading the spirited part of the soul is never an ally of reason. Hence, he should train himself not to rely on his feelings at all. The (iv-c) reading is akin to the (iv-a) reading; for if the morally bad person knows when the soul will not be an ally of reason, then he can simply prepare himself, through rigorous training, for those cases when the spirited part of the soul is not an ally of reason. On the (iv-b) reading, it is clear that the unjust person can come out the worse for ignoring his feelings, since some, but not all, of them will be in the service of reason. His problem lies in just the fact that, on the one hand, it would be a mistake for him to act as if none of his feelings were ever in the service of reason; but, on the other, he cannot discern when they are and when they are not.

My concern here is not to defend an interpretation of Plato as such, but rather to defend the view that psychic harmony, as I have stated it, is essential to living well because of its contribution to a person's happiness. This view certainly owes its inspiration to Plato even if in the end it can be shown that he held a somewhat different view.

I assume without argument that psychic harmony is of immense importance. The issue is whether we are significantly more favored to have this harmony with a morally good character than with a morally bad character. I shall argue that we are, and that this is so because (a) it is of the utmost importance that we be clear about the reasons for our actions, especially in regards to our friends and loved ones, and (b) we are significantly more favored to be clear about our reasons if we have a morally good character than if we have a morally bad character. By reasons I mean the motivational explanation for a person's actions.

The idea of being favored is to be understood in an intuitive way. Consider. A child born into a well-educated family is, other things equal, favored to do better in the academy than a child born into a poorly educated family. The very environment, including the trained resources to which she has access, and the cultural exposure that her parents provide her will undoubtedly give her an advantage. So she is favored, although it may very well turn out that a child from a poorly educated family actually does considerably better. There is nothing trivial here about the idea of being favored, notwithstanding the fact that a more rigorous rendering of this concept does not seem possible. To move to different examples, given the past performances of sports teams or two horses, one may be favored to win over its competitor. And when there is a general consensus among informed individuals that favors one team or horse over the other, this, too, is hardly trivial. If it were trivial the notion of an upset would be empty. The notion of being favored reflects the idea of what are reasonable expectations given an informed assessment of the circumstances. If a certain outcome pertaining to matters of great importance is desired and an informed assessment of various circumstances reveals that the desired outcome is significantly more likely given one set of circumstances rather than any of the available alternatives, then it is eminently rational to choose the optimal set of circumstances.

My claim is that we are significantly more favored to be clear about our reasons if we have a morally good character than if we have a morally bad character. It is in light of the remarks of the preceding paragraph that this claim is to be understood. I shall defend this claim and not the first one. The first claim reads that it is of the utmost importance that we be clear about the reasons for our actions, especially in regards to our friends and loved ones. I take its truth to be self-evident.

Obviously, it is not just in terms of their outcomes that the actions of individuals have meaning. For the outcomes of an act are but one set of criteria by which an act can be evaluated. For example, whether an act is foolish or prudent cannot be determined by looking only at its outcome. Likewise for whether an act is brave or craven. Indeed, whether or not a person's act is kind is not settled simply by whether or not it benefits another; for a person may benefit another unwittingly, thinking that he is actually causing her harm. In continually beating Frederick Douglass, his slave master did not treat him kindly, notwithstanding the fact that Douglass may very well not have shaken off the chains of slavery but for his finding the beatings insufferable. As an aside, then, even if there is no gainsaying the utilitarian thesis that the outcome of an act is most central to our evaluation of it, there is absolutely no reason to suppose that nothing else, in particular a person's motive, is remotely relevant.

What our own motives are matters to us because to love a person is to want to do the right things for her and in the right way. What the motives of others are matters because their assessment of our actions is inextricably tied to their assessment of our motives. In fact, a great many times, though not all the time, what matters most are the motives behind an action. Were this not true, we could not make sense of a parent's joyful response to the cup that his six-year-old daughter made for him in class. As an instrument for drinking water, the artifact may very well not be useful, its design irredeemably flawed. But what occasions the parent's joy upon being presented the cup by his daughter is not so much the artistry itself, although that may be ever so commendable, but rather the motives that gave rise to the cup. The father views the cup as a wonderful expression of his six-year-old daughter's love for him. An implicit assumption, naturally, is that the child has done the best she could. One does not expect a child to be a skilled potter. If, contrary to what we are supposing, the daughter were a gifted potter, then it is rather unlikely that he would be as moved were she to present to him a poorly designed cup. And this is not because the cup is not particularly functional, although that may very well be the case, but because the father would have no reason to think that the daughter would view the cup as an expression of her love for him. This is particularly revealing about gift giving between loved ones and friends, for this shows that even when a gift comes from a child the gift can be abortive as an expression of love if in a flagrant way it is not in keeping with a person's abilities or resources.

In this regard it is perhaps useful to distinguish between two categories of gifts. Some gifts are conventional tokens of appreciation, love, or affection: a box of candy, flowers, and the like. On the other hand, some gifts are intended to speak to a certain desire or need of a person or to fulfill a specific function or role in the individual's life. The latter are artifact gifts; the former, token-gesture gifts. Place settings, radios, watches, and clothes are all artifact gifts. With regard to artifact gifts, a person's resources and (in instances of handiwork) ability, as well as prevailing standards of suitability, are relevant factors. A multimillionaire need not buy her college daughter, who desperately needs a car, a custom-made vehicle. A small, nicely equipped, sturdy car would be very appropriate. By contrast, that very same car, although it makes a suitable gift for her college daughter, probably does not make a suitable wedding gift for a dear friend. I believe that the distinction between token-gesture and artifact gifts is a useful one, although obviously it is not always clear whether a gift is one or the other. In fact, the same item—say, a book —can be one or the other, depending on the circumstances. In any event, these two categories of gifts are useful for our purposes. Given different purposes, there are no doubt other equally viable categories.

Needless to say, the motive behind a token-gesture gift makes all the difference in the world in terms of the response it engenders on the receiver's part. No one who receives as a gift a box of candy or a dozen roses is apt to need them in order to achieve some further thing in life. And the odds are that the person can well afford to buy them himself. A fortiori, then, unless the receiver believes that it was the other's love and care for him that moved her to present him with flowers or candy, her gift will have little or no meaning to him. It may possibly be an affront to him. With token-gesture gifts, motives make the difference precisely because the gift itself is of little, if any, significance to one in the absence of the giver's motives being of the right sort. As a rule, they do not tax a person's resources, financial or otherwise. Thus great appreciation is not called for on that score.

Artifact gifts, of course, tend to be useful in their own right. Still, the giver's motives are of the utmost importance to us. However wonderful and useful a gift might be, no one wants to discover that the only reason why he was given it is that the giver was concerned to prove a point to others—that she has excellent taste, that price is no object to her, that she is a wonderful person, or some such thing. One feels exploited or used in such an instance. An act that was hitherto thought to be a kind one is now seen as manipulative and cruel.

As I have said, with artifact gifts a person's resources and (in instances of handiwork) abilities, as well as standards of suitability, are all relevant factors. These have to be balanced against one another in ways that I shall not attempt to address here, except to say that one implication of their relevance in connection with suitability is that quality trumps price in the following way. If a person has only a hundred dollars to spend, it is better that she pick an item for which one hundred dollars will purchase a high-quality version than that she pick an item for which that amount will purchase only a poor-quality version. Throughout I have been talking about gift giving between loved ones and friends. The degree of intimacy, of course, is itself a relevant factor. But I assume that so much is obvious.

For an artifact gift to be resoundingly received as an expression of love, the receiver must have the sense that, in the ways indicated in the preceding paragraph, it reflects a very good effort on the part of the giver. To return briefly, then, to the story of the cup that the six-year-old daughter made for her father, my remarks assume that cup is intended as an artifact gift on the part of the child. It is something that she made for him to use. It is different from her giving him a stick of bubble gum or a flower or saving for him a piece of cake from the school party, all of which, on my view, are best regarded as token-gesture gifts. That its design should be flawed is no bar to the father's treasuring the cup precisely because the father has no reason to suppose that the daughter is a gifted potter. Likewise, if she bought the cup for his birthday with money she earned selling iced tea, it would not matter that the cup's quality was substantially inferior to many he already possesses, since six-year-old children are not expected to be in the financial position to make substantial purchases. His adult friend could not get away with giving him the same kind of cup, except as a token-gesture gift. The cup with the frog in it may be cute, or the cup's message may be reminiscent of a precious moment between them.

So motives matter. As I proceed with the main argument to establish that the moral person is favored to be happier than the immoral person, I hope to show that the moral are likely to be significantly clearer about their motives than the immoral (Section 21). The outline of the main argument is as follows. (P1) The moral person has, in virtue of being such, more self-knowledge than the immoral person who dissimulates caring behavior, at least when it comes to interpersonal relationships. In particular, the moral person will be more certain than the immoral person who dissimulates caring behavior as to why he is moved to display caring behavior toward those whom he takes to be his friends and loved ones. (P2) Other things equal, a person's happiness is more secure if it stems from the self-knowledge that he possesses with respect to the realization of his endeavors. (P3) Because it is sufficiently important to us that our displays of caring behavior toward those whom we take ourselves to care deeply about be genuine rather than simulated, we will more than likely be significantly less happy than we would be otherwise, regardless of our other sources of happiness, if we are generally uncertain as to whether or not our caring behavior toward them is genuine. (C4) Therefore, the moral person is favored to be happier than the immoral person who dissimulates caring behavior. I shall simply call a person who dissimulates caring behavior a dissimulator. In the language of moral character, it goes without saying that a moral person has a good moral character and an immoral person a bad moral character. Of the argument's three premises, the first is the most controversial; the third, the least. I shall therefore begin the detailed discussion with the third one.

To begin, there can be an intrinsic or extrinsic reason qua motivational explanation for why a person displays caring behavior toward another. The reason is intrinsic if the love that the individual has for the other is the primary motivation for his display of caring behavior toward her; it is extrinsic if something else is the primary motivation. We have genuine caring behavior in the first instance and simulated caring behavior in the second. A person who wanted to win another's trust only for the purpose of obtaining military secrets from her would have a reason to simulate caring behavior. Premise 3 asserts that if a person loves another, it would disturb him greatly if it should turn out, often enough, that his caring behavior toward her were not genuine, that is, if the explanation for why he was motivated to display caring behavior toward her turned out, often enough, to have nothing to do with the fact that he cares for her. One cannot love another and, at the same time, be indifferent to one's reasons for displaying caring behavior toward her. There is hardly anything controversial about this claim. Its truth surely follows from what it means to love another.

Still, the claim is not insignificant, since there can, as it happens, be external reasons for displaying caring behavior toward those whom we love. For instance, because having close ties with some person is essential to our psychological well-being, and displays of caring behavior serve to maintain such ties, then it is certainly to a person's advantage to display caring behavior from time to time toward those with whom he has close ties. But needless to say, no one who loves another wants this to be the reason why he displays caring behavior toward her. No one wants it to turn out that he displays caring behavior to his friend or lover only because he *needs* the relationship in order to survive, rather than because he genuinely cares for the other person.

Premise 3 also speaks to the importance of our being confident that our displays of caring behavior toward our loved ones are genuine. The assumption is that because our loved ones have the highest priority in our lives, we are most concerned to do right by them. Accordingly, if our confidence is shaken in this regard, this would be tantamount to discovering that we are not being the kind of person that we want to be in our interactions with them, or at least having serious doubts about whether we are. And this would give rise to profound dismay, which would ineluctably detract from our happiness. No one could be happy if he were continually plagued with doubts about such a matter. It is one thing to wonder occasionally about the motivations behind one's actions toward loved ones; it is quite another to be plagued with doubts about whether one's motivations for displaying caring behavior toward them are generally intrinsic ones.

Let me turn now to premise 2, namely, that other things equal, a person's happiness is more secure if it stems from the self-knowledge that he possesses with respect to the realization of his endeavors. The truth of this claim can be easily made out. For while occasional luck can truly be a wonderful thing, too much of it will destroy our self-confidence. The more it turns out that the explanation for our successes is luck, the less they reflect positively upon us, since the successes cannot be credited to our own abilities, skills, and ingenuity. So, in the overwhelming majority of instances, we want the explanation for our successes to be none other than that we have properly and skillfully employed our natural assets. We want to be the author of our successes, let us say. These remarks are not merely an aside. On the contrary, they make it abundantly clear that we do not wish to be plagued with self-doubt as to whether or not we are the author of our successes. This is significant for the simple reason that, other things equal, the less a person is plagued with self-doubt in this regard, the happier he is.

Needless to say, it matters not whether the endeavors are constitutive of our interpersonal relationships. We want to do good for those whom we love. In particular, we want the good that we do for them to stem from the right motives, since from the standpoint of motives it is rightly held that we are completely successful in the good that we do for our loved ones only when our actions spring from the love that we have for them, and not, for instance, the desire to make them beholden to us or the desire to be seen by them or others as generous. Nor, again, do we want the good that we do for them to be attributed to heightened feelings of piety, an ever-present concern to do one's duty as a result of which acting out of love would seem to carry little or no weight with one. When it comes to doing good for our loved ones, the magnanimity of our deeds is not the only measure of our success. Most relevant is the extent to which our actions are motivated by love; it is just not possible to love a person and yet be indifferent to why, in general, one is moved to do good for her. Accordingly, if it should turn out too often that the motive for our actions is other than love, we would find this deeply disturbing, which would surely detract from our happiness. By the same token, when we are secure in the knowledge that we are motivated by love, our happiness is buoyed.

Ideally, perhaps, the good that we do for our loved ones should be a case of pure motives, in that the only operative motive should be our love for them. But pure motives of this sort are no doubt hard to come by and, in a world where we are apt to be subject to the influence of many factors, are surely unreasonable to expect of people. Thus, it goes without saying that motives can be mixed, that there are times when a person's actions may stem from more than one motive. Indeed, even the motive from duty (à la Kant) and some other less noble motive—the desire for revenge or the desire to be in the public spotlight or self-interest or jealousy or anger—can converge in terms of the kind of action to which they give rise. A person may be moved to bring to light the morally corrupt past of a public official not only because he morally ought to, but out of revenge or the desire to enhance his own political fortunes. A person's belief that his parents would leave their considerable inheritance entirely to him may motivate him to inform them that his sibling has forged their signature in order to obtain a number of loans. And so on. As I have said, motives can be mixed.

Bearing this in mind, let us distinguish between two kinds of mixed-motive cases. One is what we may call the primary-motive case: a person has a primary motive, that is, there is a single motive that suffices to get her to perform the act in question, and if there are any other operative motives, these are secondary in that none stands as the sufficient explanation for why the person is moved to perform the act in question. There is no incompatibility between one motive being sufficient to move a person to perform a given act and another motive bearing favorably upon her being moved to do so. The other mixed-motive case is what we may call the joint-motives case: two or more motives suffice to get the person to perform the act in question, and no single operative motive is sufficient by itself to get her to do so. In either case a motive is operative if it contributes to a person's being moved to act as she did. A distinguished professor may be moved to work with an older student primarily because he is brilliant; and although his being strikingly attractive is a plus, she would not have given any thought at all to working with him were he merely attractive. Or, a couple may attend a $250-a-plate dinner party because it is being held for their favorite charity and because an old acquaintance, who has taken up volunteer work, is hosting it, though neither consideration alone would have moved them to attend the party. Respectively, we have an example of a primary-motive case and a joint-motives case.

Now, while it may very well be unreasonable for our loved ones to expect the good that we do for them to be motivated purely out of love, there is nothing at all unreasonable or untoward about their expecting love to be the primary explanation for the good that we do for them. When duty and affection, for example, call for the very same course of action, such as saving a loved one from drowning, it is not unreasonable in the least to expect affection to be the primary explanation for rescuing the person,[6] although considerations of duty

---

[6] In fact, many would think it horrifying if things were otherwise. See, of course, Bernard Williams's famous critique of impartialist morality in his "Persons, Character, and Morality" (1976b). This line of thought is developed at length, and with great cogency, in Blum (1980).

are not entirely irrelevant. And if it is thought that considerations of duty are utterly out of place in this instance, surely this cannot be because whenever a person should be motivated primarily by love, then considerations of duty should have no bearing upon her or his actions. For as we have seen (Section 12), parents have a duty to care for their children, although it is primarily out of love that they should be moved to do so. By contrast, notice that as an explanation here for the rescue effort, joint motives is quite unsatisfactory. Although anyone who was drowning will undoubtedly be very grateful that he had been rescued, surely no one wants to learn from his reputed friend that the friend would not have rescued him but for the fact that the friend rightly took himself to have a moral obligation to do so, where it is understood that the friendship was not sufficient to move the friend to make the rescue.

In general, we find unsatisfactory a joint-motives explanation for the good that we do for our loved ones precisely because such an explanation entails that we do not have sufficient regard for the well-being of our loved ones—that their concerns, their weal and woe, do not have sufficient weight with us. Such an explanation entails that their well-being and concerns have far too little priority in our lives in view of what is appropriate when there are significant bonds of affection between people.

As an aside, one reason why impartialist moral theories necessarily miss the mark in terms of interaction between loved ones is that these theories are not able to satisfactorily account for the priority that people have in each other's lives when there are significant bonds of affection between them. These theories miss the mark because the role that love plays in our lives is not to be explained from an impartial perspective. For if the arguments of Chapter Two are sound, then the importance of love in human life is independent of conceptions of the right, since it was argued there that love—at least parental love—is indispensable to the survival of the human species.

To sum up, I began with the premise that, other things equal, a person's happiness is more secure if it stems from the self-knowledge that he possesses with respect to the realization of his endeavors. Extending this premise to our interactions with our loved ones, I observed that we want to be secure in the knowledge that we are motivated by love to do good for them, and that being secure in this knowledge buoys our happiness. I have noted, however, that although it is of the utmost importance to us that our love is what motivates us to do good for our loved ones, it need not concern us that other motives are operative as well, provided that love is the primary motive. So, despite the importance that we attach to being moved by love to do good for our loved ones, there is no need to insist that motives be pure in this regard, meaning that no other motive save love is operative. If love is the primary motivation, then it cannot be argued that our loved ones fail to have the proper place in our lives; for if love is the primary motive, then it follows from the account of primary motives given that our love for our loved ones is sufficient to move us to do good for them. Our happiness is buoyed if we are secure in the knowledge that love is the primary motive for our doing good for our loved ones.

If this much is obvious or, in light of our discussion, has now come to be, what is not so obvious is that in virtue of having a good moral character we are more favored to be secure in this knowledge than we are if we have a bad moral character. This, of course, is the first premise of our argument: (P1) The moral person has, in virtue of being such, more self-knowledge than the immoral person who dissimulates caring behavior, at least when it comes to interpersonal relationships. (P2) Other things equal, a person's happiness is more secure if it stems from the self-knowledge that he possesses with respect to the realization of his endeavors. (P3) Because it is sufficiently important to us that our displays of caring behavior toward those whom we take ourselves to care deeply about be genuine rather than simulated, we will more than likely be significantly less happy that we would be otherwise, regardless of our other sources of happiness, if we are generally uncertain as to whether or not our caring behavior toward them is genuine. (C4) Therefore, the moral person is favored to be happier than the immoral person who dissimulates caring behavior. I have defended the second and third premises. I now turn to defend the first.

21. Psychic Harmony: The Main Argument

One difference between the moral and the immoral person is obvious enough. Treating others in the way that they morally ought to be treated is foremost among the aims of the former, whereas this is not so for the latter. But equally obvious, this difference is not illuminating.

Here is another difference. There is absolutely nothing about the nature of the moral life that makes being able to dissimulate caring behavior indispensable to the successful pursuit of the moral life. Or, to put the point another way, it is manifestly false—at least as a general thesis—that however successful persons might be in leading a moral life they would be even more successful if only they were to dissimulate caring behavior masterfully. Unlike some abilities or capacities or skills such as strength of will, social perceptivity, or sobriety of thought, the ability to feign caring behavior is not a morally enabling power. The moral life thus stands in stark contrast to the immoral life. As a general thesis it is true that however successful persons might be in leading an immoral life they would be even more successful if only they were able to dissimulate caring behavior masterfully.

The explanation for this difference is quite straightforward. To treat a person morally is to benefit him or, in any case, not to treat him in an adverse way undeservingly, whereas to treat a person immorally is to harm him or, in any case, to treat him in an adverse way undeservingly. This way of putting things allows us to escape a confusion stemming from the fact that one can be undeserving both of things that are beneficial and things that are harmful to one. This wording also allows us to sidestep the issue of whether the view suggested by Plato in the *Gorgias* concerning punishment is sound: namely, that morally justified punishment, if there be any, is beneficial to the recipient. For whether it is or not, the recipient is at least not undeserving of it.

Now, it goes without saying that no reasonable person takes delight in being treated in adverse ways undeservingly; accordingly, no such person will knowingly allow himself to be so treated by another. Thus, an immoral person cannot expect others to be willing targets of immoral behavior on his part. Quite the contrary, he can assume that others will do all they can to avoid being the object of his immoral behavior. What this means, clearly, is that if a person is to be successful in his endeavors to treat others immorally, then he must proceed in a way whereby others are unable to prevent him from wronging them. A person who could make himself invisible because he possessed Gyges' ring could proceed in this way. Likewise for a person who possessed so much power that he could always get people to do what he wanted them to do. But so much for philosophical fictions. There are no Gyges' rings to be had, and no one is powerful enough always to be able to get people to do what he wants them to do. However, another way in which a person can succeed in treating others wrongly without their being able to prevent it is by first gaining their trust. And there is no surer way to gain a person's trust than by getting her to believe that one takes her good to heart, that one cares about her. A person who can masterfully dissimulate caring behavior can gain the trust of others for the purpose of his immoral ends in just this way.

I do not, of course, wish to deny the extent to which sheer power, especially physical power, is used to achieve immoral ends. Crimes of violence are real enough. Just so, criminal violence is but a part of the spectrum of immoral behavior. Much of the moral pain (from wrongdoing) that people experience in their lives has precious little to do with criminal violence, and so very much to do with feelings of betrayal, with feelings that one's trust has been violated. Much of the moral pain that people experience stems from their interpersonal relationships. It is hard to imagine an adult who, in the end, has never felt betrayed or manipulated or exploited or egregiously deceived or let down in some awful way. Wrongs of this sort sometimes leave wounds that never fully heal, cause pain from which people never fully recover. Their memory can have a haunting effect upon a person's life well after they have been committed. I do not mean to diminish the depth of the moral pain owing to criminal violence, but only to put it in perspective. As I have said, much of the moral pain that people experience stems from feelings of betrayal in their interpersonal relationships.

So, if an immoral person could masterfully dissimulate caring behavior, thereby gaining the trust of others, there can be no question but that opportunities to wrong others would abound. And feigning such behavior is precisely what the immoral life generally calls for, in the absence of a Gyges' ring or overwhelming power.

But the question to be answered, so it would seem, is this: How is the immoral person at a disadvantage on account of dissimulating caring behavior? Not surprisingly, it has been argued that the psychological toll is so enormous that it is not likely to be outweighed by the benefits that accrue to a person on account of dissimulating caring behavior. Offhand, this line of thought seems plausible enough. For the master dissimulator must take care not to let his true motives be discovered by others, as that would surely be his undoing. This means that he must always be on his guard against remarks or behavior that might reveal his true intent. And it seems reasonable to suppose that this just has to wear on him. After all, it is one thing to hide one's feelings from time to time or to hide one's feelings from some and not others. It is quite another, however, to spend a life hiding one's feelings from everyone. The psychological costs of doing the latter would, indeed, seem to be unbearably high (Foot 1958).

But this line of argument makes an assumption that I do not wish to make, namely, that the immoral person cares for no one but himself, and thus is indifferent to the harm that he does to all others in order to advance his own ends. Thus, on this view, the immoral person is prepared to treat anyone and everyone immorally because he has no feelings of affection for anyone. It has been objected, however, that this characterization of the immoral person is unfair because, as I have already noted, it is generally held that in virtue of the realized capacity to love, life itself is just that much richer. And, so the objection goes, there is no reason to think that the immoral person will not want to have this capacity realized in his life as well. The idea here, clearly, is not to have it turn out that the immoral person loves everyone, contrary to all appearances, but only that it is false that he loves no one (Kalin 1970).

On the assumption that the immoral person loves a few individuals and, therefore, would in no way seek to treat them immorally, it would be false that he would have to worry always about his true motives being revealed. In particular, he would not have to worry about that around those whom he loves. After all, since he genuinely loves them, it could not be discovered by them that his true motive for displaying caring behavior toward them is that he wants to gain their trust so that he could then treat them immorally. Now, if precisely what makes life psychologically unbearable for the wholly immoral person is that he must always be on his guard lest anyone should discover his true motives, that problem does not exist for the less than wholly immoral person. His true motives are to do good for the few whom he loves, and this he has no qualms about their discovering. He wants them to know, surely.

As a response here, those who think that the immoral life is psychologically unbearable for the sorts of reasons already mentioned might wish to insist that it does not much matter whether the immoral person must worry about being discovered by everyone or nearly everyone—the thought being that even if he has to worry about nearly everyone, life is still unbearable. I think that this response, which I shall not develop further, seriously underestimates the psychological haven that a person can find in just a few loved ones. Life's cares and burdens are so much more bearable if there are even a few individuals, sometimes only one, to whom a person can turn for mutual understanding and support, and with whom there is mutual delight in one another's well-being and flourishing. After all, not even the moral person looks to everyone for support and understanding, nor is there mutual delight between him and all others in regards to the well-being and flourishing of individuals. On the contrary, it is in but a few that the moral person finds a haven from the cares and burdens of life. He is sustained by but a few. Likewise, then, there is no reason to suppose that the immoral person cannot be sustained by but a few, notwithstanding the fact that, given the very nature of things, the immoral person will be concerned that his true motives are not discovered by most others, whereas the moral person will not have this concern.

Earlier I said it would seem that the question to be answered is: How is the immoral person at a disadvantage on account of dissimulating caring behavior? As I hope is clear, the question should now be: How is the immoral person at a disadvantage on account of dissimulating caring behavior, given that he has a few loved ones, and so there is at least one individual with whom there is mutual trust and concern for one another's well-being and flourishing? It is understood that this revised question assumes that for the reasons mentioned, the argument sketched above according to which the immoral life is psychologically unbearable fails. However, as I hope to show in what follows, there is another way in which the immoral person turns out to be at a considerable disadvantage.

My contention is that the problem for the immoral person is this: Because of his adeptness at dissimulating caring behavior (about which I shall say more in due course), it turns out often enough that, to a degree he finds disconcerting, he is less certain than the moral person is as to why he is moved to do good for his loved ones. Specifically, because of this adeptness the immoral person is less certain than the moral person that it is his love for his loved ones that moves him to do good for them. Lest there be any misunderstanding, the claim here is not that the moral person, by contrast, is never uncertain about his motives in this regard, for that is surely false. However, in the comparison between two types of individuals, in order for it to be true that one mode of living often occasions considerable uncertainty with respect to one's motives toward one's loved ones, it need not be true that the other precludes uncertainty altogether on this score. Furthermore, the claim is that the immoral person's uncertainty is directly attributable, and in a nonincidental way, to the skill that aids him in leading an immoral life, namely, his deftness at dissimulating caring behavior; whereas the uncertainty that the moral person might experience is not attributable to any skill or trait of character that serves her in leading a moral life—except of course in an incidental way.

For example, the self-examination characteristic of the moral person could lead to an uncertainty with regard to motives, as self-examination might reveal that a motive other than a moral one is the explanation for her behavior on a given occasion: perhaps it is not as much her commitment to racial equality that moves her to speak on behalf of her fellow employee (although there are compelling moral reasons for her to speak out on that account) as her enormous attraction for the person. Still, it would clearly be a mistake to maintain that because of the importance that the moral person attaches to self-examination, it is a characteristic feature of the moral life that it leads to uncertainty with respect to one's motives. The moral person can experience conflict, or undergo a shift in loyalties that takes place very subtly, or she may just be unclear about her own feelings. Needless to say, though, experiences of this sort are simply part and parcel of the human condition. The moral person does not, on account of being such, have any special liabilities in this regard.

I turn now to defend the view that the immoral person's uncertainty with regard to his motives for doing good for his loved ones is directly attributable to his deftness at dissimulating caring behavior. As an intuitive way of seeing that dissimulating caring behavior can give rise to uncertainty in this regard, I should like to begin the discussion with an example.

Consider the case of the paid mourner—an individual who earns his (or some of his) livelihood through being paid to mourn at funerals, and who can so masterfully simulate grief that it seems he has in fact lost a loved one. Although this individual is hired to attend the funerals of complete strangers, his behavior would nonetheless suggest that the deceased was a deep friend or very close relative of his, as his behavior is indistinguishable from the sort of grieflike behavior that one would expect of someone who bore that kind of relationship to the deceased. The paid mourner cries, exhibits physical weakness as the coffin of the deceased is passed before him, and so on. (It will be recalled [Section 19] that grief is a morally appropriate response that is characteristic of a person's loss of loved ones. Hence, grieving constitutes a form of caring behavior.) Of course, the paid mourner prepares himself; he puts himself in the proper frame of mind. He does not just run into the funeral from a game of tennis or what have you.

In any event, imagine that one day our paid mourner actually loses his dearly beloved sibling, and he then attends her funeral. He cries, exhibits physical weakness as the coffin is passed before him, and so on. But now observe. Even if it is true that our paid mourner does grieve the loss of his dear sibling, it in no way follows that his grieflike behavior is evidence of this. For, by hypothesis, he is capable of exhibiting this sort of behavior with regard to people about whom he cares absolutely nothing.

The significance of what is being said here should not be underestimated. Normally, a person's crying counts as quite strong evidence to others, as well as himself, that he was emotionally moved by the situation at hand. In fact, there would not seem to be better evidence of this, although other evidence to this effect can be proffered. Incoherent speech or a lack of speech attributable to what has transpired would likewise count as very strong evidence that a person was much moved by the circumstances. The tears of a person who survives a loved one are naturally and most readily regarded by everyone as all but incontrovertible evidence of the person's sorrow at the loss of the deceased. But not so for the paid mourner. In virtue of his life style, he is in no position to view his tears as evidence to that effect. The claim here is not that there is no evidence available to the paid mourner that he grieves the loss of his beloved sibling, but only that his tears at the funeral cannot play the same evidentiary role in this regard as they would for someone who could not masterfully simulate grief behavior.

It might be pointed out here that the paid mourner will be able to feel the difference between simply acting out grief in the case of a perfect stranger and actually feeling grief on account of the loss of a loved one. On this view, the genuineness of the latter will somehow be felt. While this line of reasoning is not very plausible, as we shall see, it is worth noting that it does not tell against the point that I have made. For it will remain true that, because of his life style, the paid mourner's tears, for example, at the funeral cannot play the same evidentiary role in his life that they play in the lives of others in regards to whether or not he is deeply sorry over the loss of a loved one. Thus, he is at a disadvantage in the sense that he will not have available to him a substantial piece of evidence normally available to others, and relied upon, on occasions of this sort.

In defense of the view that one can feel inwardly the difference between actual tears of grief and simulated tears of grief, it might be pointed out that people shed tears for a variety of reasons that have nothing whatsoever to do with grief. Since we speak of tears of joy or compassion, this shows, so the objection continues, that something besides shedding tears has to be the deciding factor in a person's belief that he is experiencing grief. That something else, the objection contends, is the difference that the person feels inwardly. In a sense, but only in a sense, the point is well taken. Presumably, a person who sheds tears because he is quite moved by a wedding ceremony or an honor that he has received or the courageous story of a handicapped person is not experiencing grief. The same goes for a person who is moved to tears of compassion by an account or pictures of children starving to death in underdeveloped countries or the horrors of American slavery or the Holocaust. But from this, though, it in no way follows that the deciding factor in whether or not a person is experiencing grief is some inward feeling. This is because in general, contexts, by which I mean the relevant events or state of affairs, are crucial to what feelings a person can be experiencing.

While viewing a television program or reading a book about the Holocaust or American slavery or the starving children in underdeveloped countries, tears of compassion make sense—not over lunch during a discussion of last night's ballet performance or during a romantic encounter. Again, tears of joy are in order if one is witnessing a certain kind of event—a wedding, an honor, a triumph of a loved one, or the awarding of a special honor. Tears of joy are not in order just because one should happen to wake up in an especially buoyant mood or a neighbor's husband purchased a new pair of socks. The importance of context is underscored by the observation that in order to make sense of a person's shedding tears, it is simply not enough that he has the appropriate belief (for example, some children are starving, a loved one triumphed), but the context is of the utmost importance. Likewise for tears of grief. If Mary and Paul lost their daughter ten years ago, tears of grief over lunch during a discussion of the presidential elections will make little or no sense, at least not unless there is a story to be told: their daughter's childhood dream was to be president, and it was one of the presidential candidates under discussion who told their daughter that girls, too, can grow up to be president.

All of this is just to say that, generally, inner feelings are hardly all that count in anyone's assessment of the feelings a person might be experiencing, whether it is the person's assessment of his own feelings or another's assessment of them. If a person should start shedding tears during a lunch conversation on presidential politics, it is not just that we would be unaccepting of the explanation that they are tears of compassion over the starving children in underdeveloped countries, but we would be quite confident that he, too, should not be accepting of that explanation. To be sure, it is possible to tell a story that would make this explanation palatable. Perhaps the person had escaped such misfortune himself; and, having just viewed an especially poignant scene of such children, he had not been able to distance himself emotionally from the matter before going to lunch. So, when his lunch companion briefly alluded to the profound poverty that one of the candidates had managed to overcome, the person was simply unable to maintain his composure. The story explains what, on the face of it, is wildly implausible, namely, the occurrence of tears of compassion over starving children during a lunch conversation on presidential politics. It provides a context for how tears of compassion could possibly have been occurring at the time they occurred.

The relevance of these remarks to the contention that one can just feel the difference between dissimulated grief and genuine grief is this. To begin, only if a person recently has lost a loved one does he have an appropriate context for experiencing grief in the present. The loss of a loved one ten years ago plus the occurrence of a complete stranger's funeral today does not, in and of itself, constitute an appropriate context for experiencing grief today, neither over the loved one lost ten years ago nor, a fortiori, the death of the complete stranger. But precisely what the paid mourner has mastered is the art of simulating grief—the tears, the quivering, the shaking, the pained facial expressions, and so on—in contexts in which grief on his part is not at all appropriate, since by hypothesis he routinely displays grief behavior when he is a complete stranger to the deceased. Thus, he has made the context irrelevant to his ability to appear as if he were grieving.

Second, to dissimulate grief behavior our paid mourner cannot attend the funeral shedding tears of joy, or merely tears of compassion. Thus, he cannot prepare himself by viewing a film about the starving young or about the triumph of a handicapped person or by reading a comic book. For it is profound sense of loss that he wishes his behavior to express. Thus, he must bring it about that he feels a sense of loss over someone, that he feels a sense of the anguish that comes with having lost a loved one. This he can do by dwelling upon the appropriate thoughts or by reviewing an account of a person's loss of a loved one and imaginatively putting himself in that person's place. When these considerations are taken in conjunction with the observations of the preceding paragraph, the implication is clear. The paid mourner succeeds in feigning grief in a context that is not appropriate for him precisely because he does things that cause feelings of grief on his part to be felt at least to some extent. He induces himself to experience such feelings.

This is why our paid mourner cannot just feel the difference between genuine grief and simulated grief—or, at any rate, the difference there is not the manifest one that the contention supposes it to be. For in dissimulating grief behavior the paid mourner does not merely imitate the bodily movements generally characteristic of grief-stricken behavior, in the way that a child, say, imitates an instance of his parents' behavior. Although the child moves his body in all the correct ways, his behavior fails to convey the feelings of his parents; for the child lacks the experience that would permit him to in any way engage the appropriate feelings. By contrast, our paid mourner is able to bring it about that he experiences some of the feelings of grief.

If this seems rather untenable, it is only because we generally think of the experiencing of feelings as something that happens to people rather than something that is brought about by them. This is understandable, since that is usually the case. Clearly, people usually do not set out to experience grief or shame or guilt or resentment. Moreover, it is generally true that people cannot directly cause themselves to experience this or that feeling in the way that they can directly raise their arm or brush their teeth. One does not set in motion a chain of events that yields the result that one's arm is raised or one's teeth are brushed; one simply does these things. From none of this, though, does it follow that people are unable to do things that cause them to experience or, in any case, dramatically increase the likelihood that they will experience this or that feeling. Likewise, from none of this does it follow that people can only be passive with respect to their feelings, that there can be no agency with respect to our having this or that feeling. It is certainly true, at least often enough, that if a person should dwell upon the way in which she has been egregiously wronged, she commences to feel anger and resentment. Recognizing this, many people are careful not to think too long and hard about the ways in which they have been wronged in the past. Or, to go the other way, a person who dwells too long upon the wrongs that he has done to others will most certainly commence to feel a bit of shame or guilt. Again, recognizing this, people do not dwell upon the ways in which they have wronged others.

The claim here is only that it is a mistake to think that the nature of feelings is such that people can only be passive with respect to them (Solomon 1977). I have drawn attention to this truth only to shore up the argument that the idea that one just feels the difference between genuine grief and dissimulated grief is not as easily made out as one might suppose, because the person who dissimulates grief brings it about that he has a measure of feelings of grief. I have not claimed, nor is there any need to, that most people are not passive with respect to their feelings.[7]

---

[7] The very best actors rehearse their performances (cf. Miller 1972). For example, in order to display angry behavior in a performance, actors rehearse so as to get the timing of their responses right. They rehearse to become attuned to both each other and their stage surroundings. Indeed, actors often prepare themselves for their roles by doing things that put them in the frame of mind their roles call for (Olivier 1986, pp. 26–27, 44–45, ch. 17). What they do *not* do is simply walk on stage and deliver a stellar performance.

Presumably, the more funerals a paid mourner "worked," the more difficulty he would have distinguishing simulated grief from genuine grief, since the more masterfully he would be able to simulate grief and, moreover, the more *accustomed* he would become to doing so. It is one thing to simulate a powerful emotion such as grief; it is quite another to do so with such regularity that one becomes accustomed to doing so. This last consideration gives us a way of distinguishing a paid mourner from a very capable actor. An actor who is masterfully able to simulate powerful emotions for a given performance need not, thereby, become accustomed to doing so. This holds even

The thesis that I have been defending is that the immoral person's uncertainty about his motives for doing good for his loved ones is directly attributable to his deftness at dissimulating caring behavior. So that we would have before us a vivid illustration of the truth of this claim, I have discussed at length the example of the paid mourner, it being remembered that grief constitutes a form of caring behavior. And things are worse for the immoral person generally; after all, the paid mourner's dissimulation of caring behavior is confined to a specific feeling, grief, and is for a very well-defined situation for which the paid mourner gets to prepare himself in advance. Not so for the immoral person who dissimulates caring behavior in order to increase his chances of treating others immorally. Let me explain.

There are many unexpected events in life that often have nothing to do with miscalculations as such. There are the unanticipated invitations or gifts or offers; there are the unanticipated losses that nothing could really have been done to prevent. No one can predict when these things are going to happen. But no matter how unanticipated a person's good fortune or misfortune may be, there can be no question but that a loved one's affective response should be both appropriate and spontaneous. If Smith and Chin are deep friends and Chin tells Smith that she, Chin, has just won the Nobel Prize in literature or that she has just lost her son, then Smith should respond with joy in the first case, sadness in the second, and spontaneously in either case—spontaneously because Smith's attitude toward Chin should be such that the appropriate feelings are automatically engaged, given the news conveyed to him by Chin. He should not have to deliberate about whether to have the appropriate feelings. He should not have to work them up. Indeed, anything but spontaneous joy or sadness on Smith's part, depending on the story, would give Chin reason to question the depth of Smith's friendship. At least this is so in the absence of a very good explanation. If Smith has just lost his spouse, then it is understandable that he does not respond with quite the joy that Chin would rightly expect to the news that she has just won the Nobel Prize. By contrast, if Smith has just won the Nobel Prize and

---

if, on account of having the ability to simulate powerful emotions masterfully, one is more liable to become accustomed to simulating such emotions than one who lacks this ability. A liability in this regard is, thereby, a fait accompli.

Chin informs him that she has lost her son, then sadness on Smith's part should still be forthcoming. He should certainly not respond by exclaiming that he has just won the Nobel Prize.

There is nothing mysterious about the spontaneity here. To love or, in weaker language, to have feelings of affection for a person is to have a positive attitude toward that individual well in place. A concern for the individual's well-being and some identification with his flourishing is part and parcel of that positive attitude. With such an attitude already well in place, how one should be immediately moved to react is thus less a matter of choice than what one is told. It is not possible for a person to feel joy over the suffering of someone he dearly loves. Of course, there can be mixed emotions, as when a parent's child leaves home after receiving a prestigious offer from an out-of-state law firm, or when a good friend becomes romantically involved, thus shifting his interaction with one. And it is certainly true that love is compatible with a possessive jealousy, as a result of which a person is unable to rejoice in any good fortune that might lessen time spent together. These are complexities that need not be pursued here.

The point about spontaneity bears on the issue of dissimulating caring behavior in the following way. Although the immoral person does not have feelings of affection for his targets of immorality, it goes without saying that he can be successful at dissimulating caring behavior toward them only if his behavior exhibits the spontaneity that is characteristic of a person who actually has such feelings. So, his behavior must exhibit the required spontaneity without the requisite psychological attitudes being at all in place. This brings out the enormity of the task of being a successful dissimulator.

But let us suppose that the immoral person who is a dissimulator is up to the task. Now, it will be remembered that the immoral person fakes caring behavior because appearing to be caring is the key to success at his immoral exploits. The belief that another cares for us is a necessary, though not sufficient, condition for our being willing to trust her; and, of course, what we believe in this regard is a function of our assessment of the person's behavior toward us, and so of how she appears to us. The appearance of caring behavior on a person's part is of the utmost importance to those whom the individual cares about. Other things equal, if a person behaves in ways that are characteristic of a genuine caring person, we take her to be a genuine caring person. If one genuinely loves another, then one has a reason to want to appear to her as a caring person. Likewise, if one's aim is to gain a person's trust so that one can later exploit her, then one has a reason to want to appear to her as a caring person. It is just that in the former case the appearance corresponds to a certain psychological reality—namely, one's having the requisite psychological attitudes—whereas in the latter case it does not.

The immoral person who succeeds in his immorality through dissimulating caring behavior must be so adept at doing so that nothing more than the realization that he needs to do so for the sake of appearances is sufficient to result in his displaying the appropriate caring behavior. And there is the rub. For as I have just noted, the appearance of caring behavior is of the utmost importance even with regard to those whom we genuinely care about.

Recalling that we have allowed that the immoral person cares about a few individuals, suppose it is true that John is someone whom the immoral person, call him Peter, cares dearly about, and John suffers a tremendous harm—he loses his parents, say. Clearly, it will be of the utmost importance to John that Peter display the appropriate caring behavior toward him. This truth cannot be lost on any reasonable person, including Peter. Thus, it follows that he has a reason to display caring behavior toward John, which is the same as the reason he has for displaying caring behavior toward any of his targets of immorality, namely, that John would question Peter's affection for him if he (Peter) failed to do so, and would actually break off the friendship —something that Peter would find very distressing. But this, surely, cannot be the reason why Peter wants to be moved to display caring behavior toward John—at least not if he cares dearly about John. If he cares for John, then Peter wants—surely he must want—his affection for John to be the reason why he is moved to display caring behavior toward him, and not the fact that he would lose John as a friend. Respectively, we have an intrinsic and an extrinsic reason. The problem, of course, is that precisely what Peter's mastery at dissimulating caring behavior amounts to is his being able to display the appropriate caring behavior with the characteristic spontaneity, without the requisite psychological attitude being in place, whenever he realizes that it would be important for him to do so for appearance' sake. And there can be no getting around the fact that appearances do matter here. John would be absolutely devastated were Peter not to display any caring behavior, and Peter knows this.

The claim here is not that in virtue of his ability to dissimulate caring behavior, the concern to save appearances is what must move him to display such behavior. On the contrary, it is perfectly compatible with all that has been said that Peter is moved, as he desires to be, by his affection for John. The difficulty, however, is that Peter's skill at dissimulating caring behavior makes it substantially more difficult for him to be as confident as he would otherwise be in its absence that he is moved by his affection for John. The explanation for this is rather apparent. Although Peter cares for John, it remains true nonetheless that it is in his self-interest to display caring behavior for John, since he otherwise loses John as a friend (which he does not want); and as an immoral person, Peter has mastered the art of dissimulating caring behavior whenever he deems it important to appear caring. Thus, given the kind of person that Peter is, it turns out that his affection for John is compatible with his actually being moved out of self-interest, in spite of himself, to display caring behavior toward John. Given the kind of person that he is, his love for John is not the only available explanation for his display of caring behavior in the present circumstances.

Herein lies the reason why the immoral person who is a masterful dissimulator will be less certain than the moral person as to why he is moved to display caring behavior toward those whom he loves. Although the former will often exhibit the appropriate behavior, the problem is just that, in virtue of his being the kind of immoral person that he is, there is an equally plausible explanation for his doing so that is not attributable to the love that he has for the individual in question. This is not true of the moral person in virtue of his being the kind of person that he is, as the moral life does not call for mastery at dissimulating caring behavior.

In general, when a person, say, Smith, displays caring behavior toward another, he is able to take that behavior at face value: his tears over the suffering of friend A mean that Smith was deeply moved, and he was moved because he cares for friend A. It could be, of course, that just days before, Smith had spent time comforting friend B, who had also suffered a tragic loss, and Smith is still emotionally raw from that experience. So, Smith is not altogether clear as to why he is moved to tears in his interactions with A: Is it A's suffering, or is it that he is emotionally very raw, having just spent time with B? So, we have an explanation in this instance for why the tears cannot be taken at face value that the person is moved by A's suffering. However, it is not one that is in any way cancerous with respect to Smith's motivations. The uncertainty here is not indicative of his having a way of life that casts a shadow of doubt upon why he is generally moved to display caring behavior. But not so for the immoral person who has mastered the art of dissimulating caring behavior. And this generally is the contrast between the life of the immoral person and the life of the moral person.

Because the immoral person has so mastered the art of simulating caring behavior that he is able to exhibit the appropriate behavior, including the characteristic spontaneity, without the requisite psychological attitude being well in place, it is not in many instances possible for him to take his caring behavior at face value, even toward those whom he loves. And it follows from this that the immoral person simply cannot be as confident as the moral person as to why he is moved to display caring behavior toward those whom he loves. For it will be remembered, drawing upon our discussion of the paid mourner, that precisely what dissimulating caring behavior is able to do is bring about the appropriate feelings, in the absence of the requisite psychological attitude being in place.

If the argument of this section is sound, then it enables us to explain why leading a moral life, as opposed to an immoral one, can hold an attraction for individuals regardless of their station in life. Whatever our economic or social standing might be, it matters to us, surely, that our displaying caring behavior toward our friends and loved ones is genuine. Indeed, it is arguable that our deep interpersonal relationships are the most important part of our lives or, at any rate, they should be. Accordingly, a most decisive consideration in favor of any walk of life is that it enhances or underwrites our confidence that our caring behavior toward our loved ones is genuine; likewise, a most decisive consideration against any is that it would undermine our confidence in this regard. Because of the significance that our loved ones have in our lives, because of the meaning that they give to it, we will not knowingly do anything that undermines our confidence that we interact with them in the way that we should. The claim, now, is not that we never, in fact, pursue an activity that undermines our confidence in this regard, but only that we do not do so knowingly. Things are complicated here because not only may a person misjudge the impact that the pursuit of an activity will have on his life, he may be self-deceived about it; and one wants to say that in some sense the self-deceived person knows the truth about matters. Thus, it is best to say simply that no person consciously pursues an activity that he knows will undermine his confidence that his interactions with his loved ones are genuine. In any case, there is no reason whatsoever to believe that the moral person has any special liabilities when it comes to self-deception.[8]

In a word, being moral turns out to be of great importance precisely where it matters most in our lives, namely, with regard to our loved ones. Love gives morality a place in our lives that it would not otherwise have. If you will: love anchors morality in our lives; for it is in virtue of love that doing what is right has ontological priority in our lives. It is not because we are moral that we love, as perhaps Kantians would have it; rather, it is because we love that that we are moral. And if love is part of the Good, then the Right, namely, morality, is anchored in the Good.

[8] See Robert Audi (1985). In fact, if Audi is right, then it is the immoral—not the moral—person who is especially liable to self-deception.

CHAPTER EIGHT

The Damned

Having a sense of self-worth is indispensable to our flourishing. One aspect of self-worth is what I have called self-respect (Section 18). Another is self-esteem. I wish to draw an important connection between self-esteem and morality, namely, that the significance of self-esteem can be an explanation for an individual's leading an immoral life. If the argument is sound, then in a most important respect the Kantian picture of the moral person is fundamentally mistaken. I begin with an account of self-esteem.

22. Self-Esteem

Roughly, self-esteem is the sense of worth that is tied to the conviction that our endeavors—the things we attempt to accomplish and the kind of life we attempt to lead—are worthwhile; and our endeavors are determined by the values that are constitutive of our self-concept.[1]

[1] The classical account of self-esteem is to be found in William James (1890). While James's account has been refined, expanded upon, and applied with greater theoretical precision, it would seem that his basic insights on the topic have survived critical scrutiny. On this see Brown (1965, p. 648) and Coopersmith (1967, p. 27). Rosenberg (1979) applies the notion of self-esteem to a number of important social contexts. I have profited enormously from his applications. Finally, while the language "values that are constitutive of a person's self-esteem" is my own, this way of putting the point owes its inspiration to Ziller (1976).

The conviction that our endeavors are worthwhile is secured by the esteem and approval we receive from those whom we deem to be competent to judge and appreciate our endeavors. Because we generally value more than one kind of activity or end, our self-esteem usually has more than one source. To pick three obvious and significant values, we usually want to have a successful relationship, to excel in our career, and to raise our children well. Accordingly, success at all three will contribute to our self-esteem, though one may do so to a greater extent than the others, depending on its importance to us as determined by our values. Rightly or wrongly, one may, for example, place one's career above one's children or spouse, or both. Indeed, it is possible to attach so much importance to one's career that one's self-esteem (overall) is minimally affected by the enormity of one's failure in regard to the other two.

Obviously enough, the more significant sources there are to our self-esteem, the easier it is to become accepting of less than we had hoped for with respect to a given endeavor. Most of us take great delight in being both a good parent and spouse; and it is precisely because we do that our overall self-esteem remains high even though we are not as successful as we had hoped to be in our careers. For virtually all of us, to be a failure on all three accounts would be devastating in terms of our self-esteem, as our life would seem to be all but a total failure. As for a person who really did not value these ends but pursued them only because he was swept along by the current of society, his failure on all three accounts probably would not devastate his self-esteem.

The very idea of self-esteem reveals the extent to which we are quintessentially social beings, in that it is in virtue of the approval of others that we deem our endeavors to be worthwhile. But the way to grasp this point is not as a claim that we do things only insofar as they elicit esteem and approval from others, but as the insight that in the absence of the esteem and approval of others it is not possible for us to know that our endeavors are worthwhile. Self-esteem reflects the two-part idea that we need to know that our aims have some worth, and that we cannot know this independently of the esteem and approval we receive from others.

In this regard, it is important to distinguish between explicit and implicit approval. Implicit in the social fabric of any society are judgments about the relative worth of various ends. A career in medical research is usually considered a very worthwhile career. To live in some societies is to know this if one knows anything. Thus, a person who is thinking about going into medical research need not wonder whether she is pursuing a worthwhile goal. But as to her own performance as a medical researcher, that is very much tied to the explicit approval of at least a few others in her field. If everyone in her field continually questions either the worth of her research or her results, her self-esteem as a medical researcher will surely be very low. Again, while the prevailing view may be that few careers compare favorably to a successful career in entertainment, a person's self-esteem as an entertainer will be very low if the reviews of his work are overwhelmingly critical. These remarks are merely meant to shore up the point about the significance of the esteem and approval of others while acknowledging the importance of the fact that there is a respect in which these need not be explicit.

The importance of self-esteem cannot be overestimated. People will make every effort to construct their lives in ways that enhance their self-esteem, given both the values that are salient to their self-conception and the options available to them. A person's values are perhaps the more important of the two because the successful pursuit of ends that are very much at odds with a person's values will contribute little or nothing to his self-esteem, however much he is admired by others for his accomplishments. Also, the idea that a person's self-esteem is tied to the successful pursuit of endeavors that are in keeping with the values that are salient to a person's self-concept reflects the fact that our self-esteem turns upon the successful pursuit of ends that hold an importance for us in our lives, as opposed to merely the successful pursuit of ends as such. Naturally, though, because of the prevalence of some values throughout society, some ends are more likely than others to hold an importance for all or most individuals. Successful relationships and raising children well come readily to mind here. Neither education nor religion would seem to be valued to quite the same extent.

Now, although there are many determinants of the values people have, the two that are most directly influential are the child's parental environment and her or his extended social environment. To varying degrees these two environments reflect the prevailing values of society. While it may be true that the former should be more influential than the latter, this need not be so. The former refers to parental upbringing and thus the things that a child is encouraged to do through parental approval and disapproval, as well as the opportunities that the parents make available to the child, including the things to which the child is exposed from day to day, and so the child's home environment. The extended social environment refers to the quality of the neighborhood, the schools, and so on, which in turn affect the kinds of friends and peers the child comes to have. It is certainly possible that the prevailing values of society may not be well refracted through the child's family and community, as a result of which the values that define the child's self-concept will differ in important ways from the prevailing values of society. A child who is not encouraged by his parents to learn and who grows up in a community in which everything but learning seems to be valued is not likely to place a premium upon doing well in school. Being able to attract members of the opposite gender or being able to dance or sing or play some sport well may turn out to be much more important to the child. The reason why parents and the extended social environment are so influential in this regard should be obvious: the child's initial sense of the worth of anything owes everything to these two. Quite often, the parental environment plays a greater role in this regard than the child's extended social environment; but this need not be so, as I have already noted. Whether one has the greater influence or they are both equally influential is most apparent when the values of the parental and the extended social environment are at odds with each other. Then the child will either equally value the esteem from both environments or the esteem of one over the other. The child's behavior should reveal the nature of the influence. I shall leave this complexity aside, however.

This brief discussion about the acquisition of values should underscore the centrality of a person's values in regards to what accomplishments serve to enhance a person's self-esteem. Depending on the content of a person's values, all sorts of activities or life styles can enhance a person's self-esteem. I have maintained that a person's values may differ from the prevailing values of society. In this regard, it is important to bring out that this is especially likely in the case of individuals who belong to a reasonably identifiable group against which there is widespread and systematic discrimination. It goes without saying that none of this is meant to deny that some people suffer from low self-esteem. They may not have the wherewithal to live up to the ordering of values that define their self-concept, or they may suffer from bad luck, or they may hold dearly to values that, as a result of widespread and systematic discrimination, society prevents them from realizing in their lives.

A key factor in people's having low self-esteem is that at the outset of their lives they are held up to standards that are excessively high, as a result of which they are made to feel that nothing they do is ever good enough. It is one thing not to let a child wallow in complacency; it is quite another to cause a child to feel inadequate in the name of motivation. A child should definitely be encouraged to do better, but not at the expense of believing that she or he never does anything that is good enough. It is virtually a truism that one can always do better. Certainly, though, it does not follow from this that nothing is ever good enough. One response to excessively high standards in regards to a most salient value in one's life is to turn to a different set of aims, and thus to look to a different source for the affirmation of one's self-worth.

Obviously, this involves something of a shift in the values that define a person's self-concept. The person may jettison entirely the values that he was never able to measure up to. Or, he may simply sublimate them; that is, while he yet wishes he could measure up to the other values, he lets measuring up to a different set of values stand in for his doing so. The most relevant factors in all of this are the extent to which other forms of approval are readily available and just how fixed the values are that define the person's self-concept. Having said this, let me hasten to add that changing the values that are constitutive of our self-concept is anything but easy. Given their values, most people whose marriages turn out to be unsuccessful, and who fail in their careers, and whose children become criminals suffer from enormously low self-esteem. What they invariably do not do is relinquish these values in whose lights they are a failure. To be sure, if as a rule the values that define our self-concept could be changed at a stroke, low self-esteem would scarcely be a problem.

In view of what has been said, there can be no question but that we are quite attached to those activities through which we become secure in our self-esteem, regardless of the nature of the activity. If performing an activity contributes mightily to our self-esteem and, furthermore, we are especially good at it, then we are extremely unlikely to give up that activity if the resulting void in our self-esteem cannot be immediately filled, as usually it cannot be.

To take a controversial example and to simplify things somewhat, the idea of complete gender equality has been difficult for men to accept because the self-esteem of "real" men has been so inextricably tied to the idea that it is a man's place to provide for a woman: a "real" man did this, if nothing else (Thomas 1980b). A poor and uneducated man who yet managed to provide for his spouse was nonetheless a "real" man. Thus the idea of gender equality has often been threatening to the self-esteem of men—their very self-identity—because while it entails that men are to jettison a certain role, namely, that of providing for women, which has contributed immeasurably to their self-esteem, it does not speak to the void that giving up this role creates. Gender equality constitutes not merely a shift in the tasks and responsibilities of women and men, but a profound shift in the self-concept of both, but men especially. There are men who as husbands have been able to make the adjustment, in that they have been able to give up this contribution to their self-esteem—but not easily, and not without tremendous support, care, and understanding from those individuals who have a central place in their lives, namely, their wives.

The very cool reception that many men have given the idea of gender equality nicely underscores the claim that we are quite attached to those activities through which we become secure in our self-esteem, regardless of the nature of the activity. For not only are there moral considerations that favor gender equality, there are economic and self-interested ones as well. Two incomes are better than one, and if women provided for themselves things would certainly be less burdensome for men. But because of the way bearing this burden successfully has been so central to the self-esteem of men, far from rushing to embrace the idea of gender equality, many men have denounced the idea as foolish and offensive.

The issue of gender equality is much more complicated. I have said nothing about the fact that according to this ideal, it is no longer the role of men to have power and authority over women. But my simplification is, I trust, true to the spirit of things. And the discussion nicely illustrates the point being considered. An arrangement that makes one significantly better off in many respects can be altogether unacceptable to one if it requires that one give up a role that has contributed immensely to one's self-esteem. As I have said, the importance of self-esteem cannot be overestimated.

At this juncture, I should like to call attention to one endeavor in particular, the successful pursuit of which may significantly enhance a person's self-esteem, namely, leading a moral life. That everyone should realize this goal in their lives is no conceptual bar to its enhancing the self-esteem of those who do so, any more than the idea that everyone should realize the goal of being educated is a bar to its enhancing the self-esteem of those who do so. For whether or not everyone should be moral, it is manifestly clear that neither everyone is nor, a fortiori, that anyone is in virtue of being human. And it is equally clear that some people are more successful than others at leading a moral life.[2] This should come as no surprise, for leading a moral life calls for traits of character that are not equally possessed by all, such as strength of will in the case of honesty, or the capacity for sympathetic understanding in the case of kindness. Moral insight generally is tied to maturity of thought, which tends to go hand in hand with breadth of experience. What is more, there can be no doubt that a person can take great pride in doing what is morally good in precisely the same way that a person can take great pride in any other accomplishment: a piece of good writing, the securing of an excellent deal, a successful seduction, or whatever. Thus, a person can take pride in the fact that he leads a morally good life in just the way that a person can take pride in the fact that he runs a successful business. Finally, insofar as it can be said that people are responsible for their actions, a person is as much responsible for her moral actions as she is for her other actions.

So, there is every reason to believe that the self-esteem of persons can be specifically tied to their moral life. Accordingly, if leading a moral life is a salient feature of a person's self-concept, then she can have high or low self-esteem depending on how successful she is at doing so. Or, and this gets to the heart of what I am after, it may very well turn out that a person's values are such that doing what is moral simply does not contribute to his self-esteem at all. So, from the standpoint of his self-esteem, his not leading a moral life is of little or no consequence. It may very well be true that everyone should lead a moral life, but it is false either as a conceptual point or as a

[2] For this powerful point, I am much indebted to Bernard Williams's essay "The Idea of Equality" (1962). Recall, too, our discussion of the morally autonomous (Section 1). Leaving aside the issue of whether individuals are equal in their intellectual endowments, it is clear that if individuals are, these endowments are not developed to the same extent in everyone.

generalization that everyone's self-esteem is tied to leading a moral life. It is false that among the values constitutive of a person's self-concept there must be values that entail that leading a moral life, being a moral person, is an endeavor worth pursuing.

Moral values, let us say, need not be constitutive of a person's self-concept. And the explanation for this need not start with some deep flaw in the psychological make-up of the individual: that is, the explanation for his not having them need not be some psychological flaw that prevented him from acquiring them. He need not have been psychologically deficient in ways that make impossible the acquisition of moral values. For on the assumption that the values that define a person's self-concept are determined by his parental and extended social environments, the explanation for why moral values are not among such values may be none other than that moral values were not imparted to him by his environments. If a person's only exposure to classical music was through an occasional television commercial, precisely what one would expect is that he should not come to value classical music. There would not be anything mysterious about his not doing so. And while it might be plausibly argued that this is his loss, what cannot be argued is that his not valuing classical music starts with a flaw in his psychological make-up. A similar argument, obviously, can be made for fine foods or works of art. Generally, then, although it is quite possible that a person lacks certain values in virtue of which he would be better off, it does not follow from this that his lacking these values can be explained in terms of a psychological flaw. Moral values are no exception here, notwithstanding the truth that moral values should be among everyone's values.

So a person can be deficient in his tastes and preferences without that deficiency being attributed to some psychological flaw. Let us assume, for the sake of argument, that the person who has no appreciation whatsoever for classical music or fine cuisine or the arts is deficient in his tastes and preferences. This may be simply because, as a result of his parental and extended social environments, values embracing these ends never became constitutive of his self-concept; hence, his self-esteem never turned upon having an appreciation for any of these things. The person is deficient (on our assumption) in terms of his preferences and tastes but not psychologically flawed, as he responds to his environment in precisely the ways that he should; and thus he lacks just the values one would expect him to lack given his parental and extended social environments. The psychological fit between his environment and his values is precisely as it should be. In a like manner, a person can be morally deficient in terms of values but not psychologically flawed.

To sum up, I have argued the following two related points concerning moral values and self-esteem. First, moral values are not necessarily constitutive of our self-concept, and therefore our self-esteem need not be tied to pursuing the moral life; second, the fact that moral values that are not constitutive of our self-concept need not be explained in terms of a psychological flaw on our part. In the following section, I shall speak to the implications that this argument has for the Kantian view of the connection between rationality and morality.

23. Kantian Morality and Self-Esteem

Crudely put, the Kantian view is that morality holds a natural attraction for us because, on pain of irrationality, morality has a claim to our acting in accordance with it; for the realization of ourselves as rational creatures is inextricably tied to our acting morally. In particular, Kant held that it could be demonstrably shown that on pain of being formally inconsistent each and every individual has to accept certain moral truths. Of course, if he is right, then that does settle the matter, given the ever so plausible assumption that, in virtue of their rationality, consistency is a deeply held value of rational creatures. While it seems doubtful that Kant is right, his legacy is the idea with which I began this paragraph: that on pain of irrationality morality has a claim to our acting in accordance with it.

If the arguments of the preceding section are sound, however, then this idea is very much mistaken. For one, with the possible exception of values pertaining to consistency (and things that speak to biological needs), there are no values that must be constitutive of the self-concept of persons simply in virtue of their being rational creatures; in any case, it is certainly false that moral values must do so on that account. For another, there are no endeavors that hold a natural attraction for us independent of our values; and moral values are no exception here.

It would seem that the Kantian explanation for the immoral person must always be either that he suffers from weakness of will in some way or that he does not sufficiently attend to the character of his immoral deeds. No doubt one or the other explanation is true enough in some instances. But our discussion gives us at least one other explanation: it may be that moral values simply are not among the values of the immoral person—that such values are not constitutive of his self-concept. I should like to close by focusing upon this point.

The damned, if there be any, are those whose self-esteem is so tied to their pursuits of immorality, those whose immoral endeavors contribute so immeasurably to their sense of worth, that the self-esteem they might receive on account of leading a moral life could not possibly fill the void left by the loss of self-esteem that they would suffer on account of giving up their immoral ways. Or, the damned turn out to be those whose lives are so bereft of self-respect that they will do anything that offers the hope of their having a sense of worth. These are people entirely bereft of basic psychological security, and so whose self-esteem must do double work in their lives. The problem is not so much their environment as their psychological needs. Their self-esteem must stand in for their self-respect as well. But our accomplishments, however great they might be, are no substitute for the sense of worth that I have called self-respect, nor for the basic psychological security (Section 7), owing to parents, that gives rise to self-respect. Lacking self-respect, these individuals are often indifferent to whatever means they might employ to compensate for this lack. Their lives are fertile soil for any values just so long as the successful pursuit of them would seem to compensate for this lack. Parents can directly contribute to their children's having immoral values if they (the parents) lead ignoble lives themselves, or they can indirectly contribute by failing to engender in them basic psychological security. Both proper example and love itself are necessary if parents are to have any hope of contributing to the moral flourishing of their children.

The realization of morality in our lives is not so much a function of either rationality or strength of will as it is of having the proper values instilled in us from the start. It is perhaps tempting to think that if the values themselves can be rationally defensible or indefensible, then surely it must follow that a person can be argued into morality if indeed the moral life is superior. But not so. The idea of rational defensibility is ambiguous: does it mean a demonstration on the order of a proof or a set of considerations in which it is reasonable to embrace one alternative over another? Kant was after the former, and it is plausible to suppose that it eluded him. As to the latter, the simple fact of the matter is that what we see as reasonable is not independent of the values that are constitutive of our self-concept, but is very much a function of them. There is no vantage point independent of our values from which we can assess either our experiences or the ideas presented to us.

I have maintained that the moral life is profoundly richer than the immoral life because of the way in which love resounds throughout the life of the moral person. But there is no reason to think that the sufficiently immoral person should appreciate this, although it may be true. Indeed, it is not the sort of thing that he could appreciate. If a person's experiences do not resonate with this claim, then he will surely remain unconvinced by it. And his experiences will do so only if the right values are constitutive of his self-concept. There is argument to be made for living the moral life, and those whose values allow them to experience the richness of love throughout their moral life are the ones who are in the position to make it, as they are in the position to articulate the sense of loss that there would be in the absence of the moral life; in contrast, the sufficiently immoral cannot even see this loss.

Wrongdoing cannot always be attributed to a failure of reason or to a failure to have been presented with (or to have considered) a sufficiently cogent argument. The evil of the Holocaust is not owing to a failure along any of these lines. On the contrary, the Nazis were deeply committed to perpetrating the moral atrocities of the Holocaust. They did so with great determination, skill, and ingenuity. Indeed, with enormous imagination and skill, many of the key figures in the perpetration of this moral atrocity did what they could —and with great success—to prevent the horror of their deeds from pricking both their conscience and the conscience of those carrying out their orders (Hilberg 1985; Lifton 1986). It was not their powers of reasoning that the Nazis had succeeded in deadening, but their moral sensibilities. It is because they were so successful in deadening their moral sensibilities that moral considerations—that is, moral reasons—of the obvious sort had no weight with them. No, wrongdoing cannot always be attributed to a failure of reason. Sometimes what is at the heart of wrongdoing are the sort of values that are constitutive of a person's self-concept. Or, it may be a person's desperate need to affirm his self-worth, a need that, if great enough, can render him susceptible to the most morally horrendous values. Thus not all arguments should be expected to convince.

This essay, perhaps, constitutes one such argument. It is not likely to convert the sufficiently immoral; but hopefully it will give those who endeavor to lead a moral life one more reason to continue believing, to make every effort to touch the lives of others, and to be sure that moral values are constitutive of the self-concept of their children. It is in this way that the foundation for the continuation of morality will be carved out of the rock of social life. For after all is said and done: It is not so much the arguments we give as it is the life we live that most profoundly touches the lives of others.

Bibliography

For the most part, this bibliography lists only those works that are cited in this book. Classical references are not included. In general, the original place of publication for an article is listed. However, when a reprint publication is given, page references are to this publication.

Alexander, Richard D. 1987. *The Biology of Moral Systems*. New York: Aldine de Gruyter.

Alston, William P. 1976. "Traits, Consistency and Conceptual Alternatives for Personality Theory." In Harre (1976), pp. 63–97.

Andre, Judith. 1987. "The Equal Moral Weight of Self- and Other-Regarding Acts." *Canadian Journal of Philosophy* 17: 155–65.

Archer, Richard L. 1980. "Self-Disclosure." In Wegner and Vallacher (1980), pp. 131–57.

Argyle, Michael. 1972. "Non-Verbal Communication in Human Social Interaction." In Hinde (1972), pp. 243–268.

Audi, Robert. 1985. "Self-Deception and Rationality." In Mike W. Martin (ed.), *Self-Deception and Self-Understanding: New Essays in Philosophy and Psychology* (Lawrence: University Press of Kansas).

Badhwar, Nera Kapur. 1985. "Friendship, Justice, and Supererogation." *American Philosophical Quarterly* 22: 123–132.

———. 1987. "Friends as Ends in Themselves." *Philosophy and Phenomenological Research* 48: 1–23.

Baier, Annette. 1982. "Caring About Caring: A Reply to Frankfurt." *Synthese* 53: 273–90. Rpt. in A. Baier (1985a).

————. 1985a. *Postures of the Mind*. Minneapolis: University of Minnesota Press.

————. 1985b. "What Do Women Want in Moral Theory?" *Nous* 19: 53–63.

————. 1986. "Trust and Antitrust." *Ethics* 96: 231–60.

Baier, Kurt. 1958. *The Moral Point of View*. Ithaca, N.Y.: Cornell University Press.

————. 1966. "Moral Obligation." *American Philosophical Quarterly* 1: 210–26.

————. 1972. "The Justification of Governmental Authority." *Journal of Philosophy* 69: 700–16.

————. 1974. "Moral Development." *The Monist* 58: 601–15.

————. 1984. "Rationality, Reason, and the Good." In David Copp and David Zimmerman (eds.), *Morality, Reason and Truth* (Totowa, N.J.: Rowman and Allanheld), pp. 193–211.

Bandura, Albert. 1977. *Social Learning Theory*. Englewood Cliffs, N.J.: Prentice-Hall.

Becker, Lawrence C. 1986. *Reciprocity*. New York: Routledge and Kegan Paul.

Bem, Daryl J. 1970. *Beliefs, Attitudes, and Human Affairs*. Belmont, Calif.: Brooks/Cole.

Bennett, Jonathan. 1981. "Morality and Consequences." In McMurrin (1981), pp. 45–116.

Bertram, Brian C. R. 1978. "Kin Selection in Lions and in Evolution." In Clutton-Brock and Harvey (1978), pp. 160–82.

Blum, Lawrence A. 1980. *Friendship, Altruism, and Morality*. Boston: Routledge and Kegan Paul.

Bowlby, John. 1953. *Child Care and the Growth of Love*. Baltimore: Penguin Books.

————. 1969. *Attachment*. New York: Basic Books.

————. 1976. "The Self-Reliant Personality: Some Conditions That Promote It." In Harre (1976), pp. 1–24. Rpt. in Bowlby (1979).

————. 1979. *The Making and Breaking of Affectional Bonds*. London: Tavistock.

Boxill, Bernard. 1976. "Self-Respect and Protest." *Philosophy and Public Affairs* 6: 359–70.

————. 1984. *Blacks and Social Justice*. Totowa, N.J.: Rowman and Allanheld.

Brandt, Richard B. 1976. "The Psychology of Benevolence and Its Implications for Philosophy." *Journal of Philosophy* 73: 429–53.

————. 1978. *A Theory of the Good and the Right*. New York: Oxford University Press.

Brown, Roger. 1965. *Social Psychology*. New York: Freeman Press.

Burch, Robert W. 1974. "Are There Moral Experts?" *The Monist* 58: 646–58.

Burnyeat, M. F. 1980. "Aristotle on Learning to Be Good." In Rorty (1980a), pp. 69–92.

Card, Claudia. 1988. "Gratitude and Obligation." *American Philosophical Quarterly* 25: 115–27.

Clutton-Brock, T. H., and Paul Harvey (eds.). 1978. *Readings in Sociobiology*. San Francisco: W. H. Freeman.

Cooper, John M. 1975. *Reason and Human Good in Aristotle*. Cambridge, Mass.: Harvard University Press.

———. 1980. "Aristotle on Friendship." In Rorty (1980a), pp. 301–40.

Coopersmith, Stanley. 1967. *The Antecedents of Self-Esteem*. San Francisco: W. H. Freeman.

Cozby, P. C. 1973. "Self-Disclosure: A Literature Review." *Psychology Bulletin* 79.

Darwall, Stephen L. 1983. *Impartial Reason*. Ithaca, N.Y.: Cornell University Press.

Dawkins, Richard. 1976. *The Selfish Gene*. New York: Oxford University Press.

de Sousa, Ronald. 1987. *The Rationality of Emotion*. Cambridge, Mass.: MIT Press.

Donagan, Alan. 1977. *The Theory of Morality*. Chicago: University of Chicago Press.

Dworkin, Andrea. 1983. *Right-Wing Women*. New York: Perigee.

Eibl-Eibesfeldt, Irënaus. 1972. "Similarities and Differences Between Cultures in Expressive Movements." In Hinde (1972), pp. 297–312.

Elgin, Catherine Z. 1983. *With Reference to Reference*. Indianapolis: Hackett.

Falk, W. D. 1986. *Ought, Reasons, and Morality*. Ithaca, N.Y.: Cornell University Press.

Foot, Philippa. 1958. "Moral Beliefs." *Proceedings of the Aristotelian Society* 59 (1958–59). Rpt. in Foot (1977).

———. 1972. "Morality as a System of Hypothetical Imperatives." *The Philosophical Review* 81: 305–16. Rpt. in Foot (1977).

———. 1977. *Virtues and Vices*. Los Angeles: University of California Press.

———. 1984. "Killing and Letting Die." In Garfield and Hennessey (1984), pp. 175–85.

Frankfurt, Harry S. 1971. "Freedom of the Will and the Concept of a Person." *Journal of Philosophy* 68: 5–20.

Freud, Sigmund. 1961. *Civilization and Its Discontents*. Trans. James Strachey. New York: W. W. Norton.

Friedman, Marilyn. 1988. "Friendship, Choice and Change." Bolling Green State University. Photocopy.

Fuller, Lou L. 1964. *The Morality of Law*. New Haven, Conn.: Yale University Press.

Garfield, Jay, and Patricia Hennessey (eds.). 1984. *Abortion: Moral and Legal Perspectives*. Amherst: University of Massachusetts Press.

Gauthier, David. 1970a. "Introduction." In Gauthier (1970b), pp. 1–23.

———. (ed.). 1970b. *Morality and Rational Self-Interest*. Englewood, N.J.: Prentice-Hall.

———. 1986. *Morals by Agreement*. New York: Oxford University Press.

248   Bibliography

Genovese, Eugene. 1974. *Roll Jordon Roll*. New York: Pantheon Books.

Gerstein, Robert S. 1978. "Intimacy and Privacy." *Ethics* 89: 76–81.

Gewirth, Alan. 1978. *Reason and Morality*. Chicago: University of Chicago Press.

Gibbard, Allan F. 1982. "Human Evolution and the Sense of Justice." *Midwest Studies in Philosophy* 7: 31–46.

Gilligan, Carol. 1982. *In a Different Voice*. Cambridge, Mass.: Harvard University Press.

Goffman, Erving. 1959. *Presentation of the Self in Everyday Life*. Garden City, N.Y.: Doubleday Anchor.

———. 1963. *Behavior in Public Places*. Glencoe, Ill.: Free Press of Glencoe.

Goodall, Jane. 1988. *In the Shadow of Man*. Rev. ed. Boston: Houghton Mifflin.

Goodpaster, Kenneth. 1978. "On Being Morally Considerable." *Journal of Philosophy* 75: 308–25.

Gould, Stephen J. 1977. *Ever Since Darwin*. New York: W. W. Norton.

Greenspan, Patricia S. 1980. "A Case of Mixed Feelings: Ambivalence and the Logic of Emotions." In Rorty (1980b).

———. 1988. *Emotions and Reasons: An Inquiry into Emotional Justification*. New York: Routledge and Kegan Paul.

Grice, H. P. 1975. "Logic and Conversation." In P. Cole and J. L. Morgan (eds.), *Syntax and Semantics*, vol. 3 (New York: Academic Press), pp. 43–44.

Gruen, Arno. 1988. *The Betrayal of the Self*. New York: Grove Press.

Hall, Calvin S. 1954. *A Primer of Freudian Psychology*. New York: New American Library.

Hamilton, W. D. 1964. "The Genetical Evolution of Social Behavior." *Journal of Theoretical Biology* 7: 1–52.

Hare, R. M. 1963. *Freedom and Reason*. Oxford, Eng.: Clarendon Press.

Harlow, Harry F., and Clara Mears. 1979. *The Human Model: Primate Perspectives*. New York: John Wiley & Sons.

Harman, Gilbert. 1977. *The Nature of Morality*. New York: Oxford University Press.

Harre, Rom. 1976. *Personality*. Totowa, N.J.: Rowman and Littlefield.

Hart, H. L. A. 1961. *The Concept of Law*. New York: Oxford University Press.

Hilberg, Raul. 1985. *The Destruction of European Jews*. Rev. ed., 3 vols. New York: Holmes and Meier.

Hill, Thomas E., Jr. 1973. "Servility and Self-Respect." *The Monist* 57: 87–104.

———. 1982. "Self-Respect Reconsidered." In O. H. Green (ed.), *Respect for Persons* (Tulane Studies in Philosophy, vol. 31; New Orleans: Tulane University).

Hinde, Robert A. (ed.). 1972. *Non-Verbal Communication*. New York: Cambridge University Press.

———. 1978. "Social Development: A Biological Approach." In Jerome Bruner and Alison Garton (eds.), *Human Growth and Development* (New York: Oxford University Press), pp. 1–32.

Horney, Karen. 1942. *Self-Analysis*. New York: W. W. Norton.

Horton, James Oliver. 1985. "Black Education at Oberlin College: A Controversial Commitment." *Journal of Negro Education* 54: 477–99.

James, William. 1890. *Principles of Psychology*. 2 vols. Rpt. New York: Dover, 1950.

Jensen, Arthur A. 1969. "How Much Can We Boost I.Q. and Scholastic Achievement?" *Harvard Educational Review* 39: 1–123.

Jourard, Sidney M. 1971. *The Transparent Self*. 2d ed. New York: D. Van Nostrand.

Kalin, Jesse. 1970. "In Defense of Egoism." In Gauthier (1970b), pp. 67–84.

King's College Sociobiology Group (eds.). 1982. *Current Problems in Sociobiology*. Cambridge, Eng.: Cambridge University Press.

Kohlberg, Lawrence. 1971. "From Is to Ought: How to Commit the Naturalistic Fallacy and Get Away with It in the Study of Moral Development." In Theodore Mischel (ed.), *Cognitive Development and Epistemology* (New York: Academic Press), pp. 151–235. Rpt. in Kohlberg (1981).

———. 1973. "Justice as Reversibility: The Claim to Moral Adequacy of a Highest Stage of Moral Judgment." *Journal of Philosophy* 70. Rpt. in Kohlberg (1981).

———. 1981. *The Philosophy of Moral Development*. New York: Harper & Row.

Kraut, Robert. 1983. "Objects of Affection." In K. D. Irani and Gerald E. Myers (eds.), *Emotion: Philosophical Studies* (New York: Haven Press), pp. 42–56.

Kraut, Richard. 1984. *Socrates and the State*. Princeton, N.J.: Princeton University Press.

Kripke, Saul. 1980. *Naming and Necessity*. Cambridge, Mass.: Harvard University Press.

Lifton, Robert Jay. 1986. *The Nazi Doctors*. New York: Basic Books.

Machan, Tibor. 1987. "A Classical Egoist Basis of Capitalism." In Machan, *The Main Debate: Capitalism versus Communism* (New York: Random House).

MacIntyre, Alasdair. 1981. *After Virtue*. Notre Dame, Ind.: University of Notre Dame Press.

Mack, Eric. 1971. "How to Derive Ethical Egoism." *The Personalist* [renamed *Pacific Philosophical Quarterly*] 52.

Malandro, Loretta A., and Larry Barker. 1983. *Nonverbal Communication*. Reading, Mass.: Addison Wesley Publishing.

Maynard-Smith, J. 1976. "Group Selection." *Quarterly Review of Biology* 51: 277–83.

———. 1982. "The Evolution of Social Behavior: A Classification of Models." In King's College Sociobiology Group (1982).

Mayo, Clara, and Nancy Henley. 1981. *Gender and Non-Verbal Behavior*. New York: Springer-Verlag.

McConnell, Terrance. 1985. "Metaethical Principles, Meta-Prescriptions, and Moral Theories." *American Philosophical Quarterly* 22: 299–309.

McMurrin, Sterling (ed.). 1980, 1981. *The Tanner Lectures on Human Values*, vols. 1 and 2. Cambridge, Eng.: Cambridge University Press.

Meilaender, Gilbert. 1981. *Friendship: A Study in Theological Ethics*. Notre Dame, Ind.: University of Notre Dame Press.

Midgley, Mary. 1978. *Beast and Man: The Roots of Human Nature*. Ithaca, N.Y.: Cornell University Press.

Miller, Jonathan. 1972. "Plays and Players." In Hinde (1972), pp. 359–72.

Milo, Ronald D. 1984. *Immorality*. Princeton, N.J.: Princeton University Press.

Morris, Herbert. 1976. *On Guilt and Innocence*. Los Angeles: University of California Press.

Murphy, Jeffrie. 1972. "Moral Death: A Kantian Essay on Psychopathy." *Ethics* 82: 284–98.

Nagel, Thomas. 1970. *The Possibility of Altruism*. Oxford, Eng.: Oxford University Press.

———. 1976. "Moral Luck." In *Proceedings of the Aristotelian Society*, supp. vol. 50. Rpt. in Nagel (1979).

———. 1979. *Moral Questions*. New York: Cambridge University Press.

———. 1980. "The Limits of Objectivity." In McMurrin (1980), pp. 75–139.

Nell, Onora. 1975. *Acting on Principle*. New York: Columbia University Press.

Nozick, Robert. 1974. *Anarchy, State, and Utopia*. New York: Basic Books.

———. 1981. *Philosophical Explanations*. Cambridge, Mass.: Harvard University Press.

Oldenquist, Andrew. 1982. "Loyalties." *Journal of Philosophy* 79: 173–93.

Olivier, Laurence. 1986. *On Acting*. New York: Simon and Schuster.

Pritchard, Michael S. 1974. "Responsibility, Understanding, and Psychopathology." *The Monist* 58: 630–45.

Rachels, James. 1975. "Active and Passive Euthanasia." *New England Journal of Medicine* 292: 78–80.

Rawls, John. 1971. *A Theory of Justice*. Cambridge, Mass.: Harvard University Press.

Regis, Edward, Jr. 1979. "Ethical Egoism and Moral Responsibility." *American Philosophical Quarterly* 16: 45–52.

Reiman, Jeffrey. 1976. "Privacy, Intimacy, and Personhood." *Philosophy and Public Affairs* 6.

Rorty, Amelie O. (ed.). 1976a. *The Identities of Persons*. Los Angeles: University of California Press.

———. 1976b. "Literary Postscript: Characters, Persons, Selves, Individuals." In Rorty (1976a), pp. 303–23.

———. 1978. "Explaining Emotion." *Journal of Philosophy* 75: 139–61. Rpt. in Rorty (1980b): 103–126.

———— (ed.). 1980a. *Essays on Aristotle's Ethics*. Los Angeles: University of California Press.

———— (ed.). 1980b. *Explaining Emotions*. Berkeley: University of California Press.

Rosenberg, Morris. 1979. *Conceiving the Self*. New York: Basic Books.

Roy, Jean. 1976. *Hobbes et Freud*. Dalhausie, Can.: Dalhausie University Printing Centre.

Rubin, Zick, and Stephen Shenker. 1978. "Friendship, Proximity and Self-Disclosure." *Journal of Personality* 46.

Rutter, Michael. 1978. "Early Sources of Security and Competence." In Jerome Bruner and Alison Garton (eds.), *Human Growth and Development* (New York: Oxford University Press), pp. 33–61.

Sabini, John, and Maury Silver. 1982. *The Moralities of Everyday Life*. New York: Oxford University Press.

Schoeman, Ferdinand. 1984. "Privacy and Intimate Information." In Schoeman (ed.), *Philosophical Dimensions of Privacy* (New York: Cambridge University Press).

————. 1985. "Aristotle on the Good of Friendship." *Australasian Journal of Philosophy* 63: 269–82.

Sherman, Nancy. 1987. "Aristotle on Friendship and the Shared Life." *Philosophy and Phenomenological Research* 47: 589–613.

Sidgwick, Henry. 1907. *The Method of Ethics*. 7th ed. Rpt. New York: Dover, 1966.

Silverstein, Harry S. 1974. "Universality and Treating Persons as Persons." *Journal of Philosophy* 71: 57–71.

Simon, Herbert A. 1983. *Reason in Human Affairs*. Stanford, Calif.: Stanford University Press.

Singer, Peter. 1981. *Expanding Circle*. New York: Farrar, Straus, Giroux.

Sober, Elliott. 1984. *The Nature of Selection*. Cambridge, Mass.: MIT Press.

Solomon, Robert C. 1977. *The Passions*. New York: Basic Books.

Stocker, Michael. 1976. "The Schizophrenia of Modern Ethical Theories." *Journal of Philosophy* 73: 453–66.

————. 1981. "Values and Purposes: The Limits of Teleology and the Ends of Friendship." *Journal of Philosophy* 78: 747–65.

Strawson, Peter F. 1962. "Freedom and Resentment." *Proceedings of the British Academy*, vol. 98. Rpt. in Strawson, *Freedom and Resentment and Other Essays* (London, Eng.: Methuen, 1974).

Sumner, L. W. 1981. *Abortion and Moral Theory*. Princeton, N.J.: Princeton University Press.

Symons, Donald. 1979. *The Evolution of Human Sexuality*. New York: Oxford University Press.

Taylor, Charles. 1985. "Language and Human Nature." In Taylor, *Human Agency and Language*, vol. 1 (New York: Cambridge University Press).

Thomas, Laurence. 1978. "Morality and Our Self-Concept." *Journal of Value Inquiry* 12: 258–68.

———. 1980a. "Ethical Egoism and Our Psychological Dispositions." *American Philosophical Quarterly* 17: 73–78.

———. 1980b. "Sexism and Racism: Some Conceptual Differences." *Ethics* 90: 239–50.

———. 1983a. "Morality, the Self, and Our Natural Sentiments." In K. D. Irani and Gerald E. Myers (eds.), *Emotion: Philosophical Studies* (New York: Haven Press), pp. 144–63.

———. 1983b. "Self-Respect: Theory and Practice." In Leonard Harris (ed.), *Philosophy Born of Struggle* (Dubuque, Iowa: Kendall/Hunt), pp. 174–89.

———. 1985a. "Beliefs and the Motivation to Be Just." *American Philosophical Quarterly* 22: 347–52.

———. 1985b. "Love and Morality: The Possibility of Altruism." In James Fetzer (ed.), *Sociobiology and Epistemology* (Norwell, Mass.: D. Reidel), pp. 115–29.

———. 1986. "Justice, Happiness, and Self-Knowledge." *Canadian Journal of Philosophy* 16: 63–82.

———. 1987a. "Friendship." *Synthese* 72: 217–36.

———. 1987b. "Moral Behavior and Rational Creatures of the Universe." *The Monist* 70: 59–71.

———. 1988a. "Jews, Blacks, and Group Autonomy." *Social Theory and Practice* 14: 55–69.

———. 1988b. "Liberalism and the Holocaust: An Essay on Trust and the Black-Jewish Relationship." In Alan Rosenberg and Gerald E. Myers (eds.), *Echoes from the Holocaust* (Philadelphia: Temple University Press), pp. 105–17.

———. 1988c. "Rationality and Affectivity: The Metaphysics of the Moral Self." *Social Philosophy and Policy* 5: 154–72.

Trammell, Richard. 1975. "Saving Life and Taking Life." *Journal of Philosophy* 72: 131–37.

Trivers, Robert L. 1971. "The Evolution of Reciprocal Altruism." *Quarterly Review of Biology* 46: 35–57. Rpt. in Clutton-Brock and Harvey (1978), pp. 189–226.

———. 1978. "Parental Investment and Sexual Selection." In Clutton-Brock and Harvey (1978), pp. 52–97.

———. 1985. *Social Evolution*. Menlo Park, Calif.: Benjamin/Cummings.

Vallacher, Robin R. 1980. "An Introduction to Self Theory." In Wegner and Vallacher (1980), pp. 3–30.

Vlastos, Gregory. 1962. "Justice and Equality." In Richard Brandt (ed.), *Social Justice* (Englewood Cliffs, N.J.: Prentice-Hall), pp. 31–72.

Walker, Lily Schubert, and Paul H. Wright. 1976. "Self-Disclosure in Friendship." *Perceptual and Motor Skills* 42.

Washington, Booker T. 1901. *Up from Slavery*. Boston: Houghton, Mifflin.

Wegner, Daniel M., and Robin R. Vallacher (eds.). 1980. *The Self in Social Psychology*. London: Oxford University Press.

Wertheimer, Roger. 1972. *The Significance of Sense*. Ithaca, N.Y.: Cornell University Press.

White, Robert W. 1963. *Ego and Reality in Psychoanalytic Theory*. New York: International Universities Press.

Williams, Bernard. 1962. "The Idea of Equality." In Peter Laslett and W. G. Runciman (eds.), *Politics, Philosophy and Society*, vol. 2 (Oxford, Eng.: Blackwell). Rpt. in Williams (1973).

———. 1973. *Problems of the Self*. New York: Cambridge University Press.

———. 1976a. "Moral Luck." *Proceedings of the Aristotelian Society*, supp. vol. 50: 115–35. Rpt. in Williams (1981).

———. 1976b. "Persons, Character, and Morality." In Rorty (1976), pp. 197–216. Rpt. in Williams (1981).

———. 1980. "Internal and External Reasons." In Ross Harrison (ed.), *Rational Action* (New York: Cambridge University Press), pp. 17–28. Rpt. in Williams (1981).

———. 1981. *Moral Luck*. New York: Cambridge University Press.

Wilson, E. O. 1975. *Sociobiology: The New Synthesis*. Cambridge, Mass.: Harvard University Press.

———. 1978. *On Human Nature*. Cambridge, Mass.: Harvard University Press.

Wolf, Susan. 1982. "Moral Saints." *Journal of Philosophy* 79: 419–39.

Ziller, Robert C. 1976. "A Helical Theory of Personal Change." In Harre (1976), pp. 98–142.

Index